MARKETING

A DEGREE IN A BOOK

MARKETING

JOHN JESSUP WITH JOEL JESSUP

SIRIUS

John Jessup

After leaving art school in 1969, John spent four years at Pinewood Film Studios, as a runner in the art department. He started his first job in advertising in 1973, as a junior art director, moving to a number of different agencies including Ogilvy & Mather, where he became creative group head. In 1981 John started his own agency, with Neill Barker. Barker Jessup and Partners traded successfully until 1986 when it merged with another agency. At Woollams, Moira Gaskin O'Malley, he helped win prestigious accounts including Virgin Atlantic and the RAC. He joined Leo Burnett in 1992 as

SIRIUS

This edition published in 2021 by Sirius Publishing, a division of Arcturus Publishing Limited,
26/27 Bickels Yard, 151–153 Bermondsey Street,
London SE1 3HA

ISBN: 978-1-3988-1505-6
AD008394UK

Printed in China

creative director. There, John worked on almost every piece of business in their extensive portfolio. He was responsible for award-winning work on the Kellogg's, McDonald's, Walt Disney, Proctor and Gamble and Unicef accounts among many others. In 2013 John left advertising to concentrate on his own projects including an award-winning short film and this book.

Joel Jessup

Joel has worked as a scriptwriter, show developer and author for over 20 years. Starting while he was still at college in 1998 he worked primarily as a children's writer, working for companies including Disney, the BBC, CBBC, CBeebies, ITV, Nickelodeon and Fox Kids, working on shows such as the BAFTA-winning *Foxbusters*. He wrote an animated feature film that was nominated for a Goya award with another currently in development. He also worked with various online creators in making funny viral content as well as briefly working on projects for Leo Burnett and Unicef. For two years he worked as a mentor at the School of Communication Arts 2.0. Since 2011 Joel has written seven non-fiction and fiction books and contributed research material to several others. With his father and frequent collaborator John Jessup, he also created the award-winning short film *Roake*. Married for 13 years, he lives in London with two children and no cats.

CONTENTS

INTRODUCTION: WHAT IS MARKETING?

There is a common misconception that marketing is some sort of mesmeric, dark art that the consumer, as a helpless ingénue, is unable to resist. People claim that it's full of hidden and misleading messages and half-truths, designed to brainwash people into buying things they don't need or want.

The truth is that modern marketing is actually conditioned by the consumer, and their requirements are what drive the messages from the brands, not the other way around. This book is an exploration of the techniques, skills, sciences and arts that marketers apply to the brands or services they offer. It is then up to the consumer to make their own informed choices.

The text picks its way through the jargon and acronyms and gives the reader a well-researched and balanced view of the story of marketing, from its early inception to the slickly-oiled economic powerhouse it is today. It looks into the backgrounds of successful marketing campaigns, and the odd failure, to analyse what went right or spectacularly wrong. By looking back and forward at what marketing was and has become today it shows how it has travelled from the 'science of persuasion' to the 'art of disruption'. The marketing world is populated by artists, writers, psychologists, scientists, and even philosophers, and this book will examine some of their contributions to the stories behind global brands.

As long as there has been a society there has been marketing. In Roman times the amphora became an

Amphorae were an early branded item.

early marketing tool. Initially they were just vessels for the transportation of goods; then traders in busy markets began to add their names and simple designs to attract potential customers. This way they ensured that if the customer was happy, they would know which seller to recommend to friends or relatives. Even the very simple act of using the sight and smell of freshly made food and drink in a market was itself a way of bringing prospective consumers over to their stall. These same early marketing techniques are still prevalent today. Many a passer-by today could find themself lured into a coffee shop by the delicious smells emanating from it.

People use their senses to make choices. Sight, smell, taste and hearing all come into play and marketing campaigns are designed to appeal to these senses. Modern marketing goes even further to understand consumers' preferences, compiling data on people's likes and dislikes, wants and needs. Marketers paint pictures and tell stories that will embrace each individual's personal choices, utilizing targeted marketing.

Detergent brands often rely on bright colours and eye-catching, deliberately unsubtle packaging design.

What will become clear during the course of this book is that marketing is not one-way traffic from brand to consumer. Consumers wield huge influence on the destiny of brands.

Sometimes marketing happens whether companies want it or not. In Soviet Russia products were usually sold in one uniform label, but consumers would note that certain factories produced better food and would look for and note small details on the containers, like where it was made or what the individual ingredients were, leading to an inadvertent form of branding. Consumers will seek out the qualities they are looking for in order to make an informed choice, so it's up to the brands to understand their customers' needs and deliver.

Marketing starts with the product and what goes into it, then how it is packaged, where it is distributed, how it is stacked on the shelf, its value and so on. After that comes the promotion, everything from mainstream advertising to direct mail. In the 21st century with people spending so much time on their smartphones, tablets and computers, digital marketing is having a huge impact. The emergence of influencers is testament to this emerging form of marketing.

It is not only products that are subject to marketing; there are a myriad of service-based industries all vying for the attention of the consumer. Banks, airlines and holiday companies, even local dentists are now using sophisticated messaging and content to grab the attention of potential consumers.

The practice of marketing is often called marketing management, which involves companies not only carefully controlling their own marketing but analysing that of their competitors so that they can react accordingly.

The roles of brand leaders and challenger brands are very much part of the make-up of the modern consumer's world; this book will explain how each brand finds its particular niche.

Popular culture is a powerful influence. Film, music, literature and computer games are used to promote brands and find mutually common ground between brands and their consumer. Twinning brands with the latest movie, even down to placing products within the film itself, has become part of the marketer's armoury.

The promotion and marketing of popular culture itself is a massive sector. Multinational entertainment giants like Walt Disney and Sony develop toys and products at the same time as producing a movie, so that they hit the high street at the same time as the film premières at the cinemas.

It is worth saying that marketers are not free to do whatever they please to persuade the public to buy their goods and services. They, like everyone else, are subject to laws that prevent marketers and their agents from the misuse and manipulation of the truth. The phrase 'Legal, decent, honest and truthful', governs the promotion of companies and their brands or services, and has done so for decades. These regulations and laws have evolved alongside the changes in society, with recognition of diversity and ethnicity now very much part of modern marketing content.

Ultimately marketing is about making profit. To spend money promoting products in order to maximize sales and profits is a game of risk and this book

will analyse the factors involved in this economic balancing act. Marketing can be as simple as it is complex. Brands can throw millions into promotions that fail, or cleverly use word of mouth to build an army of loyal customers. Marketers can create new terminology that explains the obvious or turns centuries-old concepts into new paradigms. This book will aim to give as complete a picture of marketing, past, present and as far into the future as possible. The world is facing huge challenges; the Covid-19 pandemic is testament to that. Marketing must adapt to meet whatever obstacles are thrown in its path.

The language, codes and symbols of marketing will be explained as we lift the lid on this fascinating and complex subject. If you need further help there is a glossary at the back of the book, as well as a list of recommended further reading.

With its purchase of the Stars Wars and Marvel brands the Disney company has consolidated its grip on the family entertainment market.

Chapter One
THE ORIGINS OF MARKETING

The Birth of Commerce • Revolution • Arrival of the Big Brands • Television and Radio Sponsorship in the USA • FMCGs

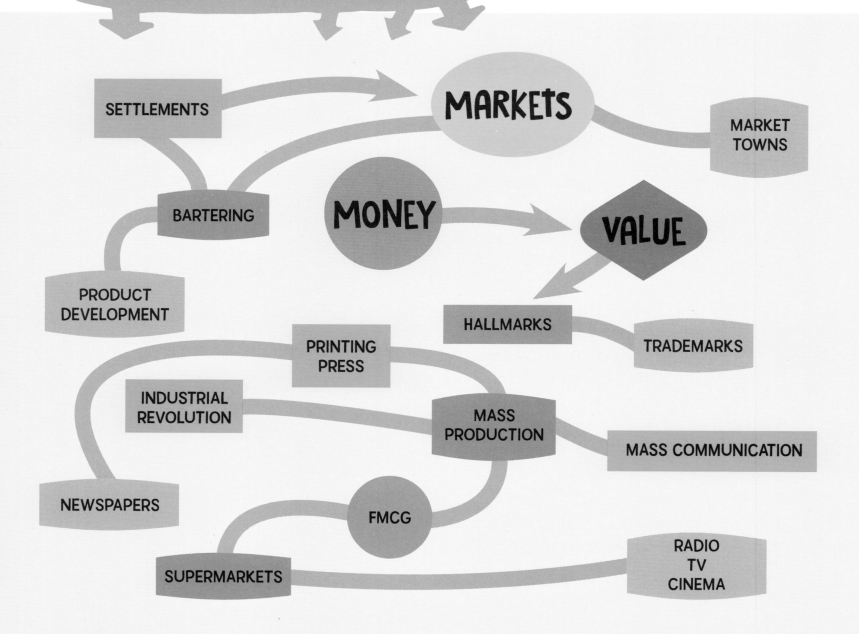

SETTLEMENTS

MARKETS

MARKET TOWNS

BARTERING

MONEY

VALUE

PRODUCT DEVELOPMENT

HALLMARKS

TRADEMARKS

PRINTING PRESS

INDUSTRIAL REVOLUTION

MASS PRODUCTION

MASS COMMUNICATION

NEWSPAPERS

FMCG

SUPERMARKETS

RADIO TV CINEMA

THE BIRTH OF COMMERCE

Marketing is not merely a modern invention. It emerged naturally out of the development of human society. Hundreds of thousands of years ago, early humans lived in small tribes of hunter-gatherers. They were nomadic, moving from place to place, so that whenever resources, particularly food, were out of season or exhausted they moved on in search of what they needed to survive. As people developed skills, members of each tribe would specialize in their particular role, for example hunters, weavers or cooks. There was no competition because everyone had their own job within their group. This was the primary form of subsistence for 90 per cent of the time that humanity has existed.

Then, roughly around 10,000 BCE, humans developed the ability to cultivate the land and grow plants, particularly grain, and domesticate animals, particularly cattle, hence there was less need to travel around. Villages and communities were established and people began trading goods as a way of acquiring things that they lacked either the resources or skills to make themselves. This was often managed by the tribes as either a gift that required no recompense, or a debt to be honoured at a future time. As communities grew in scope and size and the practice of commerce – the exchange of goods and services – began to develop, two things became necessary:

1 An established bartering system to ensure that people got a fair deal and knew the financial worth and exchange rate of certain items.
2 A way of knowing whether or not something they were giving or receiving was of good quality.

The first of these is what eventually became currency; the second is the concept of value.

The earliest form of currency, anything of value can be bartered.

VALUE ▶ *A term used in marketing that relates primarily to consumer perception, whereby a customer compares the costs or benefits of one product or service against another: 'value for money'.*

The market place

At first, around 9000–6000 BCE, commodities themselves were used as money, whether it was livestock, simple tradable goods like coffee beans or textiles, or actual items made of gold like jewellery. The value of the item was simply its actual value and not representative, although it is now known that people in India, Africa and Ancient China used the shells of the cowry, a type of sea snail, as currency. One such shell earned the nickname the 'money cowrie' from its Latin name *Monetaria moneta* and became synonymous with the concept of value exchange.

Later, storehouses and gold and silver merchants began offering people receipts for the commodities they were storing for them. These receipts became themselves a representation of value, and the actual commodities in question only needed to exist in theory. In other words, the first monetary notes.

As life became more than just day-to-day subsistence, the idea of buying things for pleasure or to improve people's way of life became more prevalent. These luxuries would be primarily limited to the ruling classes, but even when you were simply purchasing the fruits and vegetables you needed for food there would be competition among sellers and ultimately, the market.

For most of this book 'the market' will be a term meaning 'the area or arena in which commercial dealings are conducted' but at this point in history it was a *literal* market, with rows of physical stalls selling goods and wares. All across the globe, market towns grew up.

Cowrie shells were used as money worldwide up until the mid 19th century.

MARKET TOWNS

The market town is a physical representation of everything important to understanding modern marketing: products, sellers and customers; people shouting, chatting and trading; sellers gossiping and changing their approach on the promotion and pricing of goods based on live feedback; distribution and supply and demand; and the need for protection of goods and the significance of the law (market towns could only be established in the UK by custom or Royal Charter). The *Domesday Book* of 1086 listed as many as 50 towns with markets in England but around 2,000 new markets were established between 1200 and 1349, with similar expansion all across Europe. Market towns were often built near forts, castles or large houses because they would benefit both from the ability to sell goods to those households and from the protection of the local garrison.

A woodcut of Goslar, a market town in Lower Saxony, Germany.

Proto-branding

Despite this, marketing in the modern sense was not widely known. The commonly view was that in ancient history, products were generic and salesmen interchangeable. However, contemporary historians are constantly revising their view of this time and there are examples of what were considered to be marketing techniques found as far back as the Roman Empire.

While excavating the ancient Roman city of Pompeii, archaeologists discovered four interesting mosaics in the house of a garum producer named Umbricius Scaurus (garum was a type of extremely popular fermented fish sauce in 79 CE). It contained images of amphorae (which garum was stored in) that bore his personal brand and claims about his garum's superiority, saying things such as (translated from the Latin): 'The flower of garum, made of the mackerel, a product of Scaurus, from the shop of Scaurus' and 'The best liquamen, from the shop of Scaurus'

Furthermore, Monte Testaccio, an artificial mound in Rome made of an estimated 53 million broken olive oil amphorae dating from *c.* 140–250 CE, contains multiple examples of *tituli picti*, inscriptions that were either painted or stamped on each container with information about its contents, its weight and the names and districts of

Early branding

The 'Flower of Garum' mosaic was discovered during excavations in Pompeii in the 1950s.

those who bottled it. The mound has a circumference of almost a kilometre and stands 35 m (115 ft) high, testament to the demand for olive oil in Ancient Rome. However, these early examples also serve as a warning that any brand can end up on the scrap heap.

Other cultures were also practising branding to promote goods. During the Song dynasty (960–1279) in China, there was a proto-consumerist culture where many strata of society were able to purchase goods, and therefore company logos, in the form of symbolic brands and signs in shops, developed.

Aside from literally branding goods with an iron, such as cattle, the marks of manufacturers and guilds were increasingly being adopted. Metal makers would have their own personal mark to indicate their unique pieces. Taking this further, hallmarks, which have existed since at least the 4th century CE, were one of the earliest guarantees of consumer protection in Europe, only being stamped onto goods that met a certain standard. They are still used today as well as being the forerunner of other quality guarantee marks like the British Kitemark or the German *Geprüfte Sicherheit*.

Trademarks and hallmarks

Quality assurance marks: silver hallmarks, the Kitemark and the GS-Zeichen symbol

CONSUMERS ▶ *People who want or need to buy goods and or services from trading companies.*

Advertising was a common feature in ancient Roman cities.

The influence of technology

Developments in technology led to leaps forward in the scope and sophistication of early marketing techniques. In 1440, Johannes Gutenberg developed a printing press that could rapidly produce large numbers of pages full of precise text. What followed was a printing revolution that allowed books, leaflets and posters to be spread across Europe, dramatically increasing people's awareness of goods and their sellers.

People were exploring new lands, and travel became easier due to the development of more sophisticated transport like ships and carriages. The caravel, a small, highly manoeuvrable sailing ship with triangular sails, enabled fast ocean travel and the astrolabe was a breakthrough for navigation. Information about the experiences these early explorers had and the goods they encountered could be shared with their home communities. They wrote letters and told stories explaining the possibilities they saw in other people's cultures. New and exciting goods and products would change hands and would be transported back to travellers' homelands. These experiences could be termed as early market research and travelling traders were the pioneers, opening up new 'markets' for customers to try foods and homewares from around the known world.

REVOLUTION

The event that truly gave birth to the modern marketing era is widely considered to be the first Industrial Revolution, which occurred in the late 18th century in Britain. This period was marked by an upheaval in the means of production, due to many new scientific developments, such as steam and water power, a change from production by hand to machines, and ultimately mass production in mechanized factories. The population grew and, became more centralized in urban areas, with an increase in literacy and living standards, although for some, mass exploitation and child labour were also common.

Furthermore, the transport network became increasingly fast and efficient, first with canals, and then improved roads, before the railways enabled vast amounts of goods to be moved across the country. All these factors combined meant mass marketing on an unprecedented scale was not only possible, but inevitable.

NAMES TO KNOW: JOSIAH WEDGWOOD

One of the leading figures in the industrialization of pottery in the eighteenth century, Josiah Wedgwood was an early pioneer of modern marketing techniques like direct mail, travelling salesmen, catalogues and even branding to a certain extent.

His company initially produced luxury plates and tea sets for the upper classes but as his workers specialized and production became more efficient his manufacturing costs went down, enabling him to lower his prices and begin marketing his products to the middle classes. With this increased demand came the need for larger distribution and promotion.

In the first part of the 19th century, he had three travelling salesmen who would cover the length and breadth of the UK collecting orders, and showing prospective customers special catalogues with annotations about the products. They would also show them interesting half-completed samples of the products in question. He would even offer money-back guarantees and Buy One Get One Free (BOGOF) promotions before these became common. His company gave the middle classes a chance to own products they associated with wealth and prestige, making 'Wedgwood' one of the earliest brand identities.

Josiah Wedgewood used early marketing techniques to dominate the European pottery industry.

Wedgewood's blue jasperware is still hugely popular to this day.

NEWSPAPERS

The earliest newspapers are said to have been handwritten news sheets that were passed around in Venice in the mid-16th century. By the early 17th century, the first printed newspapers were distributed in Germany. In 1695, the British government relaxed their draconian censorship laws, allowing newspapers to flourish in London and then throughout the British Empire.

This early German 'newspaper' was published in 1609.

These early 20th century French ads promote everything from tea to banks.

The birth of the newspaper was without doubt a significant leap for the practice of marketing as it enabled readers not just to catch up on the news but also exposed them to recommendations for products and services and then to early advertising and promotional messages.

During and after the Industrial Revolution there was a greater need for manufacturers to distribute, place and promote the goods they were now mass producing with their new machinery and workforce. In the 18th century, advertising and promotion were already showing a high level of technical and creative sophistication, with producers able to access their consumers through newspapers, magazines, posters and even by direct mail.

ARRIVAL OF THE BIG BRANDS

However, marketing truly gathered momentum at the beginning of the 20th century, as manufacturers could use increasingly accurate market research techniques to gain a better understanding of the people to whom they were selling their goods and services. Greater improvements in the transportation and distribution of goods at a national and even international level meant a wider customer base, and having a better knowledge of the demographics of their consumers meant they were able to be more economically effective with their sales and marketing strategies.

In the USA in 1908, Henry Ford's development and refinement of mass production in the automobile industry, later known as 'Fordism', was accompanied by an equivalent leap forward in marketing, with Ford's 'Any customer can have a car painted any colour that he wants so long as it is black' slogan originating from the truth that black paint was the fastest drying and therefore necessary for the quick turnaround of his production line.

As the customer base grew exponentially, so did the ways to market to them. In the late 19th century, cinema brought the moving image to the common people but initially it didn't have the same reach as the advent of commercial radio in 1900, which allowed sellers to literally broadcast directly to their customer

THE ORIGINS OF MARKETING

base and align their interests with popular music and entertainment. In many parts of the USA, particularly the remote areas, radio was the primary and sometimes only form of entertainment.

In a stunt to prove that their slogan 'The Model T drives everywhere' was accurate, a Ford employee drives a Tin Lizzy up the courtroom steps.

Television and radio sponsorship in the USA

After World War II, television ownership became more widespread and sellers had a means to get their message in full sound and vision directly in their customer's front room, and they leapt at the chance. Both radio and TV thrived on sponsorship of their content, particularly in the USA, with celebrities also offering off-screen endorsements in ads and articles found in magazines and newspapers.

TATE AND LYLE'S GOLDEN SYRUP

Tate and Lyle's distinctive golden syrup tin is recognized by the *Guinness Book of Records* as the world's oldest branding on packaging. It has remained the same since 1885 with only slight changes due to material scarcity in the two world wars. Tate and Lyle's company name is also an interesting early example of a brand's image not necessarily being reflective of its reality because, despite their close association for over a century, Henry Tate and Abram Lyle never met in person, were fierce rivals, and the merger of their companies was only completed after their deaths.

The dead lion on the Tate & Lyle Golden syrup tin is a reference to the biblical legend of Samson.

Sponsorship

19

THE SUBTLETY OF SPONSORS

Sponsors were far from subtle. Many anthology programmes directly bore the name of the company or product in question, from the *Dupont Show of the Month* to the *Buick-Electra Playhouse*. This was considered the most effective way of building their name. However, the companies themselves would often produce both the advertising and the

Rod Serling, 1959.

actual programmes, allowing for more nuance within the show itself. Sometimes the content of the programmes would be altered to fit commercial requirements, such as episodes of *Ozzie and Harriet* being written to centre on the kitchen, so that sponsor Westinghouse could showcase its new washing machine. In an episode of *The Twilight Zone* series creator Rod Serling found himself in the strange situation where he was criticized for having a British captain on a British ship in World War II order a cup of tea, because the sponsor was Sanka instant coffee. Serling later humorously complained 'You can't "ford" a river if it's sponsored by Chevy; you can't offer someone a "match" if it's sponsored by Ronson lighters...'.

Westinghouse product advertisement from 1956.

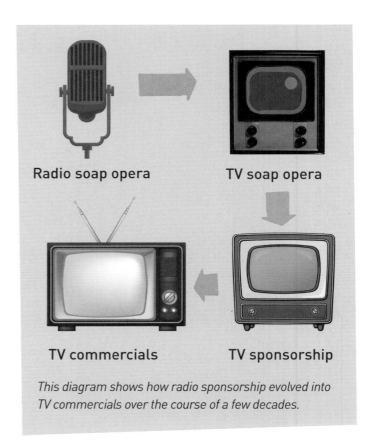

Radio soap opera

TV soap opera

TV commercials

TV sponsorship

This diagram shows how radio sponsorship evolved into TV commercials over the course of a few decades.

The term 'soap opera' originates from detergent companies sponsoring the popular radio dramas of the 1930s, because the target market for both the drama and the detergent was the housewife, who could do their chores and care for their children while listening to the exciting plot. When soap operas moved to television the promotional possibilities were increased. Promotion was integrated into the shows and sometimes spoken directly by the actors, either in character or as themselves. This later led to surreal moments such as the characters in the animated show *The Flintstones* directly advocating Winston cigarettes.

THE 1950S QUIZ SHOW SCANDAL

While many factors contributed to the shift of television and radio advertising from direct sponsorship to breaks between programming featuring pre-recorded advertising, a significant event was the quiz show scandal of the late 1950s. This was actually a series of scandals where it was revealed by the press that the producers of *Twenty-One*, *The Big Surprise* and *Dotto*, popular quiz shows of the time, had been helping certain contestants to win to make the programmes more exciting and watchable. However, it had the opposite effect, as when the truth came out it destroyed people's faith and interest in the shows. This led to new laws regulating the content of the show's production, and in efforts to restore public confidence television networks began asserting greater control over the shows themselves.

The popular quiz shows of the 1950s proved fertile ground for nefarious practices, but the truth was a stronger pull for audiences.

Commercial breaks

While live 'commercials' would often be scheduled during programming in the 1950s and 1960s, pre-taped commercials were rare, but as recording technology advanced and an increase in advertising revenue led to greater budgets, commercials became the primary method by which companies would convey their messages to consumers from the 1970s onwards. Many of these commercials were increasingly sophisticated and entertaining in their own right, with high production values, sometimes even better than the programmes they bordered. Ironically, the development of home videotape technology in the

Growth of TV commercials

KELLOGG'S

IN 1876, Dr John Harvey Kellogg was the superintendent of the Battle Creek Sanitorium in Michigan where his brother Will Keith Kellogg was also the book-keeper. The driven and single-minded J.H. Kellogg dedicated his life to improving the vegetarian diets of those at the sanitorium, his hospital and health spa for rich and famous patients, and his brother was an able and willing assistant. While the brothers were trying a new process for developing a wheat-based granola, they accidently let the results go stale. However, the brothers carried on and forced the wheat grains through rollers, with surprising results, as instead of the grains merging into one flat sheet they came out as individual flakes.

W.K. talked J.H. into serving the 'flakes' to his patients, who greatly enjoyed them, and very soon he also started to mail-order boxes of the cereal flakes to former patients of the sanatorium. This led to a massive falling out between the brothers as J.H. did not want the new cereal to leave the sanatorium. As a result, W.K. went his own way and in February 1906 he founded the Battle Creek Toasted Corn Flake Company. J.H. begrudgingly relinquished all rights to the product, and brother Will's company started in earnest to produce and market the revolutionary Kellogg's Toasted Corn Flake brand.

The name of the company changed to the Kellogg Company in 1922.

While the Kellogg Company continued to add to its portfolio of brands it also

A typical Kellogg's ad from the early 20th century.

became a frontrunner in marketing. The Kellogg's logo itself, based on W.K.'s signature and crafted by legendary typeface designer Andrew Y. Ames, is in itself an iconic brand symbol and one of the most recognized trademarks in the world. They not only produced clever promotional material, like the famous 'K E double-L, O double-good, Kellogg's best to you!' slogan, but they also set themselves above other food brands by seizing the high ground, as if their product was not just cereal but also 'A New Way of Living'.

This manifested itself through a book published by their Canadian company, with its simple message to the reader being that by eating Kellogg's All-Bran you would enjoy a constipation free life, full of energy and vitality!

Promotional efforts like this further enhanced their wholesome image amongst the consumer across all their products. They led the way in sponsorship of TV shows in the USA, being long running backers of hit shows like *What's My Line*. Kellogg's were also the first brand to put prizes in their boxes of cereal.

Tony the Tiger has been Kellogg's Frosted Flakes/ Frosties mascot since 1952.

Their influential marketing techniques didn't stop with the adult consumer; they developed some of the best-known brand icons for their children's brands, with Frosted Flakes' (Frosties in the UK) brand icon Tony the Tiger, created by legendary advertising man Leo Burnett and probably their most famous character.

FAST MOVING CONSUMER GOODS ▶ *Products that are sold swiftly and at a relatively modest price. Examples include household goods of short-term durability such as food (in packaging), drinks, confectionery, make-up and toiletries, non-prescription medication and other items that can be consumed. Also sometimes called CPG or consumer packaged goods.*

This supermarket aisle is lined with FMCGs or fast moving consumer goods.

1980s meant consumers could record their programmes and then skip the breaks, and with digital recording enabling consumers to entirely miss out breaks, advertisers are returning to direct programme sponsorship.

FMCGs

Although supermarkets were commonplace in the USA in the early 1930s, they became popular in Europe and elsewhere in the 1950s. The spread of supermarkets led to a revolution in what were called fast moving consumer goods (or FMCGs).

These products could now be made, distributed and bought at an incredible pace. The metrics of these purchases could be measured and provided to the sellers, enabling them to develop new marketing strategies and orientations on the fly. BOGOFs and point-of-sale advertising were only some of the diverse new techniques they could use on the cart-pushing shoppers.

These new developments needed new and sophisticated thinking to truly understand and enhance their possibilities. Figures like the philosopher Marshall McLuhan delved into the psychology behind marketing, but the most influential practitioners of marketing thought were people like David Ogilvy, Robert J. Keith and the 'father of modern marketing', Philip Kotler.

NAMES TO KNOW: PHILIP KOTLER

Philip Kotler's ideas and implementation of marketing techniques made him a leading figure in the field.

Born in Chicago in 1931, Philip Kotler studied economics extensively under venerated figures in the field like Milton Friedman and Robert Solow. However, in 1962, when he began teaching at the Kellogg School of Management, he chose to teach marketing as he considered it to be an inseparably important aspect of economics. Kotler was one of the early pioneers of the idea of clarifying an organization or person's marketing goals by considering the four Ps... Product, Price, Place and Promotion (see Chapter Two, pages 33–3).

He said, 'Marketing is not the art of finding clever ways to dispose of what you make. Marketing is the art of creating genuine customer value. It is the art of helping your customer become better off. The marketer's watchwords are quality, service, and value.'

When he began teaching, marketing was considered by many to be merely a peripheral consideration and nowhere near as important as actually producing the goods, but he repeatedly advocated for its importance. He reasoned that if sellers could focus on improving the lives and well-being of their customers (primarily by anticipating what they want, need and are interested in) they could massively increase their profits.

Kotler believed it was short-sighted to limit the scope of marketing to profit-based businesses, saying that it was just as important in the areas of non-profit organizations such as museums and charities, as well as for governments.

Philip Kotler has had a significant influence on modern marketing from the 1960s onwards and in the course of this book we will be revisiting some of his theories.

Summary

The key elements at the beginning of this chapter, money and value, have underpinned everything we've described and everything we will go on to explore, both in the consumer's perception of what they mean and in the seller's understanding of the symbiotic relationship between the two. Modern marketing is by its own needs as complex and sophisticated as modern humanity, but at its heart lies the same basic exchanges that happened between different tribes who needed things they couldn't make themselves.

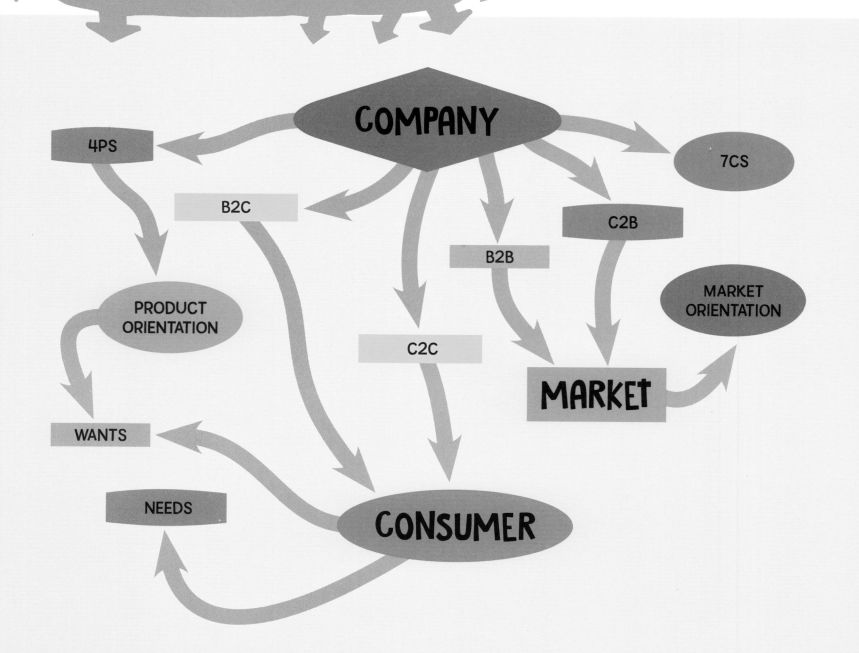

ART OR SCIENCE?

Whether marketing is better defined as an art or a science is a debate that has raged among practitioners of the marketing world for decades. This argument was made more contentious by scholars arguing about what actually *constitutes* an art or a science. The most accurate answer is that marketing falls in-between both disciplines.

In order to find the perfect 'Marketing Mix', a phrase coined by the eminent Harvard professor Neil H. Borden, companies have to weigh up the most effective combination of a number of factors. Many of the elements are of a physical nature: the cost of producing the product, pricing it, distribution, display and promotion. These have to be factored and measured to find the ideal blend, something that earlier marketing theorists would call 'a formula' as they would approach it from the field of science.

However, they then have to weigh up the subtle nuances and find creative ways to build a unique combination of all these elements for the product or service they are offering.

This is an art.

Borden considered marketing an art and likened it to a recipe:

Marketing is still an art, and the marketing manager, as head chef, must creatively marshal all his marketing activities to advance the short- and long-term interests of his firm.
Neil Borden, 'The Concept of the Marketing Mix'

Marketing: science or art?

NAMES TO KNOW: NEIL H. BORDEN

Neil H Bordon invented the term 'Marketing Mix' and was a key contributor to its importance.

Positive impact of marketing

Born in Boulder, Colorado in 1895, Neil Hopper Borden graduated from the University of Colorado in 1919, with a BA in Economics. His professor advised that he focus on teaching business administration and from 1920 he studied it for two years at Harvard University. He excelled and, once he'd obtained his degree, was appointed as an assistant dean.

Borden moved to an assistant professorship in 1925. His teaching style evolved from **Problems in Advertising**, a book of advertising case studies that he wrote in 1927, based on years of study conducted with an Advertising Research Foundation grant.

During his 40 years at Harvard Business School, Borden released several large-scale studies of marketing. During the Great Depression (1929–39) people began to feel that advertising and other forms of marketing were superfluous so he launched a particularly large study of the positive impact of marketing, which was released in 1942 as **The Economic Effects of Advertising**.

He wrote other influential books on the subject, in particular, **Advertising in Our Economy: A Condensed Version of the Economic Effects of Advertising** in 1945 and **National Advertising in Newspapers** in 1946.

Borden was elected President of the National Association of Marketing Teachers, and then National President of the American Marketing Association (1953–54), the organization that succeeded it. In 1962, he retired from teaching to concentrate on writing. He was posthumously honoured by his elevation to the American Advertising Federation Hall of Fame in 1991.

THE 'MIX' RECIPE

So where should marketing managers and other professionals in the industry start their 'Marketing Mix'? OATS is a simple acronym to kick-start a marketing plan:

'KNOW YOUR OATS'

Organize
Make the plan: Ask yourself the following questions: what resources are available and which of those are needed (money, staff, technology, stores)? What is your goal? How and when should you use the various elements? Set a timeline and make sure that each of the elements complements rather than contradicts another. Make certain that the concept is consistent.

Activate
Get the plan out into the world. If the plan is designed to activate in stages then make sure you know the timeframe for each activation. Commit to the concept of the plan without balking at possible repercussions; the analysis comes at the next part of the process.

Test
Decide the method by which the marketing team will gather results and feedback, whether by looking at sales figures or customer feedback, market share, impact on rivals or simple market research. In the past 20 years, the impact of online and digital resources have completely reinvented this stage and now almost real-time response is possible. Care must be taken not to misinterpret results or get lost in a mass of data.

Study
Analyse the results to understand if the plan worked and how it might be possible to improve it. This doesn't have to be post-mortem because of the more immediate nature of digital marketing as explained above: the test and study stages can happen simultaneously with each other or with the activation stage. Thinking and acting on the fly is the mark of a truly great marketer.

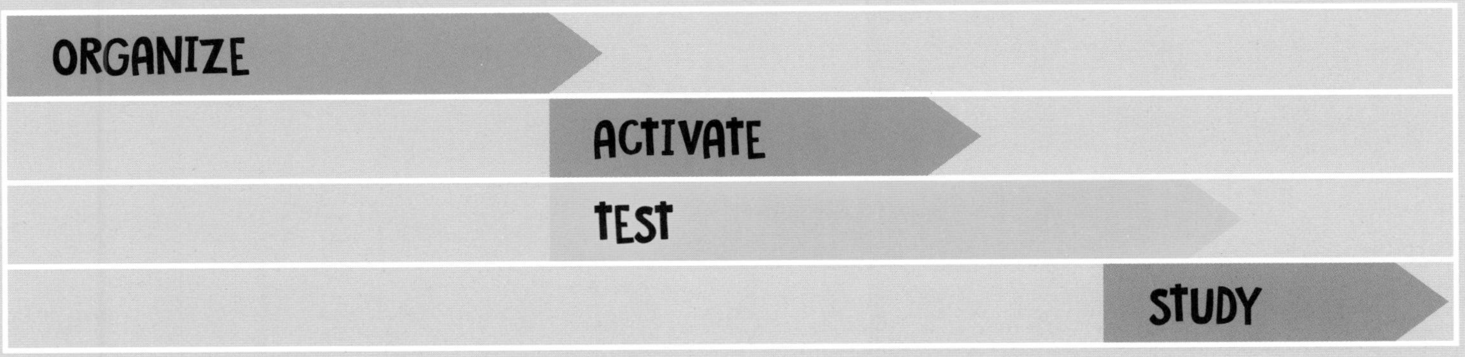

ORGANIZE

ACTIVATE

TEST

STUDY

ORIENTATION

An organization's marketing mix will also depend on its orientation. This is the decision they have made on how to focus their energies and resources. It's not the place of the marketing team to decide this but the truth is that while in the 20th century most groups were production or product oriented, in the 21st century the vast majority are marketing oriented.

ORIENTATIONS

Diagram showing various business orientations.

PRODUCTION ORIENTATION

The production-orientated organization is primarily concerned with efficiency: creating a product or service for the best possible price and then getting it to the consumer. Everything else is secondary. A company finds the cheapest materials and the most efficient design. The philosophy is that once you can offer that product, the customer will immediately buy and favour it. The advantage of this philosophy is its simplicity; while its obvious disadvantage is that it does not provide any knowledge of customers' actual needs, therefore making it impossible to build a relationship with them or improve their lives.

It's important to understand that some companies may seem entirely production oriented, but while for instance Henry Ford designed his assembly line to achieve maximum efficiency, using the fastest-drying paint etc, his primary focus was actually to get more people driving automobiles. To this end, as well as his production line, he established local dealers and automobile clubs across the USA and had a huge publicity department in his head office, all helping him achieve his business goals.

A production-oriented company will still use marketing. It's just that the focus will be entirely informational and any feedback received will be used to improve the efficiency of production more than any other element.

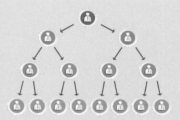

PRODUCT ORIENTATION

While production orientation is entirely fixated on price, product orientation is entirely focused on quality. Production-oriented organizations are constantly refining their business to produce the most efficient and therefore cheapest possible product, while a product-oriented group will refine their product to make it the best possible, regardless of price. Although it is called 'product-oriented' this can also be a service, for example, offering the most comfortable aeroplane journey possible.

In theory, this will give you an advantage over your competitors as your product will be superior and therefore more desirable, but history has shown that 'quality' is in fact a matter of perception and attempting to define or refine it without reference to external factors, i.e. the customer's wants and needs, will result in obsolescence and obscurity.

MARKET ORIENTATION

A market-oriented company begins by looking at the market: what people want, need or demand, particularly its target audience, and creates its product or service to those parameters. The customer is the most important element. If the customer wants the product to be cheap or conversely high quality then the elements of production or product orientation can be utilized but by analysing the market, an organization can ensure that what it offers will be popular and profitable.

This is not easy as the market is constantly changing and evolving and there is no magic formula, but standing still and waiting for the stars to align is a much less viable business model than seeing what you need to offer and then offering it. This is exacerbated by the increased flow of information in the digital age, meaning that if a company doesn't provide what their customers want, they can and will find an alternative quite quickly.

OTHER ORIENTATIONS

Organizations can adopt a sales-oriented approach, by which they use market research and other tactics to look at their possible customer base, and use it to exploit the consumer. This predatory technique is unfortunately not uncommon but it's also not particularly sustainable as aggrieved customers will inevitably create bad publicity and abandon the company. In short-term scams, like Ponzi or pyramid schemes, this is a common approach.

There is also a growing interest in a societal oriented approach, where the aim is to improve the world and society through your actions and in the hope that customers will support you and buy your products or services because you align with their personal philosophy or beliefs.

THE 4Ps

One of the best-known formulas in marketing are the 4Ps: this was an approach to marketing proposed by another of Harvard Business School's professors, E. Jerome McCarthy, back in the 1960s, and it's still very relevant to marketing today.

The 4Ps equate to Product, Price, Place and Promotion.

P1 Product

This is what the company sells in physical terms. It could be an actual item, such as food, drink, clothing, appliance and so on, or a service provided by the company.

The key to unlocking the value of this to the consumer is to find out what makes the product unique or special.

P2 Price

This is what the company charges for the goods or services. It sounds very simple. But the tricky bit is deciding the right price to charge.

It's a balancing act between finding a price that will not only drive sales but also make the most profit. Charge too much and fewer people can afford it, charge too little and it will drive more sales but a smaller profit.

Again, knowing how much the consumer values the product offered is the key to finding the right price.

P3 Place

This is where the consumer can find the product.

For consumer goods, this was once the shop, so juggling the costs of getting distribution to the right outlets for the brand needs further understanding, where the customers for it are located.

Today, more and more people are doing their shopping online, so the 'Place' is the website or browser that they are using. We will explore the intricacies of online and digital marketing in more depth later in the book.

P4 Promotion

Once the product is in place, the need is then to tell consumers how good it is, where to find it and how much it is, in other words promote the product. Advertising, PR, Point of Sale and many other tools are at the company's disposal, but we come back to the same conundrum, knowing the consumer is key to talking to them and sending the right messages to the right people.

E. Jerome McCarthy created the concept of the 4 Ps which continues to be implemented in one form or another to this day.

NAMES TO KNOW: E. JEROME MCCARTHY

Born on 20 February 1928, McCarthy began his studies at Northwestern University in Evanston, Illinois, eventually earning a PhD from the University of Minnesota with his dissertation **An Analysis of the Use of Marketing Research in Product Development**. *In 1959, he began working on mathematical models for marketing at MIT and Harvard Business School.*

He wanted to help advance the framework to think practically about the kind of problems that marketing managers frequently encountered and help solve them, as the predominant 'Functional' school of marketing thought was much more based on theory and analysis of the role of marketing in business. While the idea of a more managerial approach had been developed by others and was co-existing with the functional school, it was McCarthy's book **Basic Marketing: A Managerial Approach** *that introduced the idea of the 4Ps, with other chapters building on these ideas to create a kind of practical toolbox for any marketing manager. It was also noteworthy for bringing in elements of sociology and psychology in its analysis, whereas marketing thought mainly concentrated on economics. It was a huge success and updated editions were regularly produced by McCarthy and his co-author William D. Perreault, the most recent in 2013.*

Among his other work, he helped found the Michigan-specific Planned Innovation Institute and received the AMA (American Marketing Association) Trailblazer Award in 1987.

While the 4Ps allow people to simplify their thinking about marketing the application of them requires diligence. Making the 4Ps work effectively depends on one consistent mantra: 'Knowing and understanding to whom you are selling'. Companies invest millions in researching their consumers and their needs to get a better understanding of their preferences and lifestyles, and then when they plan their marketing mix it is a perfect fit for their brand.

Moving to the 7Ps

The 4Ps were a simple and effective springboard for most companies to conceptualize the right kind of marketing for their products, but other companies, particularly in the service sector, needed a system with more subtleties. With service companies in mind the 4Ps were reassessed in the early 1980s becoming the 7Ps, with People, Process and Physical Evidence being added to the original four.

P5 People

This is an essential ingredient for any marketing plan where there is no actual product, such as in the financial, hospitality and professional service industries. In these sectors, the people who work there are themselves the product. It's vital to make these workers, who are the face of the company to the consumer, feel an important part of the organization they represent.

P6 Process

Employees in the service industries actively carry out the interface between the company and the customer, so it's important that these key people understand the processes they need to perform when they represent the company. They should be fully aware of the strategic aims and vision of their employers so they can offer a friendly and efficient service to the customer.

P7 Physical evidence

It's not just about the people working in the service industries, it's also about the customer's environment. Physical evidence refers to all the other factors, from interior design and furnishings to the food or drinks that are served and even the uniforms. It could also mean anything the customer takes away from any establishment. Put simply, it's everything else that is not human.

Impact on service industry marketing

By adding these three extra Ps to the original four, service industry companies were now able to refine their marketing mix even further. As time has passed, however, many marketing theorists and managers felt that the

4 or 7Ps no longer reflected trends in business and society.

The 4Cs

In 1990, advertising educator Robert F. Lauterborn proposed that the 4Ps should evolve into the 4Cs.

C1 Consumer wants and needs

The increasing popularity of a market-focused business orientation led Lauterborn to conclude that focusing on what the consumer actually wants and needs would be a far more suitable first consideration. With market research and customer profiling, this is possible.

C2 Cost

The actual price of a product or service is only one part of any transaction or offer to the consumer. With the 4Cs model, cost is broken down into a number of different factors. The 'cost of time' when buying product or services, 'cost of conscience' or 'cost of guilt', for example, feeling regret for not treating their children to something nice. These factors all contribute to the overall 'cost of ownership'.

C3 Convenience

Convenience supplants 'Place' in this model because in the modern world people are not limited to going to the shops to buy their goods or services. Sometimes the opposite is true and physically going to a bricks-and-mortar

CONSUMER WANTS AND NEEDS ▶ *It's important to know the difference between a consumer 'need' and a 'want' when preparing a marketing plan.*

Need: a need can be a specific product or service, like essentials, food, drugs and household products. It can also relate to what the company is offering in the way of value regarding customer service, a fair price, even whether the consumer themselves feel valued.

Want: a want is a service or product that the consumer is prepared to buy but doesn't necessarily 'need'. Holidays, fashion, entertainment and luxury items all fall into this category, but again this could have an emotional value. In this instance, the consumer wanting to feel part of a particular brand has an emotional value and certain brands will cultivate this, fashion brands in particular.

Ultimate convenience

store is not possible. In the digital age there are so many places the consumer can go to get what they want or need. What once were mail order catalogues are now websites where consumers can shop and buy. Items can be ordered directly from tablets or smartphones or, in a brief marketing failure for Amazon, with the touch of a 'Dash' button. These developments make 'Place' virtually redundant so the ease of buying something becomes a matter of 'Convenience'.

C4 Communication

'Promotion' suggests one-way traffic between the company making and selling the product and the consumer, whereas 'Communication' suggests a much more interactive relationship, based on knowledge gained about the customer's lifestyle and needs. There is now a broader spectrum of different touchpoints between the company and its customers, including everything from traditional advertising messages to tightly targeted viral content.

Time never stands still in the minds of marketers. They are forever looking for and then exploring new and more precise ways to help companies form links between themselves and their consumer and even with other complimentary products. With this in mind, in 1979, the 4Cs in the 7Cs Compass Model was developed by Koichi Shimizu. It's a complex framework, including the 4Cs (consumer, cost, convenience and communication) and adding channel (the flow of goods), corporation and circumstances, that further advances the marketing possibilities for companies (see also Chapter Four pages 57–60).

BUSINESS INTERACTIONS

B2C is the most common model. **Business to Consumer** covers all marketing activity that takes place when companies are in the process of offering products or services to their prospective customers.

B2B or **Business to Business** is one company interacting with another company, or doing business with another. For example, a wholesale company wanting to sell to a retailer, or a financial body aiming to sell their services to a corporation.

C2C or **Consumer to Consumer** covers all marketing and sales activities between individuals, for example, if they want to sell their car or lawnmower online or even put a simple handwritten card in a shop window.

C2B, Consumer to Business, is the least common model but becoming increasingly relevant in the digital age. A prime example would be an online blogger encouraging companies to advertise on their page.

MARKETING MASTERSTROKES: THE COLA WARS

Long-term soft drink rivals the Coca-Cola Company and PepsiCo had traditionally traded marketing blows in direct competition for many decades. However, things came to a head in the late 1970s when the whole confrontation became more intense, a period known as the Cola Wars. Coca-Cola suddenly found it was losing share rapidly to Pepsi, particularly on its original Coca-Cola flagship brand. Pepsi had the upper hand, rolling out one innovative marketing ploy after another, they seemed smarter, more modern, more savvy marketeers.

The Pepsi Challenge in the mid-1970s, where consumers were asked to compare their cola to Coke's in a blind taste test, had a big impact. The Coca-Cola Company began to doubt its own products, not only were they losing brand share at an alarming rate to Pepsi, but also their own brand Diet Coke was cannibalizing the ubiquitous original Coca-Cola. They had to act, and act decisively. In April 1985, to a huge fanfare they launched a new formula for Coca-Cola commonly known as 'New Coke', by July of the same year they were forced to make an embarrassing U-turn back to the 'original' formula, such was the backlash from their loyal customers. The old formula was relaunched under the banner 'Coca-Cola Classic'

The status quo was immediately re-established, Coca-Cola was back in all its brand leader glory. It has

Pepsi and Coke's marketing conflict was dubbed 'The Cola Wars'

been suggested that the Coca-Cola Company deliberately planned the formula change as a ploy to outrage their consumers only to 'save the day' by bringing it back, though of course they deny this. Accident or marketing masterstroke?

THE WALT DISNEY COMPANY

Walt Disney understood the power of imagination and consumer engagement in creating a brand.

WALT DISNEY is such a ubiquitous brand that writing a brand biography of them seems to be unnecessary. The all-conquering Disney logo has dominated global culture for almost an entire century. In October 1923, brothers Walt and Roy Disney started the Disney Brothers Cartoon Studio and for the next few decades the name Disney became synonymous with breakthrough animated and live action movie entertainment. While Roy took care of the business end of things, Walt's imagination, coupled with some of the world's finest animators and film-makers, created blockbuster family entertainment. Walt Disney was not content to just make films; he designed theme parks and filled them with his most famous characters so children and their parents could experience what he called 'The Magic of Disney' in person.

In 1986, 20 years after Walt's death, his and Roy's animation company had become The Walt Disney Company. It is very difficult separate the man from the brand, both in name and vision, but the exponential growth since then is down to shrewd business acumen and imaginative marketing. Roy died in 1971 and the Disney brand was struggling to reach its undoubted potential in the mid-1980s, until Michael Eisner took up the reins and the company's

This statue in Walt Disney World shows how Disney's image is equally as venerated as his creation, Mickey Mouse.

These Mickey Mouse themed Campbell's soup cans show a Andy Warhol-style intersection of high and low art.

renaissance was set in motion. Apart from acquiring other leading film companies such as Pixar, Marvel Studios, 20th Century and Lucasfilm, the latter giving them control of the blockbuster *Star Wars* franchise, the Disney brand has diversified into everything from TV channels to toys, holidays and gaming. They are major players in broadcasting, owning news channel ABC, sports channel ESPN, National Geographic and direct to consumer streaming services, such as Disney+, Hulu and Hotstar. Disney Parks, Experiences and Products is a group of 14 theme parks, resort hotels and cruise liners.

The upshot of their astonishing rise to the top of the marketing pile is that in 2020 their assets were valued at $201.55 billion with a global revenue of $63.39 billion – not bad for an idea that started life as a little animated mouse sailing a steamboat.

Merchandise is available for almost the characters from Disney's many animated productions

JOBS IN MARKETING

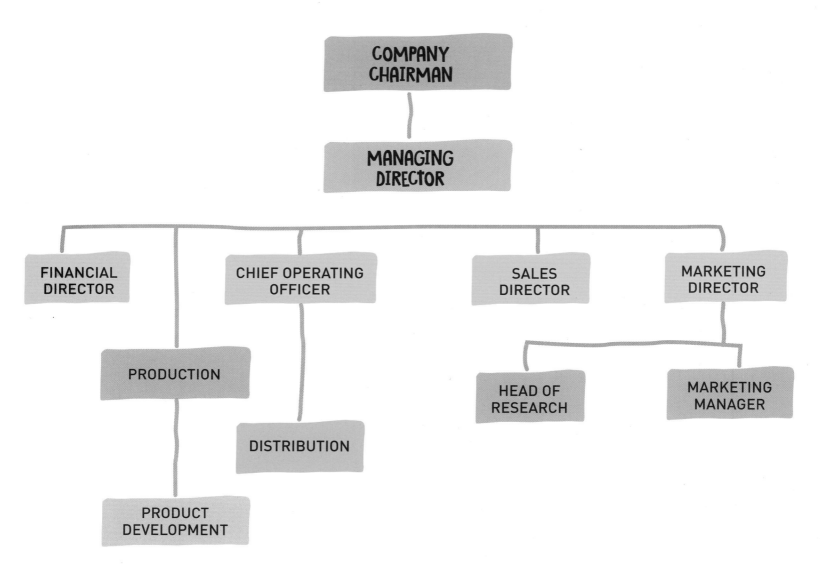

In companies that sell products or services:

Marketing manager – the bottom rung of the marketing ladder for marketing departments in companies.

Marketing director – oversees the managers and directs strategies.

Chief marketing director – the overall boss overseeing the activities of the company's marketing strategies both locally and internationally.

Social media manager – in charge of company's presence on sites such as Facebook, Twitter, Instagram etc.

Search engine optimization specialist – uses keywords, design and positioning to ensure the company comes first on any relevant search.

Email marketing manager – controls and co-ordinates email campaigns, offers and feedback.

Web content writer – writes copy for web content on websites, social media and some advertising.

Web producer – creates content for online promotion, whether it's videos, banner ads or other images or clips intended to go viral

Product manager – oversees distribution and promotion of the product as well as consulting on packaging design and any new product developments.

Marketing analyst – analyses a company or organization's campaign either during or after execution. Also gathers information about trends in marketing and buying, consult with marketing teams and help create marketing mixes.

Public relations manager – deals with PR as well as liaising with media outlets to manage press releases and news.

Brand manager – Looks after the decisions on one specific brand.

Media buyer – Negotiates with the media outlets for the best rates for clients.

Chief marketing officer – Oversees all marketing decisions for brands.

Digital marketing manager – Manages day-to-day operations concerning digital programmes.

Digital marketing director – Oversees digital operations.

eCommerce manager – Concerned with financial operations related to digital marketing.

Summary

Getting to the right marketing mix is a quest undertaken by every company trying sell their wares to the consumer. There is no magic formula, and each product or service will require the same rigour in the pursuit of a successful marketing campaign. Getting to know what makes the customer tick will give a marketer the vital insights that they can turn into great strategies. This was perfectly summed up by management consultant Peter Drucker, when he said, 'The aim of marketing is to know and understand the customer so well the product or service fits him and sells itself'.

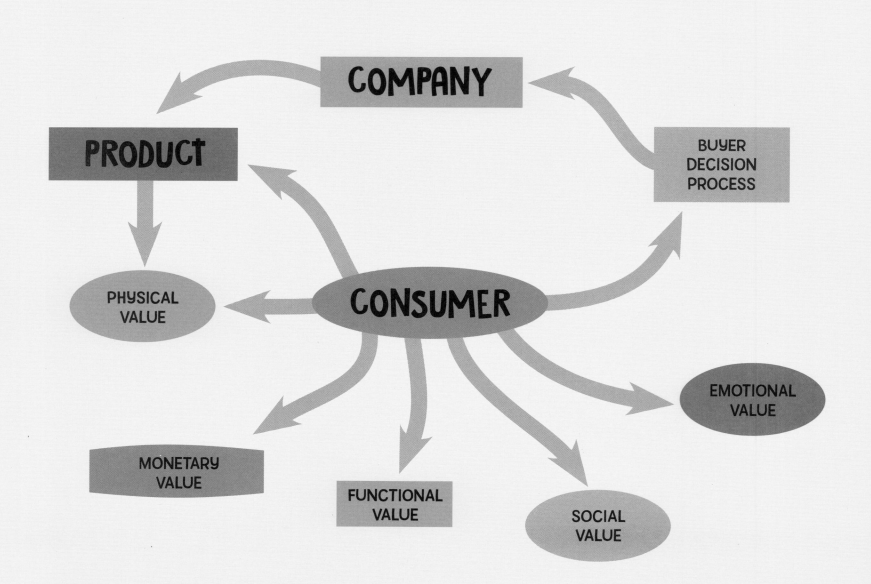

WHAT IS VALUE?

When people start to think about marketing a company, a product or a service, one of the first questions they will ask themselves is: what is its value? This is a multifaceted question that faces every marketer, because they are not just dealing with selling their wares at the right price, but also how the marketing decisions they make will affect the company's worth in both the short and long term. It's a fact that very few of the world's leading companies' CEOs started out in marketing departments. More often than not, they come from a financial background. A CEO's goal is to make the company he or she runs as valuable and as profitable as possible in order to keep the shareholders as happy as possible, and thereby keep their jobs. But it can be argued that the shareholder value of a company is not built in the finance department but in the marketing department. As we have established in the previous chapters, the key to any successful company is building a strong and lasting relationship with its customers, by understanding their wants and needs and delivering the goods and/or services to meet them.

The importance of value

THE VALUE PROPOSITION

Building a value proposition for a product or service will allow a company to market their brand successfully. To achieve this, a company will need to bring together a number of elements. Initially, they must access the resources and information they already have, the product or service itself and the value of that in physical terms i.e. cost of raw materials, production, packaging, distribution and marketing.

Then they will need to find out what the product is worth to the consumer, not just in its functional worth but its emotional or psychological value as well. The product will also have a social value, for example, when the consumer buys the item: how does it make them look to their friends and family? The worth of the brand's image must also be considered.

The Heinz baked bean can design has barely changed over the last century. Own brand products like Sainsbury's beans sometimes try to ape famous brands as much as is legally possible.

VALUE MAP

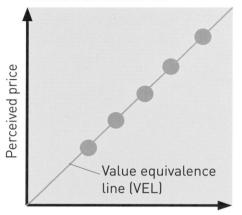

Stable market shares

Perceived price

Customer-perceived benefits

Value equivalence line (VEL)

Customer value = perceived benefits minus perceived price

Graph showing how you can calculate a product's value position in the market.

Defining value

ELEMENTS OF A VALUE PROPOSITION/MODEL

Physical value – a breakdown of all the costs involved in producing, distributing and promoting the product.

Monetary value (or Consumer Perceived Value) – what the product is worth to the consumer measured against products of a similar type.

Functional value – what it's worth to the consumer in terms of its usefulness to them.

Social value – how owning a product or using a service makes the consumer look to their peers, friends or family.

Psychological or emotional value – how the consumer feels about themselves when they buy or use the product.

Mobile phones represent many different aspects of value.

A tech company wants to launch its latest smartphone, called the Smarter phone. The company is not the brand leader in this field but believes that its new device has some features that will make it competitive.

First of all they have to work out the **physical value** of the new product, given that they have invested a lot in creating the new features while knowing that they cannot over-price it as they are perceived as a cheaper alternative

THE SMARTER PHONE

Physical value

Functional value

Social value

Perceived value

Psychological value

to the leading brand. They feel that if they price it at 10 per cent under the cost of their more expensive rival it will be competitive as the new phone actually has more features to offer.

This is intended to achieve two things: to appeal to their existing customers who will feel they are getting even more for their money, and possibly give them a chance to mop up any consumers who had bought the rival's product but felt they were not getting good value just for buying a name. In this way, the **perceived value** would be enhanced.

The new features will give the buyer increased usability so the product's **functional value** would be greater than their last offering or that of their rivals. Buyers would enjoy showing off their new phone to friends and family, safe in the knowledge that although their device doesn't have the fashionable cache of its rival, its state-of-the-art features can outperform it, giving the owner greater **social value**.

In turn, this will give the buyer **psychological value**, because not only have they got a great new smartphone with features that outstrip anyone else's and therefore feel they have made a great purchase for less money, it also makes them look shrewd and up-to-date.

There is also a further consideration when creating the value proposition: the value to business partners. By creating a product that will offer 'more for less' their business partners will also benefit both financially and psychologically as they pass on the new product to customers through their concessions.

LUCOZADE

FIRST CREATED IN NEWCASTLE in 1927 by chemist William Walker Hunt, the drink originally known as Glucozade has been through several brand shifts, managing to survive the changing modern landscape. Originally only available in its iconic orange coloured fizzy variety, Lucozade was sold as a drink to be given to the sick to help them feel better, using the slogan 'Lucozade aids recovery'. Rather than a recreational soft drink like Coca Cola, it was treated like a medicinal tonic, sold in large utilitarian glass bottles.

However, this brand identity began to lose profitability for several reasons. Its association with sickness meant it had strong negative connotations, and furthermore Britain was becoming healthier overall due to improved diets and the establishment of the National Health Service (NHS) in 1948. By the 1970s, profits were down considerably and the decision was taken to rebrand. The first attempt, in 1978, to sell Lucozade as a 'pick me up' wasn't hugely successful, although profits remained high enough that they could continue to manufacture and sell it.

It was the second rebranding, in 1983, that charted its new course. This time Lucozade was promoted as a sports drink with the slogan 'Lucozade replaces lost energy'. This new, more positive spin on its benefits was bolstered by a total pack redesign that favoured sleek curves and a bright plastic wrapper. Furthermore, the use of famous athletes, like gold-medal winning Olympian Daley Thompson, meant it was now a brand with aspirational tones rather than one with a link with illness.

This ad from the 1950s shows Lucozade's original market positioning as a palliative care drink.

They slowly introduced new flavours into the range and redesigned the packaging again in 1996, but the overall idea of Lucozade as essentially the first modern 'energy drink' remained. Later on, its health benefits began to be questioned, due to the massive amounts of sugar that the drink contained. Consequently they split the line between the soft-drink oriented Lucozade with its many diverse flavours, and the 'isotonic' Lucozade Sports with sweeteners and another redesigned bottle.

Today, Lucozade is owned by Suntory Ltd, a large Japanese conglomerate, and faces a lot of competition from caffeine-based energy drink brands such as Red Bull and Monster, but its past rebrands show that it's too early to count it out of the race.

This dynamic modern ad is more lifestyle based but still promotes the energy proposition of Lucozade.

John Dewey's studies had a much broader scope than marketing but that is where his ideas have endured the longest.

The stages that a buyer goes through as they decide to purchase has been formalized in the **buyer decision process**, originally introduced by educational reformer John Dewey in his 1910 book *How We Think*. Obviously, a lot has changed in over a hundred years and other psychologists and marketers have expanded on his original observations but the basic principles remain true:

Problem/need recognition Realize or acknowledge the problem to be solved (e.g. need warmer winter clothing) or the need to be met (food, entertainment etc).

Evaluation of alternatives Examine all the possible purchase options for this particular problem or need. This encompasses both variations within a particular solution (different brands of soup, for example) and different solutions for a particular problem (buying thicker gloves vs buying an electric handwarmer).

Purchase decision Choosing the particular purchase. Keep in mind that the idea of this being entirely motivated by one particular need, or an entirely clear-headed logical choice, is a fallacy. Any decision is influenced by a wide variety of factors, including the opinions of friends, families and public figures you admire, previous experiences with products and sudden changes in personal or financial circumstances.

Post-purchase behaviour Obviously post-purchase behaviour depends on whether the product has met the need or solved the problem, but it also depends on the customer's feeling of worth and anything that may have happened during the transaction. Understanding post-purchase care and support and alleviating any feelings of dissonance is often what separates a successful product or service from a failed one. It could be elements of the packaging that directly offers the customer help, or the creation of a special online support and aftercare service.

After-sales customer care

NAMES TO KNOW: PROFESSOR PETER DOYLE

While not famous outside the industry Peter Doyle is considered by many marketers to be one of the most influential thinkers.

Peter Doyle was considered by many of his peers to be a marketing tour de force and was influential in helping many of the UK's leading companies shape their destinies. Born in Widnes, Lancashire in 1943, he followed a grammar school education with a first-class degree in Economics at Manchester University. Further academic success followed with a Masters, then he completed his PHD at Carnegie Mellon University in Pittsburgh. He was swiftly sought out for lecturing appointments in the UK, Europe and the USA, before his appointment to the chair at Bradford University management centre, all before the age of 30.

He went on to oversee the marketing courses at INSEAD, Stanford and Warwick. His unique style had a huge impact on the students he taught, many of whom went on to lead some of the world's top companies. His research and lectures focused on the effect of marketing on an organization's success, and had a lasting impact on the industry.

Doyle's reputation as an original thinker was enhanced by his lectures and the many books he wrote on the subject of marketing. He went on to win numerous awards for his work from the American Marketing Association, the European Marketing Academy and the Academy of Marketing, and was twice winner of the president's medal of the Operational Research Society. He was also a newspaper columnist for the Guardian, and acted as an advisor to Cadbury Schweppes, Coca-Cola, KPMG, IBM, the Cabinet Office, the Institute of Directors, and the Confederation of British Industries, among others. His last book, before his untimely death at the age of 59 in 2003, was Value Based Marketing and drew a quote from Philip Kotler, who described it as, 'Destined to spark a revolution in marketing.'

OMNIPRESENT ACROSS THE UK and expanding worldwide, John Mills Limited (JML) was created in 1986 by its titular founder. It began as a small family company operating out of a basement with only a handful of employees, primarily concentrating on demonstrating its products live at homeware fairs (like the Ideal Home Exhibition) and other gatherings where they could demonstrate their merchandise to an interested audience. JML's main aim was to sell its products in a retail environment, but rather than simply putting them on the shelves of a shop, it found a way to retain the core of its 'live demonstration' model and make the brand stand out by creating a distinctive TV concession stand.

In the early days, this meant one of their employees literally driving from retailer to retailer with VHS units in the back of his car, convincing them to accept the promotional unit in their shop. Once there, it acted as a virtual live promotion, each product having its own custom-made video

JML launched an 'inventor's day' in Feb 2020 to find 'Britain's next big innovation'.

JML creator John Mills has also founded the John Mills Charitable Trust, which supports research causes.

demonstration. The products JML sells are primarily designed as assistance tools and are of particular help to people with compromised physicality, such as pensioners and those with disabilities.

JML also aligned itself with business partners with a similar customer profile such as Boots, Robert Dyas and Wilko. All their products are very competitively priced and they are famed for their selling sting 'And all for only something.99!' Many people are mistaken in the belief that JML buy cheap products from mass production centres abroad, but the truth is that the majority of their offerings are manufactured by themselves and they invest vast sums in rigorous research and testing.

JML are renowned for retailing unique and intriguing gadgets, and are constantly approached by inventors from across the world who know the company's reputation for adopting innovative ideas and designs. Even the company's executives have added ideas to the inventory, like CEO Ken Daly. He has been involved with the company almost since its inception, and its big-selling Copper Stone Pan is his brainchild. He was quoted as saying 'Honestly, it will be the best pan you have ever used, I am evangelical about these pans. It's just a brilliant product.'

JML's Rocky Mountain tumbler boasts that it keeps drinks hot or cold for longer than its competitors.

JML has distribution networks in as many as 70 countries. It's also one of the companies for which the Covid-19 pandemic has actually been a boon, with eCommerce demand surging over a three-month period, particularly through their own website. With the populace spending more time at home and therefore having greater exposure to their marketing, they saw sales increase by 20 per cent in August 2020 compared with the same month the year before.

THE BUYER DECISION PROCESS

The process that the buyer goes through before making a choice to buy involves a number of different variables.

THE BUYER DECISION PROCESS: AN EXAMPLE

Problem/need recognition A customer's trainers are old and worn. He has received some money as a birthday gift and decides to replace them. The problem here is not having footwear, either for exercise, relaxation or fashion.

Evaluation of alternatives There's a massive variety of types of trainer to choose from, from more practical/cheap options to high-profile brands and exclusive limited-edition designs. Which option is best depends on the intended purpose and the customer's opinions and values. There is also a wide variety of ways to purchase the trainers. He could use a large 'sports-fashion' retailer with bricks-and-mortar locations or an online version of the same. However, he could instead go through smaller 'boutique' online retailers that are specifically designed to sell only trainers, with special deals and exclusive 'drops' of cool designs. If budget is an issue, there is a large second-hand resale market in trainers as well.

Purchase decision The customer finds the trainer that's the type they want and within their budget. However, if they are particularly taken by a brand or design they might stretch the amount they will spend on them. They will, of course, look for a deal as well so they can maximize their purchasing power.

Post-purchase behaviour Once they are the owners of a new pair of trainers the purchaser could display a number of different attitudes. If the trainers were for a functional need, for instance sport, they will use them for that activity but will also be aware that their peers will be watching and judging them by both performance and brand choice. If the trainers were bought for fashion then they will be keen to show them off to friends and will be happy if they get commented on.

Summary

Value is something beyond a mere perception of price, it has emotional, social and psychological connotations. A company must understand every facet of the value of their product to the consumer even before they manufacture it and certainly before they market it. It is no coincidence the when we talk about humanity we talk in terms of 'human values' and it is these that the marketer should study before they make any offering to the consumer.

Chapter Four
MARKETING ECONOMICS

The Market • The 7Cs Compass Model • Chocolate Bar
Economics • The Economic Divide • Business Models
• Supply and Demand • Comparative Advantage

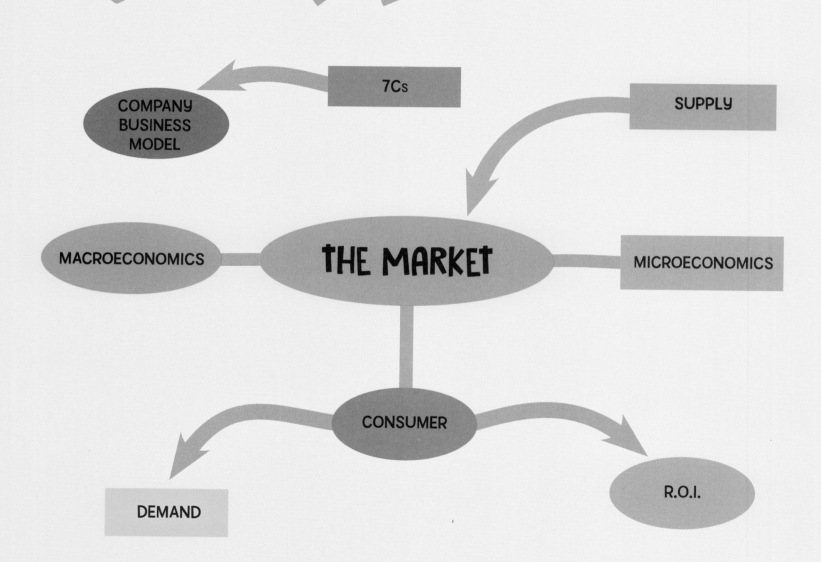

THE MARKET

As marketing is primarily about understanding money and value, a basic knowledge of marketing economics is essential to any kind of success in the field. Key to economics is the concept of 'the market'.

The marketer has to weigh up all the factors that will influence their business model, from getting the right price for their wares to securing a financially viable conduit for the resources they need to make their products or services happen.

Suffice to say there is no such thing as a completely free market, even in the most capitalist countries' government regulations will have an impact on the marketers' economic decisions.

Essentially, marketing and economics go hand in hand in the laissez-faire economic system in which a large part of the Free World operates, where consumers and their buying habits are the major influencer.

The world of marketing thrives within **free market systems,** which is defined by what the consumer is prepared to pay for goods or services and what the producer is prepared to accept.

The multinational world of marketing means that companies not only have to operate within their own countries' systems but that of many different nations and societies, and this has a profound effect on their business model.

Whatever business model companies choose to adopt for their goods or services, they have to factor in the nuances of each market in which they operate and sell their products. Inevitably, the marketers will go back to the formulas that served them well when drawing up their marketing mix.

THE MARKET ▶ *The possible audience or customer base for a particular product or service.*
▶ *The business or trade in a particular product.*

The laissez-faire system

A physiocrat gathering in 18th century Paris. The group developed the ideas behind the philosphy of laissez-faire economics

LAISSEZ-FAIRE ECONOMICS

▶ *A political philosophy frequently adopted by the free market economy. It was developed by a group of French economists (known as the physiocrats) in the 18th century in the belief that economic success was more probable if governments stayed out of the business sector.*

The many kinds of markets

DEFINING MARKETS

Markets can be defined by a wide variety of factors and boundaries:

Consumer: age, gender, economic status, social status, religion, interests, medical or psychological requirements.

Product or service: cost, type, availability, manufacturing technique, rarity, volatility, portability.

Location: country, continent, culture, government.

Process: speculation, regulation.

The 7Ps or 7Cs are a reliable way to assess a company's business model, which will in turn decide their economic strategy.

THE 7CS COMPASS MODEL

A sound economically based model analysis tool is the 7Cs Compass Model developed by Koichi Shimizu in 1979. It varies from and expands on Lauterborn's 4Cs (see pages 35–6) in interesting ways.

C1 Corporation

The factors here are the company's competitors, its own organization and investors, but also compliance with laws and regulations and its accountability, not just to the business but to its customers. Each one of these elements will have an economic consequence on both its ability to sell its products or services and on its profits. Any spending should be weighed up and balanced against these factors when constructing a business model.

For instance, your fiercest competitor decides to lower the price of their offering. Does your business model have the flexibility for you to either: follow suit and find yourself involved in a price war, or stick to your guns and hope the quality you offer and the loyalty your customers have to the brand will maintain your profit margin?

C1 **Corporation**

C2 Commodity

C2 Commodity

This means the product or service the company is offering. It's not uncommon for companies to redesign their products according to the strength of the consumers wants and needs, and this is an economic conundrum of its own. If too much is invested in a change of direction, the need to recoup the costs will put unwanted pressure on the brand and could be disquieting for investors.

C3 Cost

Cost doesn't just cover manufacturing and sales, but also the cost to the consumer, both monetary and socially. Consumers have choices to make when they are buying and their own economic circumstances can come into play, so if that particular month they are shorter of cash than normal it will test their loyalty to the name brand they prefer and they might go for a cheaper option. Similarly, if they find themselves part of a different social scene, this will have an impact on the brands with which they associate.

C3 Cost

C4 Channel

Finding the correct marketing channel for a company's products or services is a hugely important factor, beyond simply the flow of goods. Consumers can operate on many levels, from their own personal preferences to the categories and demographics they occupy.

Identifying their target consumer and the group they fit into will help the marketer find the right distribution channel through which to promote their goods and services. For example, there is very little point in advertising video games in a commercial break during an old black-and-white movie, and conversely, it's not profitable to put messages about equity release schemes in a movie about teenage superheroes.

C4 Channel

C5 Communication

C5 Communication

Communication can range from advertising and promotional messaging from companies to the way they maintain their image among their own staff. An internal campaign promoting the image they want their workers to adopt on behalf of the company that employs them can be just as effective in communicating the value of the brand as any campaign directed at the consumer.

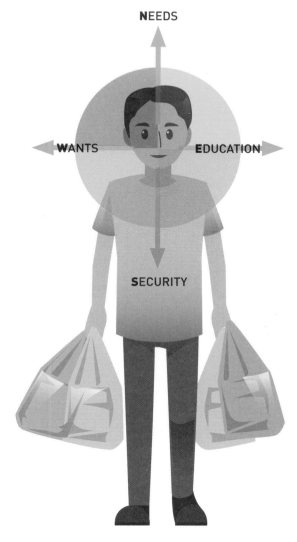

NEEDS

WANTS

EDUCATION

SECURITY

C6 Consumer

Illustrating the compass model

C6 Consumer

It is from this section that Shimizu's model gets its name, the direction of the points of the compass that indicate the consumers' particular circumstances and environments:

- **N = Needs**

This is what the consumer actually needs in their life, not merely physical needs like food, medicine and so on, but their emotional needs too, such as how they exist within their communities and social groups.

- **S = Security**

This does not just refer to physical well-being but also how comfortable the consumer feels in their life.

- **E = Education**

This includes schooling and learning but also life lessons and gathered experiences.

- **W = Wants**

Depending on financial and personal circumstance, once consumers' basic needs have been met, they can have more choice in the products and services they buy and companies have to be aware of what these are.

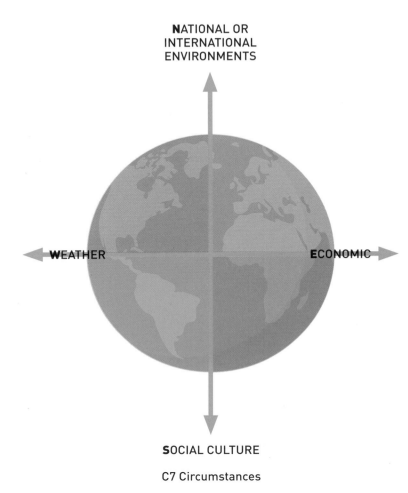

NATIONAL OR
INTERNATIONAL
ENVIRONMENTS

WEATHER

ECONOMIC

SOCIAL CULTURE

C7 Circumstances

C7 Circumstances

These refer to the circumstances surrounding companies that they often have little or no control over but are essential to consider. These could have a profound effect on their business:

- **N = National and/or international environments**
  This might be anything from the political landscape, legal machinations or even ethical influences like diversity and employment.

- **S = Social and cultural**
  Changes in society can be unpredictable as social trends change on a daily basis. Cultural differences are just as volatile, especially in the digital age where social media can be more powerful than the recognized media outlets. The proliferation of 'fake news' has become a potent part of the modern phenomenon that is social media and adds to the difficulties in predicting how consumers will react next.

- **E = Economic**
  The economic markets are a roller-coaster ride for many companies and are influenced by the same things that affect everyone. Political and social change, especially global events and upheaval, are practically impossible to forecast. Companies have to have economic plans in place to protect themselves from unforeseen circumstances.

- **W = Weather**
  This may surprise people by its inclusion as it's only become more relevant since 1979. Climate change has had a massive impact on the lives of people around the globe and consequently on companies' plans to meet consumers needs and wants.

CHOCOLATE BAR ECONOMICS

Price: Raw materials? Demand? Supply? Quality? Packaging? Distribution? Can it be manufactured in the country? If not, import cost? Manufacturing machine costs? Labour costs?

Target demographic: Children (laws sometimes apply) adults, a treat, healthy, luxury or cheap item.

Promotion costs: Advertising, sponsorship, shopper marketing, price incentives (money off, BOGOF).

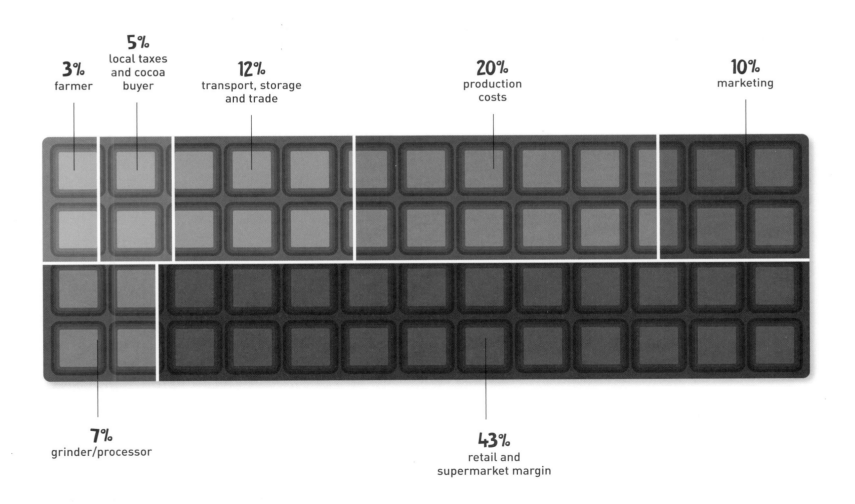

3%
farmer

5%
local taxes
and cocoa
buyer

12%
transport, storage
and trade

20%
production
costs

10%
marketing

7%
grinder/processor

43%
retail and
supermarket margin

THE ECONOMIC DIVIDE

Economics is commonly divided into two disciplines: microeconomics and macroeconomics.

Microeconomics is primarily concerned with individuals and small organizations. This reflects the smaller nature of the amounts of demand and supply being allocated by these people or groups, based on personal budgeting.

Macroeconomics, as is reflected in the name, deals with the larger issues up to and including the behaviour of huge corporations, governments and other society-spanning groups. While issues like inflation, levels of employment and growth (both financial and social) are primarily covered in macroeconomics and not microeconomics, the two disciplines are intertwined and affect each other.

For example, a financial downturn will affect the money an individual has to allocate for items beyond basic needs like rent and food, while on the macro level if enough people or firms lose confidence in a particular large organization or government it can have huge ramifications.

For most organizations' marketing mixes it would make sense to concentrate on microeconomics as that is more concerned with the behaviour of the consumer. However, macroeconomic consequences can have a huge impact, whether it's on the type of tone that's appropriate for a campaign or even the information distribution and gathering abilities you have. B2B or B2G organizations, in particular, have to pay close attention to these elements.

Micro versus macro is not a case of many boats on one ocean as much as it is an ocean composed entirely of boats instead of water.

Large international corporations

Countries

Governments

Taxation

Global policies

Large international non-profit organizations

Individuals

Families

Small organizations

Personal budgets

Personal beliefs and decisions

MICROECONOMICS

MACROECONOMICS

Micro versus macroeconomics,

BUSINESS MODELS

This is the blueprint of the structured principles and methods an organization chooses to produce and from which they receive value. This can include their purpose of existence, how they operate, who they target, what they can offer, business strategies they pursue, how their company is constructed and locates materials, and other processes. It can also encompass a company's ethos and brand. Elements such as orientation and marketing mix can play a role in the design and fulfilment of a group's business model.

Here are details of some of the most important business models:

Bricks and mortar

Bricks and mortar

One of the earliest retail business models, this refers to a business selling its wares and services in a physical location, either a shop on the high street or in other locations. In the past, it would also be used to refer to a company with factories or other production facilities as well as storage warehouses. However, in the 21st century, it's primarily used to differentiate companies with no significant online retail presence from companies that have one, and that concentrate only on in-person customer interaction, which is increasingly rare. This is especially true because companies with only physical selling locations were hugely endangered by the retail apocalypse that was prompted by companies like Amazon looking to disintermediate the market (an action taken by a company to circumnavigate middlemen in the supply chain, thus allowing them to provide goods or services directly to the consumer).

Bricks and clicks

This is now a much more common business model, being a company with both a physical and a virtual/online presence. This can be implemented through a custom website, an app for mobiles or tablets, or sometimes still ordering by telephone. The proliferation of the internet made this an extremely viable

Bricks and clicks

option for companies as they would already have access to the stock and usually some distribution/delivery method, or as an alternative the customer could order online and then collect from the physical location (known in the UK as 'click and collect'). Most formerly retail/physical companies have adopted this model so as to remain competitive with purely online retailers, and some retailers have abandoned their physical locations to become purely online.

Subscription/servitisation

As the name indicates, this business model is designed around people paying for the regular provision of a particular product or service. In the 19th and 20th centuries and sometimes earlier this would be a regular

Subscription/servitization

newspaper or magazine, mail order book or music clubs, or in some cases access to a particular location like a gym. Later, telephone companies and cable and satellite television providers would use these models. However, in the 1980s and beyond, subscription has sometimes become **servitization**, the model by which product sellers can provide extras (whether it's customer support, tailored insurance or other benefits) that complement the product. Companies like Apple and Rolls Royce use this to build brand loyalty. However, more predatory companies can use subscription in a deceptive way, in the case of early 'apps' that represented themselves as one-time purchases but were in fact a monthly subscription that the hopefully confused user would forget to cancel.

Freemium

This is an ugly portmanteau of the words 'free' and 'premium', possibly deliberate as it is frequently used as a pejorative term due to its controversial nature. It denotes when a product or service is provided for no cost, with a monetary premium charged for extra elements, whether it be extra features,

Freemium

additional services or other actual goods. This model has existed in some form in the software industry since the early 1980s. However, advances in digital distribution over the past 15 years has led to a massive expansion in its use by the developers of online games, phone games and apps. Much criticism has been given to games that have specifically been designed to try and 'hook' their user on the experience so that when a certain imaginary currency runs out they will pay premium prices to keep playing.

Franchising

This business model is usually adopted by a successful company that wants rapid expansion of their business or brand, and so will allow other companies or individuals to take on the licence of a service, skill or product they own and sell it themselves. Instead of the original company risking their own capital expanding their brand, they will let others take the risk and reap the benefits in return for fees or a share of the profits, and at a lesser risk. The franchiser always holds the legal advantage over the franchisee, so it is not an equal partnership per se. However, there are some risks involved, for instance when the franchisee does not uphold the values of the original brand it can have a detrimental effect. Prime examples of the franchise business model are fast food companies like McDonalds and Burger King.

Franchising

Peer-to-peer

The P2P or peer-to-peer model is where two individuals deal directly with one another, be it sales or distribution. It can cover any number of business situations that involve direct interaction between two persons or companies without the involvement of a third party. For example, it could be a bespoke furniture producer who will only deal with commissioned pieces. Companies such as eBay and Gumtree fall under this category, although they also sometimes facilitate business to consumer transactions too.

Peer-to-peer

Razor and blades

Razor and blade

This business gets its name from the proverbial saying, 'Give em the razor, sell'em the blades', and is associated with King Camp Gillette who invented the safety razor, although he didn't originate this business model.

In essence, it describes a principle where one item is sold cheaper or even given for free in order to support sales of a complimentary product. For example, shoe polish being given to customers who buy shoes, or free software for a computer. It's not the same as free sample marketing, which doesn't depend on a complimentary product. Razor and blade is also known in some contexts as the Aftermarket.

Multi-brand

The aim of companies that adopt the multi-brand model is to try and get the lion's share of the shelf space. They will not only produce their own unique offerings but echo their competitors, creating 'me-too' products in order to dominate the market and the shelves. It's a strategy that aims for market saturation but is not without risk as the 'me-too' products can lack the quality or provenance of their rivals. Groups such as Unilever, Kellogg's and Procter & Gamble are all big players in this business model, but it also covers virtual/software companies like Google and Adobe. This can even extend to the creation of 'blocking brands', which are designed not even necessarily for profit but as an obstacle to their competitors. For example, when Crystal Pepsi (a colourless cola) was introduced, Coca-Cola brought out Tab Clear, a similarly colourless drink but with a diet emphasis. Both products failed, but years later a former Coca-Cola marketing executive claimed their product was only intended to crash the Pepsi product by implying it was diet when it wasn't.

Multi-brand

NAMES TO KNOW: MILTON FRIEDMAN

Milton Friedman's creation of Monetarism changed the world, and polarised opinion for decades.

Milton Friedman was born in Brooklyn, New York on 31 July 1912 to a Hungarian-Jewish family. Friedman studied at Rutgers University, Columbia University, and the University of Chicago. For 30 years, he was a prominent member of the Chicago School of Economics, working alongside the Nobel prize-winning empirical economist George Stigler.

Friedman believed in monetarism, the theory that it was the government's role to control the amount of money in circulation. He supported the printing of the same low rate of money each year rather than a different amount each year. He was a strong believer in free-market capitalism and advocated for it in all his work.

During the 1970s, Milton Friedman's idea of monetarism gained popularity and in the 1980s he became an economic advisor to both Ronald Reagan and Margaret Thatcher.

Friedman believed that the government control over the economy should be limited. He supported cutting taxes, lowering government spending, getting rid of laws that limited the economy and letting parents choose which school received their tax money.

A colourful public figure, Friedman's main books were Capitalism and Freedom *and* Free to Choose. *Friedman's work was criticized by economist Paul Krugman who said, '... He slipped all too easily into claiming both that markets always work and that only markets work. It's extremely hard to find cases in which Friedman acknowledged the possibility that markets could go wrong, or that government intervention could serve a useful purpose.'*

Friedman was quoted as saying, 'The great virtue of a free market system is that it does not care what colour people are; it does not care what their religion is; it only cares whether they can produce something you want to buy.'

67

In 2020 an unanticipated shift in the level of demand due to the pandemic led to temporary shortages of common products such as toilet paper and flour.

ENGEL'S LAW

A good example of how economic insight can benefit a marketing plan is Engel's law. This theory, developed in 1857 by German statistician Ernst Engel, was based

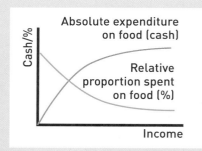

Graph illustrating Engel's law.

on an extensive study he made of household budgets. He found that as the income of a household increases, the percentage of income allocated for food purchases actually decreases, while the percentage assigned to other goods, from health to leisure activities and other luxuries, increases. While this may seem counterintuitive, the overall amount of money being spent on food still goes up, it's just that other items are now considered to be more viable. By using this law and the statistical 'shape' of its effects, known as Engel's curve, we can predict how consumers may choose to spend their money in various different economic and social circumstances and plan products and marketing based on that.

SUPPLY AND DEMAND

Fundamental to both microeconomics and marketing is the model of 'supply and demand'. On the most basic level, these are the factors that determine how organizations set their prices. In a 'perfect competition' environment, the demand for goods and services perfectly matches the supply, is a state that is called 'equilibrium'. However, equilibrium is a theoretical construct as it's impossible for a perfect competition environment (where all organizations have equal access and knowledge and resources) to exist. So, in reality the two factors frequently fluctuate.

When demand outstrips supply there is a shortage and prices increase. When supply exceeds demand it leads to a surplus and prices drop.

When demand exceeds supply new markets are often created. Organizations will then move to exploit this, but, of course, this leads to greater provision and so it swings back the other way.

Demand curves are invariably downward sloping but for some products the opposite is true. 'Veblen goods', named after US economist Thorstein Veblen, are luxury goods where the higher the price, the more they are bought, because they are being purchased as a form of status symbol. Examples include champagne or vintage cars.

'Giffen goods', named after Scottish economist Sir Robert Giffen, are fundamental goods, sometimes of inferior quality, that are considered essential to a household, like bread. When their price increases, a poor household is unable to spend its money on more expensive goods like meat and will be forced to spend more on bread to survive. However, Giffen goods can only really exist when there is no comparable product that could be substituted, and, in fact, many economists debate the existence of Giffen goods at all, calling them a myth.

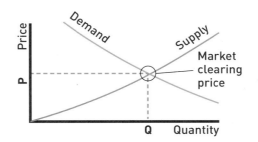

Graph demonstrating Ernst Engel's curve theory of supply and demand.

While supply is a matter of production and distribution, demand is affected by a number of determinants, some of which can be anticipated, and others can be manipulated or even created by skilful marketing. Aspects like the consumer's income, the number of potential customers and the product's existing price level are important details to learn through market research.

Other factors, such as a consumer's expectation of what their future income might be, or what price a product could have, as well as their own personal tastes and preferences, can be affected by an organization's marketing mix, whether through advertising, customer engagement or even just packaging.

Return on investment (ROI)

ROI is an equation frequently used by companies to gauge just how much capital to invest in a product in order to make the best profit. Marketers will look at all the costs relating to a product – not just the raw materials but distribution and promotion and every overhead associated with it – and then calculate its profit potential. Using the ROI formula, marketers will be able to prioritize which products will then give them the best returns. Old school marketing men called it 'Bang for your buck.'

The ROI formula

COMPARATIVE ADVANTAGE

In the late 18th and early 19th centuries, world trade was booming, and manufacturers in Great Britain were at the forefront of this boom. The economic theorists of the time gave much thought to how trading with the rest of the world would impact on the British economy. A noted economist, David Ricardo, published his own theory about what he called 'comparative advantage' in his book *On the Principles of Political Economy and Taxation*. He based his theory on a comparison between England and Portugal in the production of cloth and wine and the simple conclusion was that because Portugal could produce more using fewer man-hours they had the 'absolute

NAMES TO KNOW: JOHN MAYNARD KEYNES

JM Keynes' observations and concepts had a huge impact on the practice of macroeconomics.

Born in Cambridge, England, in 1883, John Maynard Keynes came from a background of relative privilege but also of interest in social reform, his father being an economics lecturer at Cambridge University and his mother an author and historian with a great interest in charitable endeavours.

Studying mathematics at King's College, Cambridge in 1902, Keynes changed to economics, possibly encouraged by one of his teachers, the renowned economist Alfred Marshall. After leaving with a BA and MA in 1908, Keynes worked as a government advisor for many years, attending the Versailles Treaty conference, where it was decided what reparations Germany would pay after World War I – a subject about which he wrote two books, criticizing the decisions involved.

His most famous work, and the cornerstone of Keynesian economics, The General Theory of Employment, Interest and Money, *was published in 1936. Whereas previous economists had largely believed that any attempt at interference in the market by governments was inevitably going to be counter-productive, he argued that governments should use fiscal and monetary policy to smooth the impact of contractions and expansions in the business cycle. Of course, his thinking was much influenced by the Great Depression in the 1930s.*

Keynes' theories were eventually adopted by almost all capitalist economies almost two decades after his death in 1946. He was the leader of the British delegation and was involved in the design of the international economic institutions that were being established at the end of World War II, however, he came to loggerheads with the US representatives who rejected and overruled many of his recommendations. Keynes' influence on economics started to wane in the 1970s and the validity of his theories were criticized by some of the leading American economists of the time, like Milton Friedman who questioned the ability of governments to regulate the business cycle. However, Keynesian economic

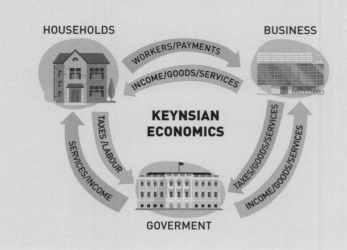

thinking would enjoy a resurgence during the financial crisis of 2007–08 the leaders of the G7 economies would use them to underpin their policies. Although famous for his economic theories Keynes was also a director of The Bank of England and a member of the Bloomsbury group of intellectuals. In 1999 John Maynard Keynes was included in **Time Magazine's** *list of the Most Important People of the Twentieth Century, they quoted 'His radical idea that governments should spend money they don't have may have saved capitalism.'*

advantage'. However, because England produced their goods at a lower 'opportunity cost' they had the 'comparative advantage'.

A modern example of comparative advantage would be an oil-producing company that also manufactured chemicals, not because they are better chemists but because they have the raw material, oil, at hand and therefore a lower opportunity cost than a non-oil producing country. It is widely regarded as one of the most influential insights in economics and the results of his findings had a huge impact on international trade and paved the way for free-market thinking. The theory is still very relevant to marketing models for multinational companies. However, today there is also pressure from consumers to source locally, which has economic consequences for businesses, the price of their offerings and therefore their marketing plans.

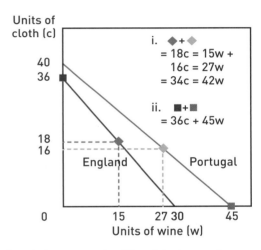

Graph demonstrating Ricardo's theory of comparative advantage.

The travel speed of tea clippers like the Cutty Sark *gave its owners the edge over their competitors in the 19th century.*

71

Ole Kirk Christiansen was a simple wooden toy maker whose marketing instincts birthed a plastic mega-brand.

MARKETING MASTERSTROKES: THE LEGO TURNAROUND

In 1932, Ole Kirk Kristiansen, a furniture maker who preferred creating toys, founded the Lego Group. The name Lego (an abbreviation of two Danish words – *Leg godt* – that translate into English as 'play well'), was chosen after a competition among his staff for which the prize was a bottle of home-brewed wine. In 1958, the iconic Lego brick as we know it now was launched and for the next few decades the Lego brand grew and grew, gaining popularity among children across the globe.

Then, around 1992, the company's business model started to come apart: their identity with kids as a 'building' toy had morphed into just another toy company that followed popular and well-worn themes of the times such as pirates and princesses.

Their traditional designers were replaced by 'Innovators' headhunted from design colleges around Europe, who despite their creative acumen, knew little about toy design and even less about Lego's tradition with building. The new designers not only took longer to get their ideas from drawing board to the shops but their simplification of the toys with fewer pieces to increase playability further alienated the hardcore fans of the Lego brand. Lines like Lego Pirates, which had enjoyed strong success since 1989, were axed in 1997. This change of direction hit the company hard and in 1998 Lego posted its first ever loss of £23 million, prompting it to shed more than a thousand staff – a traumatic event for the family-run business.

The following year, Lego made a radical change of direction and moved away from its policy to keep design ideas in-house by purchasing licensed intellectual properties. Lego Star Wars and Winnie the Pooh (for their pre-school Duplo range) were the first on to the market, followed by Harry Potter in 2001 and Indiana Jones in 2007.

While these changes had a positive impact on sales when they were in tandem with the release of the blockbuster movies, this soon tailed off once interest in the films had waned and in 2004 Lego posted a colossal shortfall of £174 million, which, according to one of its top executives, almost bankrupted the company. A rethink was vital as children were now spending less time playing with physical toys and more time with computers and screens, and Lego realized that they were not making toys interesting enough to lure them away from their new pastimes. The company had become stretched and unwieldy. A change of management saw them appoint a CEO from outside the Kristiansen family for the first time ever, although they retained ownership of the business. Lego immediately went about reviving its brand, shedding burdensome franchises, like the four Lego Theme Parks (which it sold to Merlin Entertainments), and bringing manufacturing (80 per cent of which had been outsourced) back under its control.

The company returned to its core products, reintroducing

By the year 2021 over 400 billion lego bricks had been produced.

Duplo for its littler customers, while also remodelling operations, trimming staff and modifying its distribution network. This immediately started to pay dividends with an astonishing turnaround in sales: in the USA alone, Star Wars and Indiana Jones toys saw an increase of 32 per cent and globally sales were up 18.7 per cent in 2008. Further innovations, like board games and the introduction of Lego Ninjago, helped the company leap further ahead. Despite a recession, Lego registered sales and profits twice the size of any of its competitors, registering £99.5 million profit in 2009. Lego weren't resting on their laurels and in 2014, the group, along with Warner Bros, released an animated feature film, *The Lego Movie*, in which an ordinary Lego figure saves the world. It not only performed brilliantly at the box office but also garnered great critical acclaim. More and more marketing masterstrokes have followed on the heels of the movies and in 2019 The Lego Group posted a profit of £1 billion – not bad for a company that still prides itself on being family owned.

Lego master builders pride themselves in creating ever more inventive designs.

Summary
Economics is a complex and multi-faceted subject and it is the aim of this chapter only to show it in relationship to marketing. Any successful company will find their financial and marketing departments working arm in arm, but it's important to keep in mind that appreciation and knowledge of each other's disciplines also involves keeping parts of them separate.

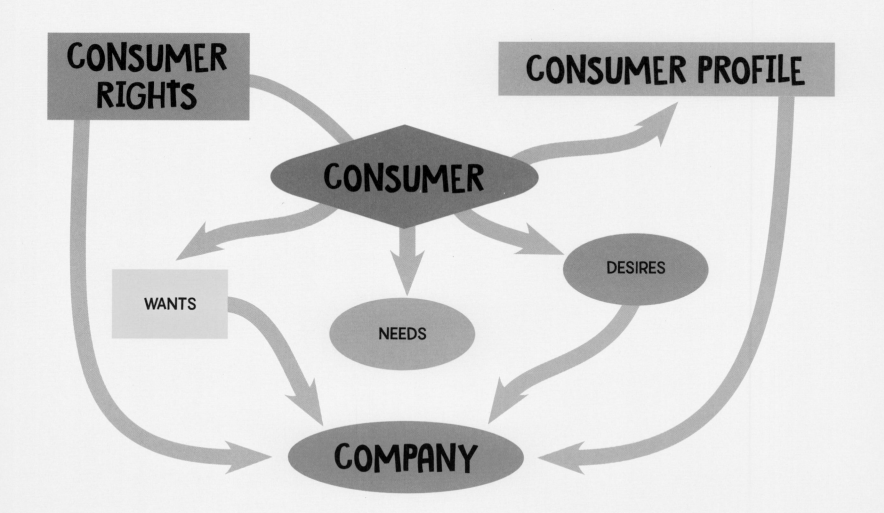

CUSTOMER MOTIVATIONS

Apple founder Steve Jobs said, 'Get closer than ever to your customers. So close that you tell them what they need well before they realize it themselves,' and he's not the only successful marketer to drive home the message of how important it is to know all you can about the consumer. When 'the market' was a literal market, it wasn't hard for sellers to know their customers because they had a much smaller number of them, but as the world developed and 'the market' became global, it became harder for producers to know who their customers were.

While detailed analysis of a customer's life is possible and desirable, you can put together a useful profile simply by looking at someone's needs, wants and desires.

Creating a customer profile

Needs

In this context a 'need' is defined as a basic element that people need to survive. Survival for some simply means continuing to live, so for them this only covers basic elements like food, water and shelter. However, beyond physical requirements there are also psychological needs, such as human affection and contact, and the chance to 'better' yourself, whether it's through education and information gathering or, for instance, improving your health and fitness by taking up exercise.

People are often uncertain whether a desire is a need or vice versa.

MASLOW AND MAX-NEEF'S HIERARCHY OF NEEDS

This is a theory proposed by psychologist Abraham Maslow in 1943. He suggested that, beginning with fundamental physiological needs like food and shelter, each human has to fulfil a certain number of needs at that level before they begin seeking the next level, moving up from safety to a sense of belonging, then to genuine self-actualization at the top. In original interpretations of the model, it was considered that you had to have fully achieved a level before you could move up to the next one.

More recent interpretations from scholars suggest that the levels overlap somewhat. While the simplicity of Maslow's pyramid is appealing and many find that it resonates with what they know, it doesn't actually have a solid scientific basis. Maslow himself admitted that he lacked sound data on the subject.

Some 40 years later, in 1986, Chilean economist Manfred Max-Neef proposed a different taxonomy. Max-Neef's theory differs from Maslow's hierarchy of needs mainly because it is based on **human scale development** – also the title of his book – which focuses on development by the people for the people and is founded on three pillars: fundamental human needs, increasing self-reliance and a balanced interdependence of people with their environment.

Neef's theory set itself as a much more democratic insight that empowers people to make their own decisions, organize their own communities and have a hand in the planning process to make sure it meets their needs. These are the fundamental ideals that most consumers all over the world now enjoy as a right.

Abraham Maslow's hierarchy of needs.

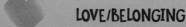
SELF-ACTUALIZATION

ESTEEM

LOVE/BELONGING

SAFETY NEEDS

PHYSIOLOGICAL NEEDS

Wants

In a marketing sense, wants are when a person's needs are directed towards a particular product or service. A person might need shelter, but want to live in a particular kind of house, or need food but want to eat sushi or pizza. Needs tend to be universal to the human experience, while wants are often culturally defined, whether by country, age, gender or other group affiliations. These decisions, while often considered by the consumer to be based on logic and necessity, are often emotional or based on 'gut instinct', what people commonly understand to be true. There's also the herd instinct of buying the same that others do, either out of a sense of belonging or a simple personal recommendation.

The difference between wants and needs

Cars such as this Mazda – promoted in this late-1960s ad as if it were a potential lover – are often very high among people's desires.

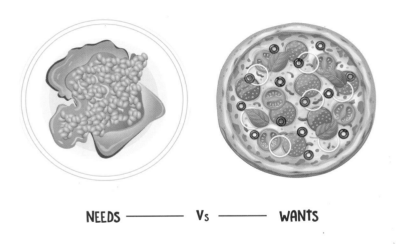

NEEDS —— Vs —— WANTS

Desires

As opposed to wanting or needing a product or service, in marketing, a desire is something a consumer would love to own but not necessarily actively seek to buy. Understanding people's desires is just as important to marketers as fulfilling their wants or needs. For example, if someone desires a luxury car but can only afford a more basic and affordable model, it's up to the marketer of the more basic model to reassure the purchaser that it will still give them the kind of emotional status they crave.

Brand Bio:
APPLE INC.

APPLE IS CURRENTLY A COLOSSAL, multinational technology business. It's one of the so-called Big Tech companies, alongside such giants as Amazon, Google, Microsoft and Facebook. Legend has it that Apple was founded in 1976 by Steve Jobs in his parents' garage in Los Altos California, along with friends Steve Wozniak and Ron Wayne. After developing their first kit-based computer together (the Apple 1), Wayne departed and it was left to Jobs and Wozniak to take the company towards new technological horizons.

Revenues grew exponentially with Apples II and III and the Macintosh in 1984. In the following years, the company went through turbulent development with first Wozniak and then Steve Jobs leaving. Apple lost considerable market share to Microsoft in the mid-1990s, only for Steve Jobs to return and put them back on course with several clever marketing decisions, allowing Jobs to cement his status as 'the godfather of all that was brilliant in electronic technology' (and marketing) before his untimely death in 2011.

Steve Jobs was synonymous with the brand for many years Here, he unveils a new titanium G4 Powerbook during his keynote address at the MacWold Expo in January 2000.

Beautifully designed products such as iPods, Macbooks and iPhones, plus breakthroughs in software innovation, propelled the company to become the first publicly traded US company to be valued at over $1 trillion in August 2018. However, it wasn't just a focus on innovation that led Steve Jobs to the pinnacle of his profession, it was his insistence on understanding the people who bought his products.

His mantra was that those who bought Apple computers and phones weren't consumers, they were people, with dreams, hopes and ambitions 'Don't sell products, sell dreams.' He championed the misunderstood, the

people whom he claimed thought outside the box, like himself, 'Here's to the crazy ones, the misfits, the rebels, the troublemakers, the round pegs in the square holes … the ones who see things differently.'

This could be seen as self-mythologizing but he was also dedicated to delegation, hiring people and trusting them to help him build his business. As he put it, 'Technology is nothing. What's important is that you have a faith in people, that they're basically good and smart, and if you give them tools, they'll do wonderful things with them.' Such was his aura that the brand he built became indistinguishable from his personal brand, making the consumers feel that they were not just buying a machine, but a piece of Steve Jobs himself. Even after his death, the Apple brand is associated indelibly with him, for better or worse, but his focus on the importance of people has had a lasting positive effect.

A presentation about the iPhone 11 by Kaiann Drance, senior director of worldwide product marketing for iPhone in September 2019 shows the strength of the brand image. Apple's new product presentations are hotly anticipated events, often watched live online worldwide.

The 35th US President John F Kennedy signed the consumer bill of rights on 15 March, 1962.

THE CONSUMER RIGHTS BILL

Before the 1950s, there was little or no protection for consumers from unscrupulous companies, and it was nigh on impossible to receive any kind of recompense for faulty or dangerous products. In the late 1950s, consumers had gathered together to find a common voice, and consumer groups pressured manufacturers to establish legal product liability, whereby consumers could seek restitution for any personal injury caused by a product. However, none of it was set into law and there was plenty of wriggle room that enabled companies to avoid their responsibilities to the customer.

On 15 March 1962, President John F. Kennedy presented the *Consumer Bill of Rights* in a speech to Congress. It is widely assumed that he was the architect of this game-changing legislature but it was actually the brainchild of Helen Ewing Nelson, a consumer protection advocate, who drafted it for JFK.

In its original form, it contained four 'Rights': the right to safety, the right to be informed, the right to choose and the right to be heard. These were set in motion and made law by the Kennedy administration. In the following years, the bill was refined and extended to eight rights, shown opposite.

CONSUMER RIGHTS

The same principles have been adopted by countries around the world and companies and producers are now required by law to adhere to these standards.

- The right to satisfaction of basic needs – to have access to basic, essential goods and services such as adequate food, clothing, shelter, health care, education, public utilities, water and sanitation.

- The right to safety – to be protected against products, production processes and services that are hazardous to health or life.

- The right to be informed – to be given the facts needed to make an informed choice, and to be protected against dishonest or misleading advertising and labelling.

- The right to choose – to be able to select from a range of products and services, offered at competitive prices with an assurance of satisfactory quality.

- The right to be heard – to have consumer interests represented in the making and execution of government policy, and in the development of products and services.

- The right to redress – to receive a fair settlement of just claims, including compensation for misrepresentation, shoddy goods or unsatisfactory services.

- The right to consumer education – to acquire knowledge and skills needed to make informed, confident choices about goods and services, while being aware of basic consumer rights and responsibilities and how to act on them.

- The right to a healthy environment – to live and work in an environment that is non-threatening to the well-being of present and future generations.

CUSTOMER PROFILE – EXAMPLE
Age: 38
Gender: Female
Marital Status: Married
Children: 2, a 7-year-old girl and a 4-year-old boy
Job title: Middle management role in a large multinational retail chain
Income: £48k PA
Husband's occupation: Teacher
Location: South-east London
Hobbies: Baking, reading, avant-garde theatre
Purchasing habits: Online shopping. Occasional day out shopping at a high-end department store with a friend

BUYER BEHAVIOUR

People are constantly making decisions: what shall I wear today? What perfume should I wear? What will I have for lunch? Many of these questions will involve buying decisions and will be made without giving them much thought. However, it is these seemingly insignificant decisions that keep marketers up at night because decoding how they are made is needed to boost revenue.

Despite the fact that the customer profile to the left is likely to be fairly typical, imagine for a moment this person's goals and motivations. She is most likely to want a flexible work regime so she can spend more time with the family. Ultimately, she would like to run her own business from home, which would give her the perfect work/life balance.

Her challenges or pain points are most likely to be maintaining a happy home lifestyle with two young children and a busy husband. His teaching job does allow more time on term breaks and holidays so he can do more child care. However, he also has to use some of this time to mark pupils' work so that impacts on them both. She also wants do well at her job, which she enjoys, but is torn between her home life and giving more time to her job. She would quit her job to spend more time with the family but her husband's teaching job is not very well paid so they need the money she brings in.

Even a consumer with a fairly normal profile is subject to a huge number and variety of influences in their buying decisions including personal, psychological and social factors.

Consumer buying behaviour

Different types of buying behaviour are motivated by a number of factors. The four primary types of buyer behaviour can be broken down based on two key elements:

1) The level of involvement the consumer has with the purchase, either high or low. This can be the practical involvement of doing research and making decisions, or the emotional involvement of their own values and beliefs.
2) The amount of variety available (or sought) within the products or services in question. In this situation, it doesn't matter how much actual variety there is but rather how much the buyer perceives it.

1 Habitual buyer behaviour

The most frequent type of buyer behaviour, this is when a product is bought so frequently that the buyer tends to stick with the brand they are most comfortable with, such as bread or milk. However, considering that these products are necessities if their brand is unavailable for any reason they will instead buy the nearest approximation of that, or even something totally different. Their involvement is low and brand loyalty only works to a certain extent. When people ask for Coke in a restaurant and don't care that they're given Pepsi, this is habitual buyer behaviour as to many consumers the word Coke means the same as cola.

For companies, this behaviour has to be mitigated by making sure their product is widely available and prominently displayed, as well as trying to ingrain the idea that their product is special and not like other similar offerings.

According to Coca Cola more than 1.9 billion people drink their product every day.

2 Variety-seeking buyer behaviour

These low involvement, high variety interactions are found when a consumer often buys a certain product but as a treat rather than a necessity, and therefore will deliberately try lots of different varieties of a brand as a novelty. Whether it's a chocolate bar or an energy drink the price is not high and therefore the buyer is happy to switch between products just to keep things interesting. Companies can benefit from this behaviour to a certain extent by introducing new products (or variations on products, like orange-flavoured chocolate) to the market, in the hope that a customer might try it just for variety's sake. It's then the marketer's task to ensure the new customer sticks with their product through careful branding and frequent promotion.

While buyers will often try different products their brand loyalty will remain solid.

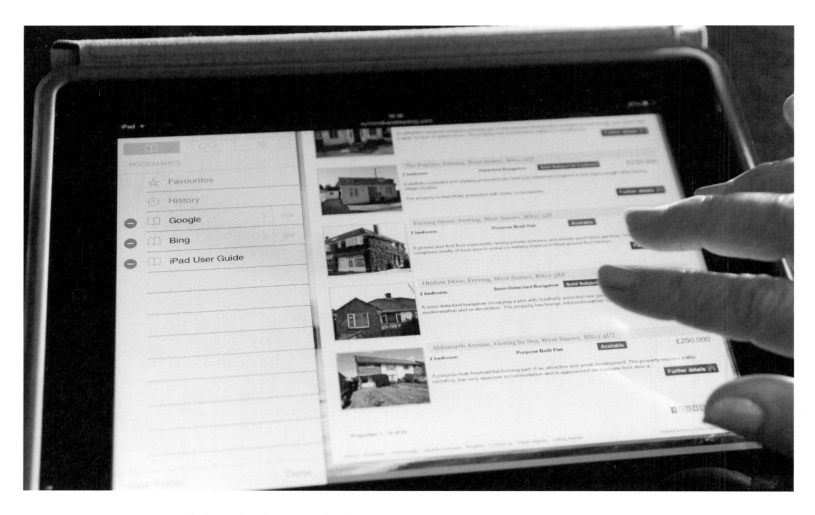

When looking for a new house the primary characteristics are size, location and local amenities.

3 Complex buyer behaviour

This type of behaviour occurs when the consumer is looking to buy an expensive product, like a car or a house, and there is a wide range of choice. The consumer will research the subject, possibly using online or other resources, as well as relying on their own knowledge and values. They may consult with friends and family, and draw on their own experiences with previous similar products. What a marketer needs to remember is that this is as much an emotional form of involvement as it is an intellectual one. While the buyer may think they are behaving entirely logically, they are in fact driven by a set of pre-assumed attitudes and often will just be looking for 'evidence' that already confirms their beliefs and desires.

4 Dissonance-reducing buyer behaviour

The other side of high involvement buying behaviour is when the product in question is specialized and therefore there is not the same variety of options. Maybe they are trying to buy a specific engine replacement for a car or a new graphics card for a computer. They will research the limited possibilities and try to discern what, if any, the differences are. It's possible that the buyer will become tired of attempting to work this out, especially if they're outside their area of expertise, and end up buying what seems to be the most popular option as a default. Marketers can mitigate this by ensuring that their products' unique benefits are explained in clear, understandable language, and thinking about how they can make their particular product stand out in the pack, whether through design or other marketing tools.

Defining unique benefits in specialist products

Modern engines require increasingly specialized parts and therefore are less accessible to tinkering from amateur mechanics.

NRS SURVEY GROUPS

A – *Upper middle class: higher managerial, administrative and professional.*

B – *Middle middle class: intermediate managerial, administrative and professional.*

C1 – *Lower middle class: supervisory or clerical and junior managerial, administrative and professional.*

C2 – *Skilled working class: skilled manual workers.*

D – *Working class: semi-skilled and unskilled manual workers.*

E – *Non-working: state pensioners, casual and lowest grade workers, unemployed living on state benefits only.*

NRS gradings are also often clustered into two groups, ABC1 and C2DE, intended to represent 'middle class' and 'working class'.

DEMOGRAPHICS

For much of the 20th century the most commonly used demographic framework was the social grade offered by the National Readership Survey (NRS), a group established in the UK in 1956 by the Institute of Practitioners in Advertising (IPA), the Newspaper Publishers Association (NPA) and the Periodical Publishers Association (PPA). The NRS was designed to provide these organizations with information showing the reach and audience of more than 250 newspapers and magazines they produced, but in practice many different companies and organizations used the groupings as shorthand for certain demographics.

The NRS claimed that it was never meant to delineate every aspect of people's social lives or beliefs but instead act as a simplistic way to describe certain target groups. The grading system is still widely used, particularly by political pollsters, but it lacks any detail about individual beliefs, background and motivations and can therefore only ever provide a scattergun approach.

In the 1950s, the kind of targeted research and information gathering that is possible nowadays did not exist. The principal methods of market research were surveys, actual sales figures, focus groups and analysis of elements such as club membership and coupon usage. Marketers sometmes still use NRS although it has largely been supplanted by other, more sophisticated systems like ACORN, MOSAIC and the National Statistics Socio-economic Classification (NS-SEC), which is the official system in the UK. They all offer a series of nested subcategories that more closely reflect the reality of people's economic and social position. Their research is not based on censuses or surveys but instead uses alternative sources. Marketers can use pre-existing data from these groups or commission bespoke data sets from them, specifically tailored to the product or service for which they are planning.

Different types of market research

Furthermore, in the 21st century, the information available to marketers is in-depth and detailed thanks to data capturing software and tools that record consumers' lifestyle habits – from the time they spend on social media or online shopping. Consumers lives, shopping and entertainment preferences provide detailed insights enabling the marketers to create an accurate, targeted approach for their marketing plans. However, wise marketers must always keep in mind that what people buy or do online is not a totally accurate reflection of a person's character and beliefs.

Data capture and marketing

As an example of how marketers see the people who are loyal to their particular brands, let's take a look at the supermarket segment. At the top end you have Waitrose and Marks & Spencer, in the middle Tesco and Sainsbury's and at the bottom end Asda, Aldi and Lidl. While Waitrose will expound the high quality of their products knowing that their consumers will pay the price to get the best, Asda know that their customers are more interested in value because they don't have the same kind of disposable income as those who shop at Waitrose.

Customers and the brand

So what does a typical customer of Waitrose look like? The answer is most likely to be something like: A/B, professional or middle management, homeowners, large disposable income or a retiree with personal pension.

KELLOGG'S NUTRI-GRAIN UK LAUNCH

In 1997, the Kellogg's Company launched its Nutri-Grain Breakfast bar in the UK. Kellogg's, the leader in breakfast cereals across the world, had been long established in the UK, opening its first office in London in 1925. Over the years, consumers' eating habits had changed. Instead of being able to sit down in the morning to breakfast, for example, many workers would bring food from home to eat as they travelled into work or when they got to their desks.

Kellogg's had already successfully launched Nutri-Grain (a baked breakfast bar with a fruit filling) in the USA, and working professionals in the UK had a very similar morning routine to their American counterparts. Company executives decided that the marketing mission for Nutri-Grain was to convince consumers to take breakfast 'on the go' and that the media package should mirror the target market's morning journeys. The consumer profile was busy, young professionals who were not time-rich in the mornings, preferring an extra half an hour in bed to sitting down to breakfast. The messaging was carefully managed so the posters and print ads would capture their attention only on their way into the centre of the big conurbations where they worked. They carefully analysed each city to identify where sales of traditional breakfasts were lowest so that they knew where to focus the messages. Major road arteries were also targeted and only locations that were facing the journey into town were chosen as poster sites. Posters were also placed within 50 m (55 yards) of the CTNs (Confectionery, Tobacconists and Newsagents) where the Nutri-Grain bars were sold, to capture impulse buyers.

The radio campaign was based on the listenership of urban radio stations, especially in the mornings, so a tailor-made 'Daypart' campaign, based on dividing the day into different broadcasting blocks, could be best utilized. The bars were also handed out free to commuters arriving at major railway stations across the UK.

After the first six months of the campaign had established usage of the brand, supermarket posters,

trolley advertising and a major TV campaign were added to the media mix on the most popular shopping days to further drive bulk buying for the home. The simple message 'Good Food on the Go' was endorsed by Kellogg's credentials in producing nutritious breakfast cereals.

The success of the UK launch of Nutri-Grain was down to an understanding of how consumers' habits are constantly adapting to the environment in which they find themselves. This shows that any company, no matter how big they are, wishing to grow with their customers needs to embrace these changes or get left behind.

DAYPART ▶ *Dayparting is the act of segmenting broadcast days into distinct time slots, reflecting the demographic of each period. For example daytime television is mostly viewed by people who stay home during that period such as child-carers or the retired. Streaming services have complicated this practice.*

Summary

The consumer's wants, needs and desires should be at the front of any marketer's plans. Understanding how to meet these fundamentals is the quest that every company embarks on even before they start to manufacture. It is no coincidence that the most successful companies have always put them first. To quote Laura Ashley, 'We don't want to push our ideas on to customers, we simply want to make what they want.'

MARKETING AND THE LAW

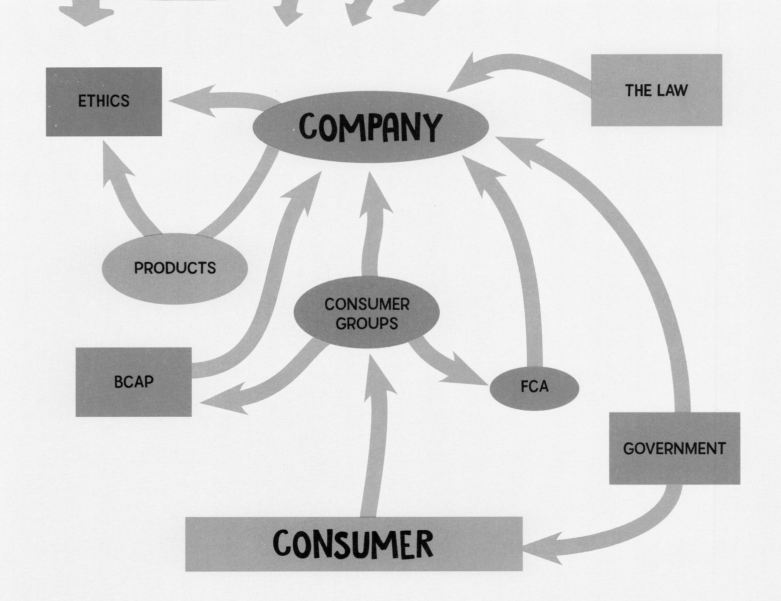

SNAKE OIL SALESMEN

Marketing, like almost every aspect of modern life, is closely regulated to conform with the laws of the land. It's not only the consumers who are taken into consideration when the authorities are drawing up the rules and laws to protect them: businesses have to be protected from other businesses, so the complexity of the legalities are a bit of a minefield for anyone running a company or setting a new one up.

Government guidelines

However, the governments of most countries in market economies have very clear guidelines for marketers and how they promote and sell their products or services. Each industry sector has its own set of regulations and the consequences of breaking them can result in anything from the banning of promotional material to severe fines and possibly, criminal proceedings.

Back in the early 19th century, snake oil salesmen were a prime example of the dubious marketing practices that were commonplace during modern marketing's infancy, making outrageous claims that their products could practically work miracles. When these elixirs were first introduced to the unsuspecting consumers, the purveyors of these 'cure alls' were able to obtain patents for their products, which contained anything and everything from opiates to arsenic, hence the term 'patent medicine'. A combination of ignorance and medical malpractice allowed these concoctions to flourish and it wasn't until the early 20th century that the non-existent benefits of these treatments were fully exposed and subsequently they were taken out of the reach of unsuspecting consumers, by food and drug legislation.

In the early 20th century snake oil salesman peddled their dubious cure-alls all over America before the US Bureau of Chemistry found the liniment they sold to be of no medical value in 1916.

The Great American Fraud *was Samuel Hopkins Adams' 11-part series about snake-oil merchants, and it devastated them.*

A vintage poster from the UK for Karswood Creosote, claiming to be a miracle cure for everything from influenza to whooping cough.

THE FCA AND THE BCAP

Today, the term 'snake oil salesmen' has become synonymous with deceptive marketing techniques, and not just in the pseudoscientific and homeopathic sectors. It's a common sobriquet for anyone attempting to hoodwink the consumer into buying their products or services by deception, whatever the industry sector.

For many decades after its inception, marketing continued to be rife with these unscrupulous practitioners preying on the general populace. It wasn't until 1906 that the US government created the FDA, Food and Drug Administration, after a series of articles from author Samuel Hopkins Adams exposed the dangers in the false claims of patent medicines, which probably harmed more people than they helped. Dubbed 'muckraking journalism', his exposés and the subsequent clamour from irate consumers encouraged the US government to lay down stricter regulations for any marketer making claims about their products. This paved the way for countries around the world to examine similar malpractice and lay down their own sets

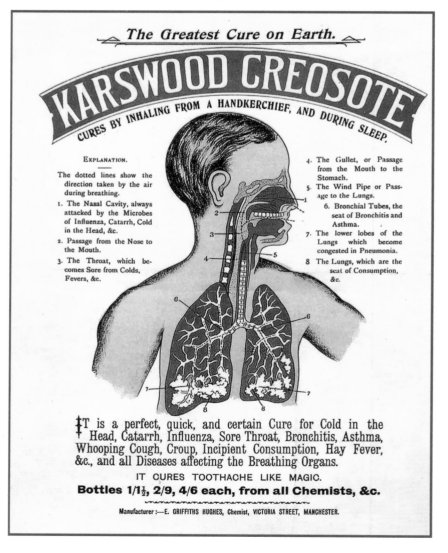

of rules in order to protect consumers. When advertising commercials first hit the screen in the UK in 1955, the content was controlled by statutory government legislation. By 1961, commercial television was readily available to an ever-growing audience and the Advertising Association decided that a more stringent code of practice was needed, and that they would implement it themselves.

Following discussions among the various industry bodies, they realized how important it was for the consumer to trust the messages that they were exposed to in newspapers and magazines, on billboards and above all on television. As a result, the first CAP (Committee of Advertising Practice/BCAP for broadcasting standards) was formed, and through this action they were able to avoid an American-style government body that would regulate their marketing messages by statute.

CAP was formed by a combination of all the interested parties, advertisers, advertising agencies and media agencies as a consequence of a report to the British parliament by the Molony Committee.

Defining standards for marketing

THE MOLONY REPORT

The final report of the Committee on Consumer Protection, which was chaired by J.T. Molony QC, was presented to parliament by Baroness Burton of Coventry in 1962. It concluded that there was a need for a strong organization to deal with consumer protection and complaints. Up until then, the Citizens Advice Bureau had dealt with the public's complaints about deceptive marketing, but it was woefully underfunded and lacked the expertise to deal with many issues. The new body would have to centre on consumer protection and complaints and would need to be properly funded and manned by people with the expertise to understand what the public was facing in terms of misleading messaging.

The committee came to the following conclusion: 'We are satisfied that the wider problem of advertising ought to be, and can be, tackled by effectively applied voluntary controls. We stress, however, that our conclusion depends on the satisfactory working of the new scheme, and in particular on the continued quality and independence of the Authority at its pinnacle.'

The Advertising Standards Authority, set up in 1961 to regulate the industry in the UK.

In the USA regulation falls to the FTC or Federal Trade Commission.

THE ASA

In 1962, the IPA (Institute of Practitioners in Advertising) launched the ASA (Advertising Standards Authority), an independent advertising regulator. It was set up to protect the consumer from any messages that didn't follow the guidelines in the CAP's code of practice, and had the authority to remove any advertising that didn't comply.

In 1974, Shirley Williams, then the Minister for Consumer Protection, spoke at the Advertising Association Conference, criticizing the system for not doing enough to tackle misleading advertising and not being visible enough. It was then decided that they needed better funding to give the body more power.

A levy of 0.1 per cent on all advertising space costs was approved by all parties and was managed by the newly formed Advertising Standards Board of Finance, ASBOF, tasked with collecting the fee. The levy not only funded the ASA in its activities, but it also meant it was able to promote itself and thereby be more visible as it went about its work.

It was further beefed up in 1988 with the introduction of the Control of Misleading Advertisements Regulations, which provided the ASA with legal backing from the Office of Fair Trading (see opposite). For the first time, the ASA was able to refer advertisers, who made persistent fallacious claims to the authorities, meaning they would be subject to legal action.

The CAP and ASA now had a much higher profile not only with marketers and their advertising and media buying agencies, but also with the consumer. They had a champion and were more easily able to complain about any advertising they felt was misleading.

However, further changes were needed as more and more messages were broadcast on TV, and in 2004 after 40 years of successful self-regulation on non-broadcast messaging, the CAP and ASA were tasked by the government to further regulate TV.

The newly formed Office of Communications (OFCOM) delegated regulation responsibility to them and they formed BCAP, the Broadcast Committee of Advertising Practice, with new codes to help regulate all broadcast advertising.

BCAP has further strengthened its codes to tackle online advertising, video on demand and any streaming that might carry advertising messages. In of 1962, the ASA dealt with around a hundred complaints. Today, it deals with more than 30,000 every year. However, 97 per cent of all advertising comes safely within the guidelines.

The code of practice is readily available to download from the CAP or BCAP websites and is updated each year to reflect the constant changes and challenges that modern society faces.

THE OFT AND THE FCA

The Office of Fair Trading (OFT), a non-ministerial government department, was established in 1973 to strengthen consumer protection, especially in the financial and consumer credit industries. It had other roles, including enforcing competition law to ensure an even playing field among financial companies.

Their common purpose was to make the markets work fairly for consumers and ensure equitable trading in vigorous competition conditions, but the ultimate aim was to prohibit the unfair practices, rogue trading, cartels and scams that had dogged the financial services industry. By enforcing better work practices and more transparency in the monetary sector, the OFT was able to improve consumer awareness and confidence and so improve the industry to the benefit of all. They did this by dividing their structure to cover the two separate segments of the market, forming a Public Markets group and a Goods and Consumer group. Although each department specialized in their own sectors they were easily able to co-ordinate when looking at the market as a whole, and therefore make the necessary recommendations to improve it.

It used a combination of education, communication and criminal enforcement to control and manage the industry and make it a safe place for companies to operate and consumers to shop. In the following years, legislation was introduced to further strengthen the OFT, in particular the *Enterprise Act* of 2002. In 2006, after much consideration, it was decided that OFT would be restructured to operate as two separate departments since it had been decided that this was a more efficient way to manage consumer and competition law.

The department had some notable victories, not least of which was taking on the credit card companies by investigating the charges that were imposed on their customers. In their report, they said that anything over £12 was punitive and unlawful and that this amount was a fair reflection of the costs sustained by the credit card company, who up to then were able to charge whatever they liked. The OFT won their day in court and the credit card companies were forced into line.

In 2016, the Financial Conduct Authority (FCA), took over the regulation of the consumer credit industry from the OFT.

In 2013 the FCA or Financial Conduct Authority, took over all regulatory powers concerning the banking and credit industries from the OFT or Office of Fair Trading.

UNDERSTANDING THE PARAMETERS

Successfully marketing a brand doesn't require marketers to be lawyers, but it does mean that they have to understand the parameters within which they are working to make sure their actions are both legal and ethical.

The Frank Statement

In 1952, *Reader's Digest* published an article about the increasing number of studies connecting lung cancer with smoking. Called 'Cancer by the Carton', it caused a huge uproar as at the time the magazine was the primary source of health news for many Americans. The article caused cigarette sales to plummet, which hadn't happened since the Great Depression.

At the end of 1953, the CEOs of 'Big Tobacco' (all the major cigarette companies) secretly assembled in New York City to meet with the premier PR company, Hill & Knowlton. They crafted a piece of marketing called 'A Frank Statement to Cigarette Smokers', which was then published in 448 newspapers on 4 January 1954. While it was only a part of a large organized campaign of disinformation and political manoeuvring that lasted for almost 50 years, it had an incredible impact with real-life deadly consequences.

The Frank Statement ('Frank' being an ingeniously deceptive choice of adjective with its resonance of both honesty and bluntness) made four claims:

1. The medical research had shown lung cancer had many possible causes (technically true but smoking was a major one).
2. That there was no agreement among authorities what the cause was (increasing numbers of scientists agreed it was smoking, but Big Tobacco sought, somewhat successfully, to sow dissent).
3. There was no proof cigarette smoking was one of the causes (a blatant lie).
4. That any statistics linking cigarette smoking to cancer could also link cancer to a wide variety of other aspects of modern living, and that a lot of scientists were sceptical

The Frank Statement from 1954, was designed to dispute claims linking smoking to lung cancer.

about the results. (In reality the tests had been designed to eliminate other factors from consideration, and any scientists who disputed it were primarily being paid by the cigarette companies.)

It then went on to reassure the public that smoking was safe and that the companies would work with scientists on any future studies, creating the Tobacco Industry Research Committee (TIRC) to fund and further investigate any possible cancer connections. In reality, the TIRC was merely a public relations tool that deliberately just funded scientific work on elements of cancer *not* connected with tobacco. If any link was found it would be suppressed.

By boosting the voices of sceptical scientists, the industry was able to undermine real progress in this field and muddy the waters for decades, all in the supposed name of protecting people. At the bottom of the Frank Statement, the CEOs signed their own names, giving it a human connection and an air of authority, banking on the trust that the public still had in them, and literally putting their own names on the line.

It paid off, as for decades, combined with manipulative advertising and political interference, the cigarette companies were able to grow their market and suppress or discredit genuine evidence of the link between smoking and cancer.

However, as evidence grew, and various whistle blowers exposed their behind-the-scenes machinations, a massive number of legal actions against the companies led to the Tobacco Master Settlement Agreement, a landmark document in 1998 that settled the case between the four main cigarette companies and the attorney generals of 46 US States, and had colossal regulatory and financial repercussions.

Big Tobacco's decision to pursue the course of action started with the Frank Statement ultimately led to considerable dissolution but not total destruction, and in fact many critics have claimed the same 'marketing plus funding sceptics' techniques have been used by other industries promoting or involving dangerous or destructive products, such as sugar and oil.

A Philip Morris ad from the 1950s. The tobacco industry even promoted 'modified risk' nicotine products, such as roasted, menthol, and ventilated products, implying that they were less harmful.

Impact of the Frank Statement

MARKETING MASTERSTROKES: DEATH CIGARETTES

In 1991, European laws governing the sale and promotion of tobacco products were tightened, meaning that warnings on packets of cigarettes had to cover a significant proportion of the visible surface, much to the dismay of the tobacco industry.

The same year, young entrepreneur and ardent smoker, B.J. Cunningham, decided to launch his own cigarette brand, and far from trying to find clever ways around the draconian regulations, he decided to embrace them.

The ironically named Death Cigarettes blatantly proclaimed the health hazards of smoking tobacco on its packaging, including a skull and crossbones logo as further proof of intention.

Positioned as 'The Honest Smoke', young smokers, tired of being lied to by the big tobacco companies, immediately took to the brand. To this post-punk audience, it was a two-fingered poke at the establishment.

If the name and the skull and crossbones logo weren't clear enough, P.J. Cunningham's aptly named Enlightened Tobacco Company PLC emblazoned its own warning alongside the legally required ones: 'MANUFACTURER'S ADVICE: Cigarettes are Addictive and Debilitating. If You Don't Smoke, Don't Start. If You Smoke, Quit.'

At its launch, the only way to purchase Death Cigarettes was by mail order, via Luxembourg, in order to circumnavigate the UK Customs and Excise authorities.

The promotional material carried on with the gallows humour, with slogans like 'Death Cigarettes, it's your funeral!' 'Serial Killer!' and 'Blow Yourself Away!'

The brand quickly acquired cult status and established a loyal following among young, rebellious smokers, but despite a gallant battle by Mr Cunningham against the tobacco giants, which went all the way to the European Courts of Justice, Death Cigarettes breathed their last in 1999.

Some say that Death Cigarettes exploited the situation to make a fast buck, but you then have to ask yourself that had the tobacco industry adopted the same nakedly honest approach to the deadly perils of smoking tobacco, instead of conducting decades of deceit, how many lives would have been spared?

A bench with the logo for Death Cigarettes, using reverse psychology and humour to promote the product.

LEGAL, DECENT AND HONEST

In the marketing world today there are a great many regulatory bodies to give guidance and lay down laws that protect the public, but at the end of the day marketers have a duty of care to their consumers and therefore a responsibility to act in a legal, decent and honest way.

FICTIONAL TEST CASE: PUFFY CHOCCY PARCELS

A food company, let's call them Ce-Real Deal, wants to launch a new cereal brand exclusively for kids, made from reconstituted corn puffs and smothered in milk chocolate. They decide that there is a huge gap in the market for this kind of cereal, especially for pre-school children. They know that they have the line capacity in their factory to manufacture large quantities of the product, and they set up a taste committee to make sure that the recipe satisfies even the fussiest kids.

They approach their pack designers to create a box that the kids will find as irresistible as the product itself. The design department comes up with what they think is a sure-fire way to grab the children's attention so they pester the life out of their parents to buy it for them.

The brand will be called Puffy Choccy Parcels and the box will be adorned with a character, Puffy the Naughty Flying Squirrel. They go to the advertising agency with their new product and marketing model and brief them to create a TV campaign. They want to target the kids during children's TV hour in the afternoon with a series of commercials about the exploits of Puffy, who will encourage the young viewers to be like him: as naughty as possible until their parents give in and buy them this cereal *(contd)*.

Ce-Real Deal company executives argue that the launch will be a sure-fire hit, as the combination of the highly indulgent cereal and the engaging Puffy will grab kids' imaginations. What could possibly go wrong?

While both the cereal company's execs and agency's whizz kids are busy congratulating themselves on their brilliant strategy, there's a dissenting voice in the room: a young marketer who had misgivings from the start and decided to do some research into the ethics and legality of this new brand.

He points out a number of questionable actions taken by the company and their advertising partners:

- 'First of all the product itself. Irresistible it may be, but that is mainly because it's full of sugar, fat, saturates and salt.'
- 'There's 40gms per 100gms of sugar in Puffy Choccy Parcels: that represents 40 per cent of the actual product. A recommended serving for children is 30gms and most kids eat more than that, so before they have even left home they will have had over a third of their daily allowance of sugar.'
- 'The traffic light product warning system on the front of the pack for this product would be a row of red!'
- 'Then there's our friend Puffy the Naughty Flying Squirrel. Cute as he is, he runs against every code of practice laid down by BCAP to protect children.'
- 'By encouraging them to pester their mums and dads to buy the product we would be breaking the law and furthermore current regulations state that broadcasters cannot allow any advertising of this sort during children's programmes.'
- 'It's not just the Food Standards Authority (FSA), BCAP and the World Health Organization (WHO) that are telling us that this product is wrong for small children, we have to ask ourselves, would we serve this to our own kids?'

NAMES TO KNOW: HELEN LANSDOWNE RESOR

Helen Lansdowne Resor's success in the advertising industry opened doors for many other female creatives.

Born in Kentucky in 1886, Helen Bayless Lansdowne was raised by a working single mother and, following her example, become a bill auditor at an advertising agency in Cincinnati. She moved on to writing newspaper ads for the Commercial Tribune and then worked as a copywriter for a small agency called the Street Railways Advertising Co.

However, it was her work at J. Walter Thompson Co., as their first female copywriter, that she began to influence and then reinvent the nature of advertising, particularly adverts aimed at women. She joined the group in 1908 and quickly distinguished herself on several high-profile campaigns. She introduced the Woodbury soap 'Skin you Love to Touch' slogan in 1911, injecting sensuality and even sexuality into the product's promotion. This was at a time when Victorian values still persisted and these sentiments were considered immoral. Despite pushing against the boundaries and laws of decency of the time, this campaign was a huge success. It's also an early example of psychological techniques in advertising, decades before this kind of approach became more commonplace.

She married Stanley Resor, who became president of J. Walter Thompson after he bought the company in 1916, and together they turned the agency into something innovative and, at the time, progressive. When she joined, advertising copy tended to be entirely descriptive, focusing on outlining the product and its benefits in a very pragmatic style. Helen Lansdowne Resor was at the forefront of a new movement of copywriters who sought to make copy more emotive and conversational. Consumers had already become aware of the 'tricks' of advertising text, often finding the claims and boasts that they featured unbelievable. Resor sought to bring believability back with subtle word choices and an element of romanticism. The copy's voice was cleverly matched to the content of the women's magazines that carried it.

She established a Women's Editorial Department at J. Walter Thompson, overseeing an entire team of female copywriters. They reinvented the image of women in advertising, pushing back against the traditional views of women as simply child-rearing homemakers. In Resor's copy, women were portrayed at work, playing sports or simply just enjoying themselves outside of a family environment. It was controversial but it worked because a new generation of self-declared modern women recognized their own lives and aspirations in the new images. In the 1930s, there were actually more women copywriters than men at the company.

This wasn't a mission of feminist reinvention, although Resor was also a staunch suffragette, fighting for women's voting rights in New York. It was simply practical marketing, taking time to understand the consumer and give them what they needed. Women had a place in the creative marketing industry because Resor fought for them but also because companies, like J. Walter Thompson, understood that they were the best people to write for their target market. Subtler copywriting also enabled them to skirt round laws restricting what could and couldn't be said or shown in advertising at the time.

Despite her many achievements Resor still suffered from the impact of institutionalized sexism, never officially holding the title of vice-president despite operating as such and working at the agency until the 1960s. Posthumously inducted into the Advertising Hall of Fame in 1967, Lansdowne Resor's success was attributed by fellow copywriter Nancy Stephenson to her 'brilliant mind that darted and dipped and swooped with terrifying speed and accuracy.'

This soap ad created by Helen Lansdowne Resor was controversial for its time because of its sexual overtones, but hailed by feminists for its portrayal of a woman in charge of her own destiny.

Summary

There is a responsibility to the consumer from all companies to make their products to the highest quality and to market them responsibly. If marketers are in any doubt that the consumer needs to be respected there are laws and rules, regulated by dedicated legal professionals, that will ensure they are protected. The phrase 'Legal, decent, honest and truthful' should always be at the top of any marketer's mind.

Chapter Seven

DIVERSITY, ETHICS AND SOCIAL RESPONSIBILITY

Meeting Standards • Corporate Social Responsibility • Recycling • Diversity • The Impact of Trade on Marketing • The PEST Analysis

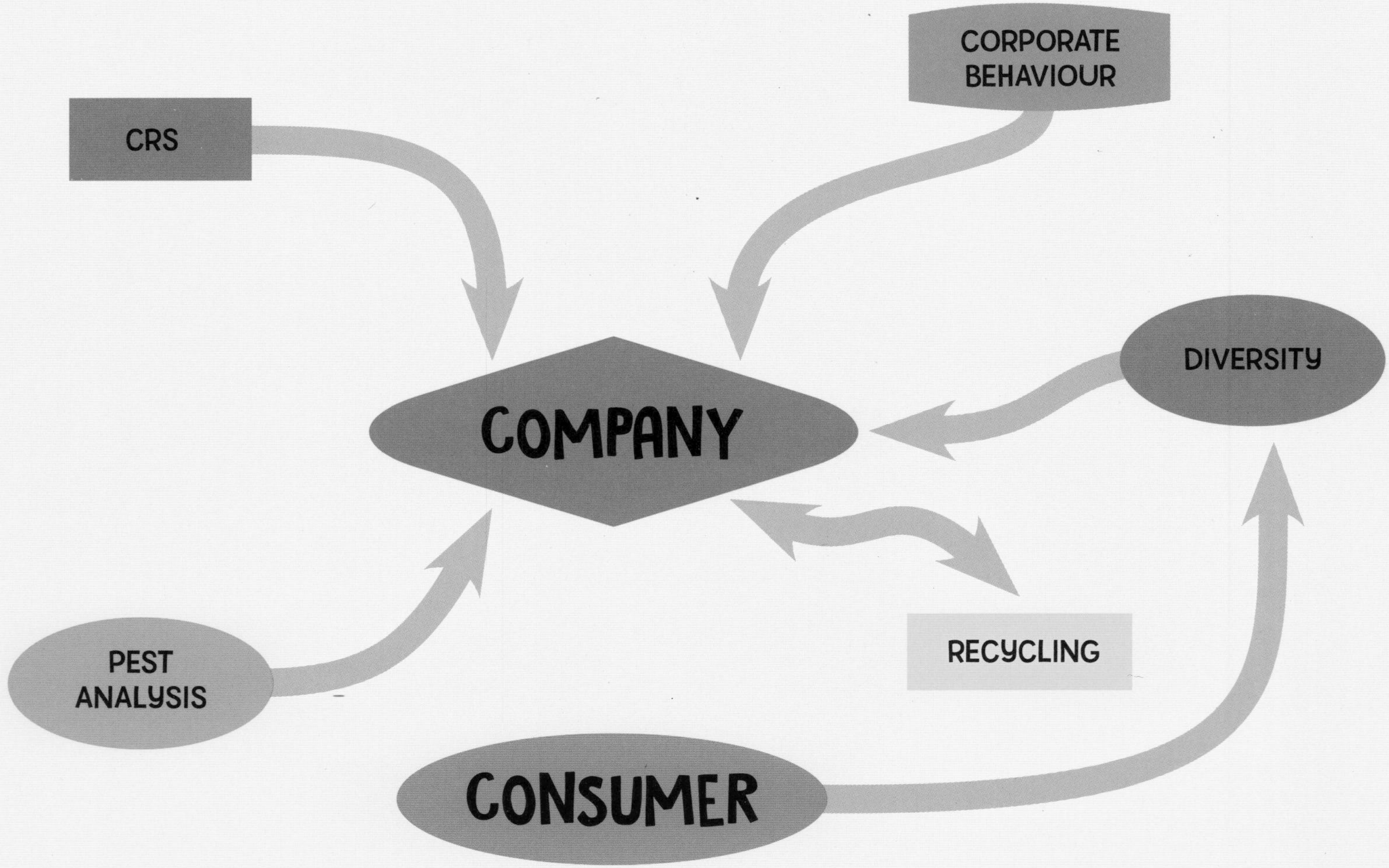

CORPORATE BEHAVIOUR

CRS

DIVERSITY

COMPANY

PEST ANALYSIS

RECYCLING

CONSUMER

MEETING STANDARDS

Every company in the world will have a view of where the products or services they offer fit into society, and now more than ever it is critical that their offerings meet the standards that are set for them. The ethics of a brand are not just for regulators to administer. Each producer has a duty of care to make sure that what goes into their wares, and the marketing that will promote them to the consumer, can withstand the closest examination.

The advent of the World Wide Web has given people the tools and knowledge to scrutinize every purchase they make. This greater awareness has brought every social, ecological and environmental issue that will condition the consumers' choices to the forefront. Marketing has always reflected the society around it, and this chapter will examine the problems and opportunities that the new age of enlightenment has brought to modern marketing, and how some of the lessons of the past have shaped it.

Everyone is responsible for standards

Rainforests across the world are increasingly facing threats such as smuggling, poaching and significant deforestation and some detractors of McDonalds' have sought to link the firm with that.

McLibel protestors Helen Steel and Dave Morris outside McDonalds' headquarters in 2005.

Responding to ethical challenges: the McLibel case

Companies the world over are under a public magnifying glass about the way they conduct themselves ethically. There are also independent environmental, social and consumer organizations who are actively scrutinizing their marketing practices. The bigger the company, the bigger the challenges, and it is how a company responds to being held to account that colours their continued relationship with the people who buy their products or services.

In the late 1980s, McDonald's found that their whole marketing ethos was under attack from environmental activists, who distributed leaflets accusing them of malpractice on many issues, from animal welfare to exploiting employees. The resulting lawsuit, known in the media as the 'McLibel case', lasted ten years, and although it eventually came out in McDonald's favour it was seen as Goliath triumphing over David. For any company, rebuilding their reputation after it has been muddied has to be carefully planned and executed as they cannot be seen to be making a knee jerk reaction in the face of adversity.

Since the turn of the 21st century McDonald's marketing messages have included constant updates and details about what they are doing to help reduce the impact their products have on the environment. This includes incentives like recycling the cooking oil they use into bio-fuel to power their vehicles, changing from polystyrene to recycled paper packaging and getting rid of plastic toys from their Happy Meals. In one of their latest announcements' they claimed that the targets they are setting on the reduction of greenhouse gases in their businesses will be the equivalent of taking 32 million cars off the road by 2030.

By talking about positive environmental actions like these, large companies are now appearing to be more transparent about the undoubted negative views that some consumers have of them as well as trying to address the concerns that they may have.

CORPORATE SOCIAL RESPONSIBILITY

Being a good citizen is not just confined to individuals; companies across the board have a duty of care to the world in which they operate. This self-regulating practice is known as corporate social responsibility (CSR), and corporations big and small are expected to participate.

The aim of this policy is for organizations to demonstrate their philanthropic, sociable and charitable natures. It can be supporting NGOs (see right), with their work in the developing world. It can also mean smaller actions such as donating monies to help grass-roots soccer at a local level. In this way, businesses are getting more actively involved in schemes that help the community at large.

By diverting some of their profits to ethically responsible causes, their actions are seen by consumers, employees and shareholders favourably, therefore CSR is not just an altruistic strategy. In marketing terms, it can reflect a positive light on everything else the company does and, as such, be an essential part of any organization's business plan. These contributions are in reality important investments that will in the long run turn into profit, not just monetary but in public relations terms as well.

The CSR strategy of a company can be defined by a number of different factors – anything from the environmental views of the senior management, to offsetting their global carbon footprint. The Covid-19 pandemic has thrown a bright light on how companies responded to this health crisis; not just the physical issues it created, but also the mental and social impact on communities. Although all these good deeds are useful for a company's image, they should be wary of taking it for granted that the consumer will be blindly impressed by them. In a recent study carried out by Cone Communications, 65 per cent of respondents stated that they would research any brand's stance on an issue before taking it as read.

RECYCLING

The idea of reusing or recycling the component parts of objects or packaging first entered common consciousness during the two world wars. Resource scarcity meant that people would have to reuse common materials. The British government released pamphlets like 'Make Do and Mend', and ran scrap drives encouraging people to donate waste metal for melting down and using in munitions.

NGO ▶ *Non-governmental organization, for example, UNICEF, the Red Cross and Médecins Sans Frontières (MSF) International. They are usually non-profit and often formed by private citizens but can wield immense influence.*

NGOs have had a huge impact in tackling social and environmental issues around the globe.

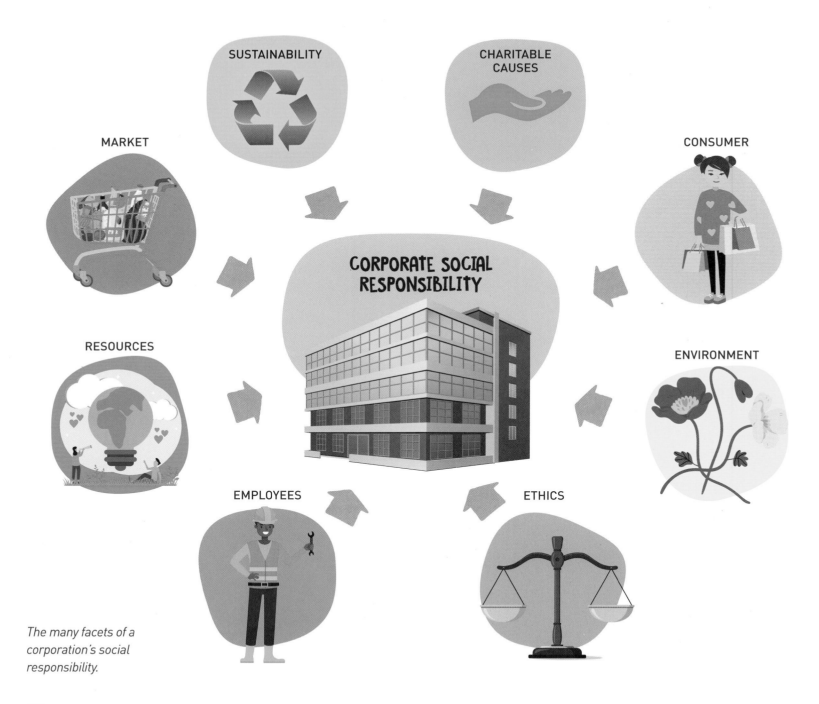

SUSTAINABILITY

CHARITABLE CAUSES

MARKET

CONSUMER

CORPORATE SOCIAL RESPONSIBILITY

RESOURCES

ENVIRONMENT

EMPLOYEES

ETHICS

The many facets of a corporation's social responsibility.

However, it was the rapid growth in the use of plastic that created a true environmental crisis from the 1960s onwards. Glass was also an issue (the first bottle bank was seen in the UK in 1977). Then, paper, from newspapers and other wood-pulp materials, was widely recycled. But it was when single-use plastic items began swamping landfills that the problem became endemic. Large amounts of lightweight plastic rubbish were even being blown by air currents to form an enormous trash island in the centre of the Atlantic Ocean.

While for decades the public were either unaware or uncaring, in the 1980s and 1990s increasing environmental consciousness lit on recycling as a tangible act to make people feel they were actually helping. In 2003, it became law across the UK that councils had to provide every homeowner with a bin for recycling.

Companies needed to take a lead in this area, as much of their product's packaging were either non-recyclable or used a very small percentage of recycled material. There was an ethical marketing advantage for businesses that could boast fully recycled product elements and a sustainable production loop. Many companies sought to be seen as environmentally friendly but in some cases were simply playing lip service to the idea, 'greenwashing' their reputations.

Separating rubbish for recycling into groups such as paper, plastic and tin cans allows consumers to feel they are personally contributing to environmental efforts.

Organizations are now making pledges and assigning targets for levels of recyclability and signing on to global commitments. For example, Coca-Cola have said that they aim for 50 per cent of their primary packaging to be recycled materials by the year 2030. This is combined with a reduction in packaging size, charges for plastic bags and the use of recyclable materials for common items, i.e. paper straws. For some companies that's not enough, for instance, innovative recycling company TerraCycle now operates a specialized service whereby individuals and businesses can donate traditionally unrecyclable materials to their centres, where they are broken down into very basic component parts and reused by partner organizations.

Up to now, recycling has been the most recognizable, acceptable mainstream practice of environmentalism but has become criticized for being both inefficient and possibly ineffective. Interest in recycling has definitely declined due to companies feeling they cannot profit from it, alongside concerns over recyclable waste being sent abroad and then not properly treated.

Companies may need to take a more radical approach to lessen their impact on the planet.

Advances have been made in the cause of diversity but there is further to go.

A diverse workforce and customer base

DIVERSITY

The subject of diversity is the most hotly debated and probably the most misunderstood issue facing marketers today. Whenever a company seeks to launch a new product or reposition an existing brand there are many considerations to be undertaken regarding the consumers at whom it is aimed.

There is no easy, all embracing image or set of words that will satisfy everyone. A marketer can feel they have addressed every possibility only to find that in doing so they have left out, or even worse, offended a huge segment of the target audience. Demographics such as gender, ethnicity, sexual orientation, age and physicality are all relevant, and this is on top of the usual groups based on work, financial status and geography. Tiptoeing through a minefield of background data to come to the right position has become the norm for every company planning their strategy for their marketing model. There is no simple answer. What it *does* mean for the marketer is studying the available data and then going deeper.

The challenge for every company is not just that they have to consider the make-up of their customer base, but they need to look at their own workforce too. If they are a company that has truly embraced a diverse policy of recruitment they will have a much better chance of understanding the people who are likely, or not, to buy their products. Just paying lip service to what is in reality the future of all marketing practice is only likely to alienate more people than it attracts.

LGBT ▶ *LGBT stands for Lesbian, Gay, Bisexual and Transgender. It represents the interests of individuals who identify with these groups. Sometimes it is extended to LGBTQIA+, adding Queer, Intersex and Asexual people to the group, but often the four-letter acronym is taken to stand for the totality of sexuality and gender identity.*

The original LGBT Pride flag was designed in 1978 by US artist Gilbert Baker.

It's not enough to tweet support for LGBT rights or BLM, companies have to act on it. Amani al-Khatahtbeh – author, activist and the founder of a blog for Muslim women, MuslimGirl.com – simply put it, 'We want products made for us, by us.'

BLM ▶ *Black Lives Matter is a movement protesting against incidents of police brutality and all racially motivated violence against black people. It has become a broad coalition of movements and organizations and seeks primarily to achieve criminal justice reform.*

THE IMPACT OF TRADE ON MARKETING

The Fairtrade symbol is a familiar logo on many products available in supermarkets and elsewhere. To the consumer, it may mean they are making a more ethical purchase, but in a lot of cases consumers themselves may not be aware of its actual significance, beyond a simplistic-sounding slogan alongside pictures of happy farmers. For this reason, some have accused it of being a pure marketing device when the reality is better and considerably more complex.

For centuries, travellers from Western countries have patronized local sellers in other regions. In the 1950s, they noticed that despite producing commodities of good quality and quantity, the farmers and product makers were finding it hard to earn enough to continue working, let alone make a profit. These travellers decided to try to personally export the products and take them to North America or Europe where they might be able to get better prices, then bring the money back to them.

This system needed to be regulated to ensure no one got exploited. For this reason, Fairtrade USA was founded in 1997 to formalize and oversee a way that large companies could pay sustainable prices to farmers and other suppliers. Tea, coffee and chocolate companies were the first adopters but eventually a wider and more diverse group of businesses signed up to the Fairtrade system. The money from Fairtrade deals is used by the communities for projects like schools and medical facilities to improve the lives of the workers and their families. Fairtrade is not just about supporting workers producing raw materials but also the millions of 'home workers' crafting items that end up on sale in the more affluent western economies. Rebecca van Bergen, founder and executive director of Nest, a non-profit organization that supports women artisans globally, sums it up simply. 'Fairtrade is about ensuring that workers in a company's supply chain are being treated and paid fairly.'

Most cocoa and coffee farmers earn less than $1 a day, and many have never even tasted the sweets and drinks that their beans make.

ETHICS TEST CASE: TOOTHSOME TOOTHPASTE

The marketing department of a large multinational company has identified a gap in their portfolio, an ethically sound, teeth hygiene brand. They decide that the gap should be filled by a vegan, animal cruelty-free, chemical-free, organic, all-natural ingredients, toothpaste. As well as the ethically sound product, the packaging would be completely biodegradable, and anything that isn't would be completely recyclable.

The new brand will be called Toothsome, a play on the words 'tooth' and 'wholesome', and any images used in both the packaging and the promotional material will be completely inclusive of all gender, LGBT, ethnic and age groups. Of course, they have not forgotten that the product must be effective so their research and development lab have made sure that Toothsome

promotes strong oral hygiene, and will deal effectively with plaque, which will mean healthier teeth and gums. Having satisfied themselves that they have ticked every ethical and efficacy box, the team confidently takes Toothsome to their CEO for what they feel will be the formality of his approval to launch.

After the all-singing, all-dancing presentation of Toothsome, which includes the catchy tag line, 'What's good for your teeth is good for the World!', the beaming marketing director asks the CEO what he thinks. The CEO has one question, 'Why?'

The assembled group of marketers are a little taken aback, surely, it's obvious? They go on to explain again all the ethical, ecological and social benefits of Toothsome, and the CEO cuts them short with the same question, 'Why?' The marketing director thinks he sees where this question is leading and pipes up, 'We are a large multinational company and many of the products we sell have recently come under fire from various consumer groups and ethical activists'. He continues, 'By launching such a PC brand we can be seen to be doing our bit for the do-gooders and the eco brigade and so deflect any criticism away from our other brands.'

After listening patiently, the CEO tells the marketing team that he will not approve Toothsome. 'I'm afraid that a company like ours launching a brand like this will be seen for what it is. A lame attempt to cash in on a market

trend that we could never hope to access in our current position. We need to show the consumer that we are making genuine strides towards a more ethically sustainable future.

'I respectfully suggest, that if we want to do something worthwhile with this budget we could, for instance, use it to offer children from poorer backgrounds free dental care in their communities, without any strings attached. This will show that the company really takes local issues to heart.' At this point those present at the meeting are all nodding furiously at the CEO, who goes on to say, 'But before we do any of this, I intend to overhaul all the company's ethical policies, production methods, products, staffing and recruitment ... starting with the marketing department.'

CORPORATE BEHAVIOUR

▶ *This is the standard that a company sets for itself as a whole and then ensures that it is adhered to at all levels and in all marketing communications. For this reason, corporate behaviour will influence every part of the organization's operations. The role it plays in the day-to-day running of a business will depend on the size of the company. In marketing terms, corporate behaviour will also be a decisive factor in the business's dealings with the consumer, and for the customer they will see consistency of the company's values in the messaging and promotions of a brand or service. This kind of ethical stance means a fairer, more honest approach to business both with their staff and their customers, and as such will reflect favourably on the products and services they offer.*

NAMES TO KNOW: ANITA RODDICK

Anita Roddick acted according to her own ethics but also recognized the power of the green economy.

Body Shop founder Anita Roddick was born on 23 October 1942, in a bomb shelter in Littlehampton on England's south coast. Having initially trained as a teacher after leaving school, she went on to get a job with the United Nations (UN). The extensive international travels her job required enabled her to visit many places where people were struggling, either from environmental or social issues. She also noticed the natural ingredients they used to care for their skin and hair. In 1976, she opened 'The Shop' as it was originally called, in Brighton, selling products sourced from places she had visited and created using the same local principals and recipes.

It was intended to provide an independent income for her family while her husband worked in South America, but Roddick also wanted to create an alternative to what she saw as the profit-driven hair and make-up industry and she saw a potential market for a more ethically minded cosmetics store that told the customer the story of the product's origins.

Some of the elements that made The Body Shop an immediate success were what Roddick claimed 'brilliant accidents', rather than the result of a calculated marketing plan. For example, they offered refillable containers (actually urine sample bottles), which they encouraged the customers to return and have refilled. This was not just for environmental reasons but also because The Body Shop couldn't afford any other containers.

It opened a second branch six months later and continued building on its ethos and success, until by the early 1990s it had over 600 branches across the globe. The company was a pioneer in banning the use of ingredients in their products that had been tested on animals, then went further by campaigning to eliminate animal testing across the entire cosmetics industry. In 1990, they created a charitable foundation that financed projects worldwide with the aim of helping disadvantaged children and adults.

Anita Roddick also personally worked with multiple charities, including Greenpeace. She advocated in cases of unfair confinement and swore to use her personal fortune to help.

For a long period, The Body Shop was synonymous with environmentalism and ethical consumption, its shops designed to seem natural and makeshift, and other brands and services followed suit as 'green' causes became increasingly popular. In the late 1990s, it also launched campaigns to combat self-image problems in women, keeping itself at the forefront of representation.

In later years, the company was accused of 'greenwashing', or representing itself as more charitable than it actually was, with critics claiming they gave no money at all to

causes in the first 11 years of its operation. Further controversy followed when The Body Shop was sold to L'Oréal in 2006, as L'Oréal had continued to sell products in China despite the government requiring that cosmetics be tested on animals. However, Roddick insisted the sale would allow her to influence L'Oréal's decisions from the inside.

For her work, Anita Roddick was given an OBE in 1988 and was made a Dame in 2003. She died of pancreatic cancer in 2007 and by her request almost her entire fortune was given to charity.

A familiar presence on the high street, The Body Shop has been impacted like many retailers, by the growth of online shopping.

115

THE PEST ANALYSIS (POLITICAL, ECONOMIC, SOCIO-CULTURAL AND TECHNOLOGICAL)

There are many factors that can influence a company's corporate behaviour, both internal and external forces can have an impact. By tracking and analysing these macro-environmental factors on a regular basis an organization can adjust its behaviour accordingly. It is a useful business tool that will enable businesses to handle growth, decline and their position in the market. There are also other factors that can come into play and be added to the analytical framework, as seen in the chart below.

An analytical framework

- **Political** How the company interacts with government and other municipal bodies and their policies. For example, lobbying for exemptions to laws might not be looked upon favourably by customers.
- **Economic** How a company contributes to the overall monetary system in which it operates. If a company exploits loopholes to avoid paying tax it might alienate possible consumers.
- **Socio-cultural** How a company interacts with the culture and society of its customer base and the world around it. Showing that they are sensitive to people's concerns and can reflect the diverse make-up of society in their own company would be beneficial.
- **Technological** How a company uses technology, whether pre-existing or in development, with regard to its impact on people's lives and the environment. Choosing to use renewable energy sources in their manufacturing shows an awareness of climate issue

PESTEL or PESTLE:	**which includes legal and environmental themes**
SLEP:	**includes legal themes**
STEPE:	**includes ecological themes**
STEEPLE and STEEPLED:	**includes ethics and demographic themes (occasionally written as PESTLEE)**
DESTEP:	**includes demographic and ecological themes**
SPELIT:	**includes legal and intercultural themes, often used in the USA since 2005**
STEER:	**which considers sociocultural, technological, economic, ecological and regulatory factors, but does not specifically include political factors**

PEST ANALYSIS VARIANTS

POLITICAL

ECONOMIC

SOCIAL

TECHNOLOGY

THE CO-OP

This vintage tin from the Cooperative Wholesale Society depicts the Crumpshall Biscuit Works near Manchester.

IN 1844, THE ROCHDALE SOCIETY OF EQUITABLE PIONEERS, an organization of wholesale food retailers, introduced the idea of distributing a share of their collective profits to all its members – a scheme that became known as the dividend or Divi. By 1872, this equitable model had been accepted by many more retail bodies and so the 'Co-operative Wholesale Society' (CWS) was established. Stores sprang up across the UK, all supplied by the Co-operative society, and very soon they were diversifying into every form of high street commercial interest, from banks and insurance to legal services. All these mutual amenities were available to members to help them build their businesses and customer base.

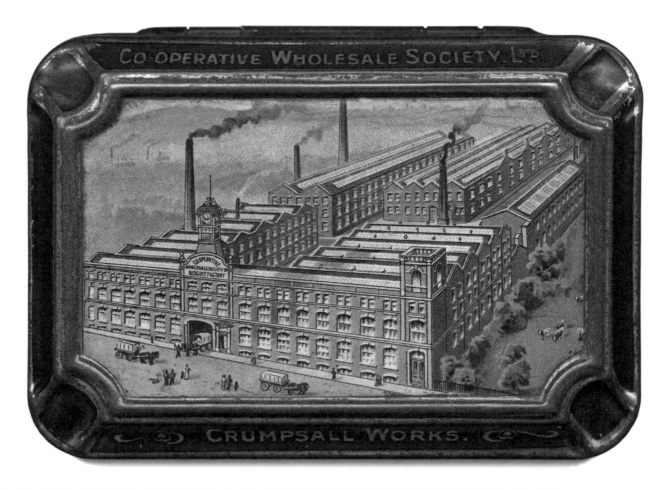

In 2016 Co-op deliberately returned to its distinctive 'clover-leaf' logo from 1968.

The CWS were not the only co-operative in the UK. There were many others, all with the same basic principles: to give their members a collective strength and more muscle with their marketing practices. For over a century, co-operative societies were the backbone of high street retail and wholesale traders, and there was a great deal of rivalry.

In 1968, the Co-op introduced the familiar 'clover leaf' branding for all its stores and produce, as a mark of their obligation to a co-operative approach to business. The CWS underlined its ethical approach by taking actions that would set it apart from some of its high street rivals. For instance, it boycotted South African produce during the Apartheid years. The company labelled this and other commitments as 'the Co-operative difference'.

In 2000, the members of the CRS, Co-operative Retail Service (formed in 1957 as CWS's retail division and by then its biggest rival), decided to dissolve and then merge with the larger company to form the Co-operative Group Ltd.

According to their manifesto, the Co-op has long held an ethical stance in all its business activities, taking a number of initiatives. These included allowing women the same democratic rights as men within its society, displaying important nutritional information on its products and being the first major UK retailer to champion the Fairtrade movement. It also claims a significant role in raising animal welfare standards, installing renewable energy-generating systems and playing an active role in local community projects (1 per cent of members own-brand spending goes to local causes). In 2020, the Co-op Group reported an upturn of 7 per cent on the yearly figures of £10.9 billion, signifying that ethical doesn't necessarily mean unprofitable. At a time when almost every company is trumpeting its newfound global conscience, it's interesting to note that the foundations for the Co-op's ethical marketing approach were laid down over 160 years ago.

MARKETING MASTERSTROKES: PATAGONIA

In the late 1950s, Yvon Chouinard, a well-known rock climber, began selling his own brand of outdoor and climbing apparel. He also imported rugby shirts from Scotland after finding that they were useful for preventing climbing ropes from chafing his neck. In 1965, he teamed up with another climber, Tim Frost, who helped him to improve his products and meet the ever-increasing demand for them.

By 1973, they had opened the first Patagonia brand shop in Ventura, California. From the beginning, the brand had a reputation for the ethicality of its products and their corporate actions. It was one of the

Yvon Chouinard was a well-known rock-climber when he founded Patagonia Outdoor Clothing and Gear in 1973.

first companies to use recycled materials to make clothing, turning waste plastic bottles into jackets and fleeces as early as 1993. It continues to enhance its environmental and social reputation with innovative staff incentives, hailed for its family friendly policies around maternity leave.

In 2012, it was awarded 'Certified B Company' status for being an organization that the State of California sees as meeting 'rigorous standards of social and environmental performance, accountability and transparency'. Patagonia pledges 1 per cent of its total sales to environmental causes, through 'One Percent

For The Planet' – an organization of which Chouinard was a founding member.

In 2016, they went even further, committing 100 per cent of their Black Friday sales to environmental causes – a total of $10 million. In 2017, it launched its most ambitious marketing plan so far, offering customers the opportunity to part-exchange their used clothing, provided that it is in reasonable condition, for new clothing. They then took the used clothing, repaired and washed it and resold it under their Worn Wear label. They also created a programme called ReCrafted, which took scraps of material from used Patagonia gear and turned that into clothes.

The mountain image on the Patagonia sign is based on Monte Fitz Roy, on the border of Argentina and Chile.

Patagonia sees itself as an 'Activist Company' and to this end in 2018, they announced that they would cheekily donate the $10 million they received in tax cuts from the Trump administration to groups committed to fighting climate change.

Patagonia continues to lead the way in corporate ethics and standing up for environmental issues. Its mission statement is testament to that: 'Build the best product, cause no unnecessary harm, use business to inspire and implement solutions to the environmental crisis."

Patagonia prides itself on its clothing, which is often made from recycled materials.

Summary

The ethical values that each and every business in the world are held up to are not definitive, they are part of a constantly shifting social landscape that companies must adapt to.

To negotiate all the twists and turns in this roller-coaster world successfully, marketers must be on their toes. Above all, they must listen and relate to the people driving these changes: the consumers.

Chapter Eight

MARKETING RESEARCH

Doing the Research • Quantitative Research • Qualitative Data

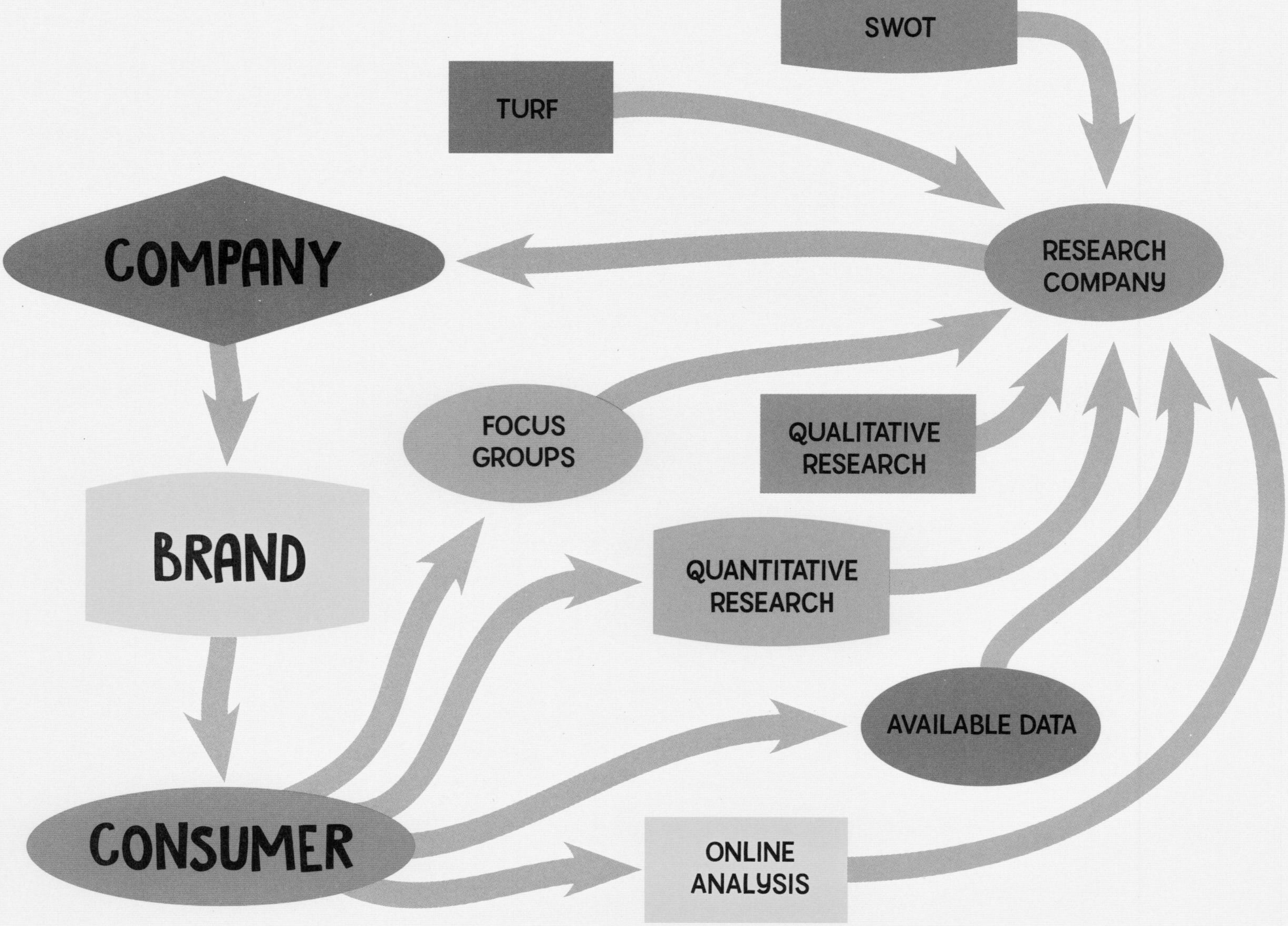
SWOT
TURF
COMPANY
RESEARCH COMPANY
FOCUS GROUPS
QUALITATIVE RESEARCH
BRAND
QUANTITATIVE RESEARCH
AVAILABLE DATA
CONSUMER
ONLINE ANALYSIS

DOING THE RESEARCH

Marketing research is a vital stage in any company's planning: without it they are virtually working blind. Knowing the consumer's wants, needs and feelings enables companies to design their products and create their marketing campaigns with more certainty. Collecting and analysing the data from research gives organizations a clearer picture of who and what they are dealing with. This information gathering falls into two main categories: quantitative and qualitative.

QUANTITATIVE RESEARCH

Quantitative research is primarily about the gathering of large amounts of data to give a company an overview of the market for their goods or services. The information about existing or future customers is either readily available, and needs analysing, or is gathered using a number of tried and trusted techniques. Just about every product has some kind of consumer feedback mechanism, through which marketers can gather the necessary insights into how much the brand is liked and how well it is performing. Through number crunching the collected data then analysing the results they can see the future of the product and adjust it accordingly to survive and prosper in the ever-changing market. Seeing the bigger picture is the goal and there are a number of ways to reach it.

One challenge early market researchers faced was the public's reluctance to offer personal information in the street.

Surveys

For the vast majority of marketing history, the most commonly used method of gathering information for quantitative research studies was via surveys. Traditionally, canvassers could be seen standing outside supermarkets holding clipboards and trying to get consumers to stop and answer a few questions about their shopping basket. It could also come via a phone call during which an agent asked, 'Can you spare us a few moments to answer some questions about…?'

Now it might come as a questionnaire attached to an email, or a text after a hotel visit, restaurant meal or even a hospital visit. The survey might take the form of a one to ten rating system, asking, 'How likely are you to recommend our service to a friend or family member?'

Areas such as Times Square are useful for gathering large amounts of data due to its popularity with tourists.

The image of the person with the clipboard stopping passers-by is becoming less relevant but is still a popular cliché.

These surveys are very specific to particular target audiences and as such can give the marketer an accurate picture of the usage and popularity of a brand across all its users. They can also be cross-referenced with other figures to see how competitive a product is or how a service is performing in competition with rival offerings. It is a less effective process than an in-depth analysis of a product, but will give the marketer enough viable data to make an informed conclusion.

Correlation research

If a company needs to find out how their brand is performing in relation to a competitor or another of their own companies, they might employ correlation research. This involves discovering the impact of one on the other by comparing two or more variables of the data they have collected. Once they have a view from the research, they can adapt, alter and manipulate the product or service to perform better in the market. These correlations can take the form of positive or negative positions and as such the reaction will reflect that. It will give the marketer the platform to produce more effective campaigns and marketing strategies.

An excellent example would be Galaxy chocolate bars learning what their market share and position is, based on the performance of Cadbury Dairy Milk, their chief rival and the market leader.

Causal-comparative research

This research method relies on the comparison of two or more different factors to determine the cause-effect relationship between multiple variables. It is also known as *ex post facto* (after the fact) research as the cause being studied is always examined in retrospect. It is mostly used in education and behavioural sciences but is increasingly used in marketing. These analyses are made using raw and available data.

Cadburys continued domination of the chocolate market is aided by their use of careful correlation research.

For example, a soft drink company might want to use sweeteners in its products to increase their health benefits but worry that a change in the taste will cause them to lose business. Causal research will allow them to determine if that is the case. It also applies to price rises in products or indeed any changes companies may want to make to their product, service or marketing.

Soft drink companies often find themselves questioning changes to their ingredients and its impact on their customers.

SWOT ANALYSIS ▶ *SWOT (Strengths, Weaknesses, Opportunities and Threats) analysis is used by companies to assess these factors in a business and see how they can best use them to their advantage. For example, a car company might have great engineering and reliability but the designs of their cars might be deemed as ugly and unappealing, like the Volkswagen beetle in the 1950s. In the USA the marketers turned the ugliness factor on its head and promoted the Beetle as cute, quirky and individual, compared to the flashy automobiles that were being sold there at the time, and it became a big hit.*

After a few years, it starts to look beautiful.

"Ugly, isn't it?"
"No class."
"Looks like an afterthought."
"Good for laughs."
"Stubby buggy."
"El Pig-O."

New York Magazine said: "And then there is the VW, which retains its value better than anything else. A 1956 VW is worth more today than any American sedan built the same year, with the possible exception of a Cadillac."

Around 27 miles to the gallon. Pints of oil instead of quarts. No radiator. Rear engine traction. Low insurance. $1,799* is the price. Beautiful, isn't it?

This series of award-winning ads by Doyle Dane Bernbach for the Volkswagon Beetle showed a masterful understanding of SWOT.

TURF analysis

(Totally Unduplicated Reach and Frequency) is mostly used in the research and understanding of a certain target market. It was originally used by companies to determine how many and what kind of people were watching, listening or reading their messaging so they could estimate the media budget. An example nowadays would be a fruit juice company trying to figure out how many different flavours or varieties of ingredients to offer possible customers in order to understand the potential of the market. They might consider launching seven different flavours but, in reality, only four might be bestsellers. Using the TURF algorithm, they will get the data they need to optimize the range they offer and save themselves expensive and wasteful manufacturing costs.

Public taste in fruit flavours is fickle, but there are certain perennial favourites like orange and strawberry.

Cross tabulation

Cross tabulation is a way to compare statistics and their relationship to a brand's sales performance in particular geographical areas or even consumer behavioural patterns. Using a chart with the relevant statistics entered and broken down into the area variables, a company can compare the data and get a picture of how their brand is performing among certain groups or in different localities. They then know where they need to concentrate their efforts for better sales.

Comparing data

CROSS TABULATION CHART

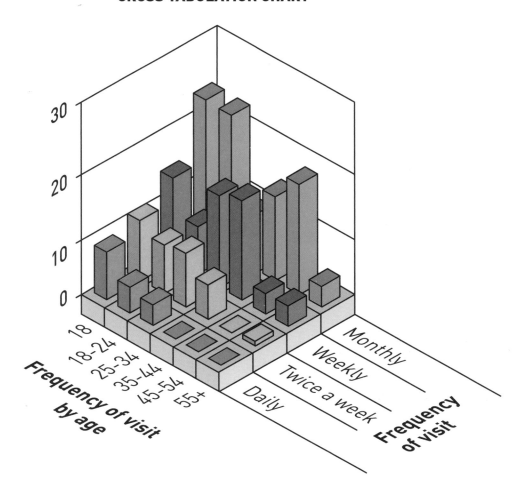

MARKET RESEARCH SURVEYS

These are not new to marketing, but, the advent of the internet has made them much easier and more accessible to today's marketer. Although there is some evidence of research surveys before his arrival on the scene, Daniel Starch is recognized by many as the first to professionalize the process. He invented the Starch Test in an attempt to measure the effectiveness of advertisements in newspapers and magazines back in the early 1920s. This involved door-to-door canvassers asking householders to recall any advertising they had seen in any publications they had read, and the impressions it had made on them. For the first time, companies could compare the effectiveness of their messaging against their rivals'.

George Gallup took market research to new levels of precision and efficacy when he founded the American Institute of Public Opinion. His pioneering work in polling techniques allowed him to break down the US electorate into demographic groups, which he then represented proportionally in a sample group of 3,000 people. It gave him the reliable data to confidently and correctly predict the outcome of the 1936 presidential election, with a win for Franklin D. Roosevelt. Subsequently, the Gallup Poll became a household name and was able to predict anything and everything in a consumer's daily life from politics to car sales.

Austrian-born psychologist Ernest Dichter (see pages 204–5) is known for his breakthrough work in motivational research, and the application of psychoanalytic processes. His theories revolved around brands having a 'soul' and therefore a human connection to the consumer. After World War I, his studies in consumer behaviour changed the way large multinational organizations saw their brands, and therefore advertised them to their customers.

In the early 1960s, Paul E. Green, a marketing professor, developed conjoint analysis, a predictive technique that works by ranking data based on surveys carried out with consumers on their likes and dislikes, and then applying it to their marketing strategies.

During the next decades, further advances were made in the collection and analysis of information gathered from consumer research surveys. Then, in 1995, the first weblog analysis software was launched. Named Analog, it was able to count how many views certain websites achieved but also from where the hits originated. It

George Gallup, originator of the Gallup Poll and numerous other key research sampling techniques.

paved the way for even more advanced systems like Google Analytics, which launched in the early 2000s.

Introduced in 2003, Net Promotor Score (NPS) is a metric used to measure how satisfied consumers are with a product or service, and gives companies the opportunity to compare their performance against their competitors'. The acceleration of technology and the massive rise in smartphone usage now gives researchers unparalleled access to detailed data and the ability to pinpoint consumers' needs and wants.

In just 100 years, marketing research has been transformed from an informed guessing game to a powerful and vital tool that gives companies targeted and accurate insights and enables them to deliver. Astronaut Neil Armstrong summed it up perfectly, 'Research is creating new knowledge.' Something with which all marketers would agree.

The first footprint on the moon. Astronaut Neil Armstrong's boot print after he stepped out onto the moon for the first time.

Conjoint analysis

This is a technique to determine how consumers make their complicated buying decisions. People are usually asked to complete a survey and the company will use the results of this to readjust their offerings. An example might be that a television manufacturer might conclude from the research that the customer is impressed by the screen size availability of their range but has issues with the audio quality. The company must then decide that in order to compete it might have to invest in better sound systems. However, that investment could impact on them being able offer the range of screen sizes they had before, and therefore could have a negative effect on their current customer base.

In the early 2000s many thought the trend would be towards larger and larger TV screens, but the creation of smart phones led to a paradigm shift towards smaller ones.

QUALITATIVE DATA

Qualitative market research is not an alternative to quantitative, it needs to be used in combination with it. Quantitative research gives a larger picture, covering

demographics and mass groups, while qualitative data gives closer, more personal insights that otherwise might be missed by the numerical approach.

Beginning in the 1950s, research techniques from psychology, sociology and ethnography began being turned to marketing purposes.

In-depth Interviews

One-on-one interviews can be conducted on a range of subjects with a wide variety of people, both from the target market and from a larger group. The personal nature of these interactions allows the interviewer to gain a much deeper understanding of the respondent and their views, beliefs and ideas, than they can glean through surveys or other quantitative research techniques. It's also the best way to get truthful responses regarding more sensitive topics that people might feel uncomfortable broaching in more formal surroundings. There is also the advantage of being able to analyse the subject's body language, which can also give clues to their preferences. While the vetting process for these interviews and the related costs might be higher than other techniques, there is significant benefit to using it. For example, a company may be looking to make big changes to one of its product lines or need to understand why its target audience may not be buying as much as they did, and quantitative techniques were not providing more insightful answers.

Qualitative data gives closer, more personal insights.

Focus groups are also used extensively in film, TV and other entertainment research.

One-on-one interviews allow the subject to relax and be more honest.

Focus groups

This technique involves gathering relevant groups of people, possibly subsets of a target market or a cross-section of the general public. They are then probed along specific investigative lines and/or shown relevant materials and asked for their opinions. As with in-depth interviews, the framework of the questions and the guidance of the discussion will be carefully crafted to particular aims. However, the benefit of focus groups is that interaction between the participants can often prompt new insights and useful new directions that may not have been anticipated. Focus groups can only really be effective if the setting is informal or at least designed to seem that way, and that is its disadvantage when set against the in-depth interview model.

Projective tests

This type of test, usually conducted on a one-to-one basis, is where visual, aural or textual stimuli are used to get rapid unfiltered responses from participants. The Rorschach inkblot test developed in 1921, in which the participant is shown a series of ten inkblot cards and asked what they see in the inkblot image on each one, is the most well-known example, although it is now considered unreliable. Projective tests can be very effective in the field of marketing research, especially in areas where companies need an insight into people's underlying or instinctive reaction to their products.

The Rorschach inkblot test was developed in 1921.

Another example is the brand personality test, where the subject is asked what personality they would assign certain brands if they were a human. This allows companies to understand people's perception of their brand (or their competitors' products) and either reflect that in their marketing or aim to change it if the company finds the results unfavourable.

Online analysis

Obviously, with caveats, all of the above techniques can now be conducted virtually online using video conferencing, although their effectiveness compared to the actual physical version is hotly debated. However, an increasingly online world offers a variety of different types of new qualitative research techniques, which, if used carefully, can be very fruitful. For instance, a word search of a product or service can simply be conducted on one of the many social networking sites such as Twitter or Facebook. Often people will give immediate responses to product rollouts and marketing campaigns on these apps, serving as enormous focus groups and allowing marketers to get an idea of how their marketing is working in real time. This has to be done carefully, with the knowledge that people's responses in these spaces might not be totally truthful, whether consciously or unconsciously.

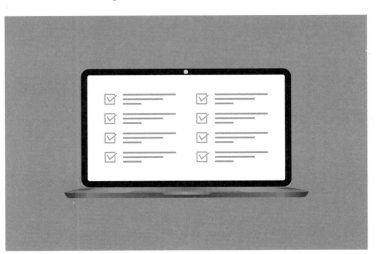

The internet and research

Online analysis is increasingly the primary method of modern data gathering.

MARKETING MISHAPS: HOOVER FREE FLIGHT PROMOTION

In the early 1990s, the UK was heading into a recession and companies across the country were struggling to find ways to prop up their dwindling profits. Hoover had long been the global brand leader in electrical, domestic cleaning products, so much so that the word 'Hoover' had become a generic noun for 'vacuum-cleaner'.

Although Hoover had American roots, it was at the time one of the UK's most trusted brands, holding a 50 per cent share of the market for many decades. However, its dominance was under threat from newcomers like Dyson. It had tried to keep ahead of the opposition with daring but ill-fated new product innovations, like 'talking vacuums' that told the consumer when it was ready to empty. Hoover's profits had been taking a hit for a few years shrinking from $147 million in 1987 to $74 million in 1992 and therefore it was already looking for ways to improve.

In the UK, Hoover teamed up with a cheap flights company called JSI Travel, who had also been feeling the effects of the recession, and devised a 'Free Flights' promotion with the promise, 'Two free flights! Unbelievable!'. JSI would sell the flights in bulk to Hoover and handle the travel arrangements, and Hoover had the opportunity to get rid of the excess products gathering dust in their warehouses.

All the consumer had to do was purchase a minimum of £100 of Hoover products to qualify for the 'free flights'. The idea was passed in front of risk assessment professionals, who advised them against doing it. One said, 'To me it made no logical sense. Having looked at the details of the promotion and attempting to calculate how it would actually work, I declined to even offer risk management coverage.'

Undaunted, Hoover decided to proceed, arguing that only a tiny fraction of purchasers would actually bother to navigate the complicated steps needed to take up the offer. Furthermore, they felt consumers were likely to spend much more than the £100 minimum, which would offset any outlay anyway. The promotions people at Hoover added extra insurance by making the terms and conditions almost impossible:

1: When a customer purchased a Hoover appliance for at least £100 at select department stores, they then had to mail in their receipt along with their application within 14 days of making their purchase.
2: Hoover would then send back a registration form, which had to be completed and returned within another 14 days.
3: Hoover would then send out a travel voucher. The customer then had only 30 days to choose three combinations of departure airports, dates and destinations.
4: Hoover retained the right to refuse the combinations selected by the customer, subsequently insisting that the customer select a further three alternatives.
5: Hoover also reserved the right to refuse the alternatives and offer a combination of their own choosing. This meant that the customer's flight would take place on a date and from a location that might well be inconvenient.

The initial offer was for return flights to European destinations and the uptake was an immediate success, so much so that Hoover sold almost their entire stock of £119 upright cleaners from the select department stores, and so had to increase production at its factory, employing more staff to meet demand.

Buoyed with the initial success, in November 1992 Hoover decided to upgrade the promotion to include free flights to the USA, which seemed to them to be a logical escalation. However, consumers soon realized that for the price of the cheapest Hoover product, just over £100, they could get a round trip to the USA (worth around £600 at the time) and so applications soared. Some buyers didn't even bother to pick up the product they'd purchased, so good was the deal.

Hoover had reckoned on a maximum of 50,000 applications but had now received more than 300,000, and although they had made around £30 million from the scheme the cost of honouring the flights was estimated to be over £100 million. Hoover were now desperate to extricate themselves from what was turning into a financial catastrophe of epic proportions. They made the process to receive the flights even more complicated and when that didn't stem the tide, they cancelled it. The consumers who had bought into the 'Unbelievable!' promotion were left angry and confused by Hoover reneging on the deal. They formed pressure groups to pursue legal action against them. One group even bought shares in Maytag, Hoover's holding company, so they could lobby its executives at the AGM.

The fallout of this marketing disaster was as unbelievable as the promotion itself. Several of their top executives were axed and the company's European division was sold to a competitor, Candy. Court cases carried on until 1998 and, in a final ignominy for Hoover, the royal family removed its prestigious royal seal of Approval after a damning BBC documentary in 2004. It just goes to show that no matter how trusted a brand, ill-considered marketing and badly researched schemes can bring even the mightiest companies to their knees.

Hoover's mis-step shows how critical it is to consider all possible angles and outcomes of a marketing strategy.

Brand Bio:
NETFLIX

NETFLIX WAS FOUNDED as a mail order-based DVD rental service in 1997, when DVDs were first introduced to the market. It then grew exponentially over the following decade, going from 300,000 subscribers in 2000 to 26 million worldwide in 2011. The increasing number of DVD players in households drove this growth, but it was when Netflix first considered a streaming service in 2005 that it started its journey to the massive multimedia conglomerate it is today.

Netflix's content platform had a small start and was considered merely an addition to its DVD service for years, due to low download speeds and confusion about how to access their service. This confusion was compounded in 2011 when they decided to separate their DVD rental and streaming services (an excellent idea in the long run) and rebrand their DVD rental service as 'Qwikster' (an ill-considered idea and a name customers disliked). While their streaming service was clearly the future of their business, rebranding the original service that had got them to where they were seemed like a slap in the face to their loyal customers. They quickly reversed that decision.

From that point, as streaming technology increased and their service included now-common elements such as recommendation algorithms, Netflix's online platform increased in popularity with over 203 million paid subscriptions across the globe since January 2021.

To supplement its growing library of TV and film, in 2011 Netflix began acquiring original content, starting with *House of Cards* in 2013 and then increasing its investment in unique productions to the extent that in 2017 it announced its intention for 50 per cent of its library to be bespoke programming. Signing exclusive multi-year development deals with talent as diverse as Adam Sandler, Barack and Michelle Obama, and *Stranger Things* creators the Duffer Brothers, positioned Netflix not just as an entertainment service but something akin to a film and television production juggernaut.

Netflix's decisions are guided by how it can measure the metrics of its audience precisely as they use its service. Despite this, its attitude to content creation can't be described as conservative as it has partnered with a wide variety of companies and produced elements as different as Japanese manga and hard-hitting documentaries. It has also been shrewd with how it interacts with and approaches the culture it has created, choosing to embrace the phrase 'Netflix and chill' rather than balk at the explicit nature of its true meaning.

The growing number of other streaming services has meant that some of the content available to Netflix is now corralled in other apps like Disney+ and Amazon Prime, but at the moment it retains its market dominance, with its logo and even its UI design being recognizably iconic. With its new interactive specials, it looks to continue to be a significant player in entertainment platforms. Whereas in the past, marketing research was a separate part of marketing, Netflix's platform allows it to conduct research 24/7 as a normal part of its operations.

People use Netflix because it can recommend content they want, and Netflix uses its customers' feedback to make that possible.

Netflix's ability to constantly monitor its audiences' behaviour has allowed it to dominate the market.

NAMES TO KNOW: CHARLES COOLIDGE PARLIN

Charles Coolidge Parlin's pioneering research showed the importance of intensive data gathering.

(1872 – 15 October 1942)
Considered by many to be the founding father of market research, Charles Coolidge Parlin's path into the world of marketing was unusual. He spent the first years of his working life as a high school teacher. In 1911, at the age of 38, Parlin had an interview at the Curtis Publishing Company for a position as a researcher in their advertising department. When asked what qualifications he had for the position, he replied, 'I think the most valuable one is not knowing anything.'

He was hired with an unspecified title for his work, so he created one of his own, calling it 'commercial research', which later became market research. His first project was working on a new magazine, Country Gentleman, *aimed at America's huge farming sector. However, at the time there was very little knowledge of the agricultural sector readily available so Parlin embarked on a huge study.*

He conducted six months of interviews with agriculturalists, the very people who would be

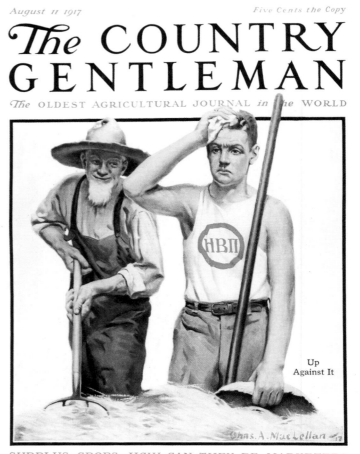

An early edition of Country Gentleman, *the magazine for which Parlin conducted his first intensive research project.*

buying advertising space in Country Gentleman, *and produced a 460-page survey. It gave the publishers an in-depth insight into the farming industry, their machinery and techniques and, crucially, the farmers themselves.*

His next research project would see Parlin conduct a study on what he called, 'The market for almost everything in the nation's one hundred largest cities'. It involved over a thousand interviews and the findings would unearth eye-opening conclusions about how the US commercial market worked. This pioneering report, called 'Department Store Lines', drew distinctions between convenience and shopping goods and suggested that marketers should focus on selling shopping goods in order to maximize profits.

His early reports and studies founded many of the principles that the marketing industry holds dear today, and central to these was the importance of understanding the consumer. After many years working for Curtis Publishing, and a phenomenal number of hugely important studies into many of the USA's industries, Parlin partnered with Donald M. Hobart to start his own research company, National Analysts. Although it was technically a division of Curtis, it operated independently, setting the standards for research companies and techniques worldwide.

Such was his impact on marketing and market research that the Charles Coolidge Parlin Marketing Research Award is the oldest and most prestigious honour in this sector, cementing his reputation as the foremost pioneer in his field.

Summary

Consumers decide the fate of a brand, and for the marketer, knowing what they think is fundamental to the success of the products and services they are offering. Research is probably the most valuable tool at a marketer's disposal: it forms the backbone of their marketing strategy. In 1597, Sir Francis Bacon prophetically stated, '*Scientia potentia est*', meaning, 'Knowledge is power'. More than 500 years later, that statement still holds true.

Brand Strategy • Brand Evolution • Brand Personality • Brand Icons • Brand Associations • Brand Tribalism • Brand Consistency • Brand Differentiation

BRAND EVOLUTION

COMPANY

MULTI-BRAND

BRAND ICONS

BRAND STRATEGY

BRAND EXTENSIONS

NEW BRAND

BRAND AWARENESS

BRAND AMBASSADORS

CONSUMER

TRIBALISM

SOCIAL MEDIA

BRAND PERSONALITY

Many of the most famous brands are almost immediately recognizable from their logos.

Big brands

BRAND STRATEGY

Branding is something that is so intrinsic to modern marketing that everything a company does to define its own unique brand will determine its success or failure in the marketplace. Careful planning and a thorough understanding of who they are, what they do and how the consumer sees them must go into any brand strategy for every company.

A company's brand strategy will depend on four considerations:

BRAND STRATEGY

NEW BRAND

PRODUCT LINE EXTENSION

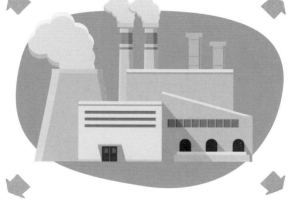

BRAND EXTENSION

MULTIBRAND

1. Is the brand a **product line extension?** In other words, does it resemble any product that the company already offers? If it bears the same brand name, it will be targeting the same market as the existing brand. It's an often-used strategy, as usually the existing brand already has a loyal customer base, and it would stand to reason that there would be some interest in a variation of it. An example of a product line extension would be Marmite XO (Extra Old). This is a very similar spread to the usual dark, salty Marmite, but it has a stronger taste than the original and is marketed in the style of a rare whisky. By piggybacking of the reputation of an established product, and doing careful research on taste, a company will have a ready-made market of interested consumers.

Marmite X-0 left the shelves in 2009 but was reintroduced 10 years later to great approbation.

BRAND VS. BRANDING ▶ *It is worth drawing a distinction between a **brand** and **branding**. A brand is what consumers see as a company's product or service or the company itself, whereas branding is what the company does to present the brand to the consumer and influence choice.*

2. **Multi-brand** is a variation of a product line extension, but instead of the brand having a single brand name, a company may offer the same kinds of products (foods, toiletries etc) under different brand names. This is a strategy aimed at targeting different consumer categories, with the same product but branded and packaged differently. Supermarkets will often employ this strategy. Tesco has a range of food items at the quality end called 'Tesco Finest', which are aimed at customers looking for a more special food experience, but visitors to their supermarkets will find a very similar range offered under the regular Tesco label for people looking for value. Both would be good quality, but by presenting and packaging Tesco Finest in a more premium way they can charge a premium price.

Tesco offer products at different price levels with different quality, but all under the same Tesco brand name.

Porsche are extremely careful that any brand extensions fit their high-end engineering image.

3. **Brand extensions,** involve offering a bigger range of products under the same brand umbrella. This strategy will depend on a deep understanding of the brand's ability to sustain the stretch of credibility involved. The people who often inhabit coffee shops are quite likely to be wearing jeans, but would they buy coffee branded by Levi's? A good example would be Porsche, famed for their sports cars, producing sunglasses. Their design and engineering credentials would support the quality, and it would be an opportunity for someone who couldn't afford the car to enjoy some of the cache that goes with the Porsche badge.

A completely new line

4. The final strategy would be developing a **new brand,** whereby a company introduces a product to a market that they have never been involved with before. This would mean starting from scratch with product, packaging and brand name. The groundwork has to be meticulous in order to give the new brand a chance of success. It is also the costliest model, as everything has to be created: the production line, the product, the packaging and the marketing model, all have to be set up.

BRAND AWARENESS ▶ *This describes how familiar a brand is to the consumer by name. Creating good brand awareness is a key step whether a company is launching a new product or reviving the fortunes of an existing one. It's the task of the marketer to identify the qualities a brand has that distinguish it from the competition, then maximize that potential.*

BRAND EVOLUTION

In the fast-moving world of modern marketing, a brand that stands still can often be left behind. However, that doesn't mean that a company has to completely change its offering in order to prosper. By carefully monitoring the market and how they fit into it, they can effect a brand evolution rather than a revolution. For example, in the UK, Barbour has, for five generations, been the chosen waterproof clothing brand for country folk and royalty. Today, they have not lost any of their status as the premium weather-defiant wear, but they have also found a new following among the younger market. A mission statement on their website tells you all you need to know about Barbour's evolution: 'Barbour remains true to its core values as a family business which espouses the unique values of the British Countryside and brings the qualities of wit, grit and glamour to its beautifully functional clothing.'

BRAND PERSONALITY

One of the initial steps for a company reviewing their current brand or creating a new one is to establish their brand personality. These are the characteristics that define the brand in human terms – the things to which the consumer can relate.

Barbour have successfully managed to court both a traditional country market and a trendy youth market.

An interesting exercise that marketing people sometimes employ with clients in search of their brand's personality is to get the individuals involved to look at themselves as a brand. They ask them to write down any physical or emotional trait that singles them out, anything from the colour of their hair to which sports team they support. By recording their individual qualities, they define what makes them stand out among their peers.

The same technique can be applied to creating a brand's personality. What are the consistencies that the consumers relate to in a brand, the things they find appealing and the features that they can identify with?

For example, Primark might identify themselves as 'Affordable fashion for all the family'. Their personality would hinge on the accessible nature of their shops and clothing, also on the fact

THE IDEAL PARTNERSHIP

An example of a brand ambassador who is now inseparable from the brand he represents is sports presenter and former England footballer, Gary Lineker. He has been associated with crisp manufacturer, Walkers, since 1994, appearing right across all their promotional material.

What is it that makes this partnership ideal? Walkers Crisps have always been made in Leicester, the city of Lineker's birth, and he started his footballing career at Leicester City Football Club, who he supported as a boy. Then he went on to

Gary Lineker, England footballer, BBC presenter and the public face of Walker's Crisps.

Walkers' brand value increased by £40.5 million in 2020.

make his mark as a free-scoring striker at other English and European clubs, like Tottenham Hotspur and Barcelona, as well as winning 80 England caps. So, for Walkers Crisps, Gary Lineker was the ultimate local boy made good, and as Walkers present themselves as a local brand that has become famous across the nation, he works well as their public face. It has worked very well for him, too, cementing his public persona as an approachable nice guy, and netting him a new contract with Walkers in 2020, that is worth £1.2 million.

the customer can buy something for everyone in any season. Therefore, their brand personality might be seen as: 'A loyal family friend who is always there when they're needed.'

Another clothing brand, like Zara, would see their main advantages as 'Confident, unpretentious style and a shopping experience that gives the customer a feeling of a little exclusivity'. Therefore, their brand personality could be: 'The classy friend with whom they like to be seen'.

Marketers will often find a real person to represent their brand and what it stands for: these are called **brand ambassadors**. It is not just a case of picking a celebrity to endorse a company, product or service. Brand ambassadors have a much more important role as they represent the brand in physical form. They're people who are inextricably linked to the brand and what it stands for, someone the consumer would believe to represent the qualities of the brand and in that way, trust. Brand ambassadors will be used in advertising and promotional messaging. In online activities, they are often influencers with large, devoted followings.

BRAND ICONS

While brand ambassadors are a figurative personification of a brand, you can often have a literal version with brand icons, or mascots. More than just a logo, they are quite often characters created to adorn packaging or in stores.

Icons and mascots

Classic examples created in the USA in the 1950s include Tony the Tiger for Kellogg's Frosted Flakes and Ronald McDonald, while in the UK the Guinness Toucan originated in 1935 and was a huge success.

Just about every Olympic Games has produced brand icons to help promote them, with mixed results: who can remember the two that they used to promote the 2012 London Games, Wenlock and Mandeville? If they are carefully crafted and nurtured by marketers they can endure for decades, if not, they are forgotten in an instant.

BRAND ASSOCIATIONS

Creating memorable and likable qualities for a brand is important for any company and their relationship with the consumer. These qualities are the factors that will differentiate them from the competition and are aptly named **brand associations**, providing the consumer with a reason to favour their product over a rival's.

A consumer's emotional response to a product or service is as much a trigger for them to buy as a practical reason for making the purchase. The marketer has a better chance of creating the right brand associations if he understands the consumer's relationship with their brand. They will study all the reliable data from qualitative and quantitative research, as well as sales to find the right associations.

American sneaker brand Converse All Star had been the chosen footwear of generations of teenagers. Converse knew that their products, basic canvas tennis shoes, would be worn until they fell apart, partly because students were cash strapped, partly as a badge of rebellious youth. They identified their brand personality as, 'confident, genuine, hardworking, tough, unselfish and passionate.' In their advertising campaign they happily featured wornpout, scruffy All Stars that had been personalized by their owners with a tagline that simply said, 'So ugly, they're cool' – a personification of the counterculture image they represent. By completely understanding the emotional attachment millions of teenagers have to their favourite sneakers, no matter how battered they are, they found the perfect brand association to sell new shoes to a new generation.

The Guinness toucan was created in 1935 by advertising agency S.H. Benson, and the poster copy was written by crime author Dorothy L Sayers.

Converse All-Star basketball sneakers are known as Chucks, due to their association with basketballer and brand ambassador Charles H. 'Chuck' Taylor.

A crowd of supporters in Manchester United's stadium at Old Trafford fully reflects the club's strong branding and its associated brand tribalism.

The brand book

BRAND TRIBALISM

The Converse All Star campaign also identifies with another form of brand consciousness, known as brand tribalism. A brand tribe is a group of consumers who collectively associate themselves with a brand. This group will actively seek out others who share their interest in a brand or product so they can share their common passion. They fall into all kinds of categories, from sports tribes to fashion and music.

Brand tribalism can cross the borders of each social group, uniting young and old, wealthy and working class, because of their shared interest. Now that the internet dominates people's lives, the spread of brand tribalism crosses international barriers, uniting people from totally different countries and cultures.

The ultimate expression of tribalism can be found in football. Once upon a time fans of a certain club would be restricted to the area where it was located, but the globalization of the game has meant that clubs now have followers across the world. The marketing machines that drive the fortunes of the biggest clubs means they now have customers in their millions, where it was once just a few thousand, and football tribalism has become brand tribalism.

Manchester United's fan base has grown from the 70,000 who would come to Old Trafford on a Saturday afternoon in the 1950s, to an estimated 1.1 billion worldwide at the last count. This gives them massive leverage with the sponsors whose branding adorns their kit and their stadium. Manchester United's latest partner is TeamViewer, a software company, who have just signed a £235 million contract to be the main logo on their shirts. They are arguably the most valuable sports brand in the world, worth more than £4 billion – proof that their marketing team has been as successful as the football team.

BRAND CONSISTENCY

Whatever the brand identity, applying it in a consistent way is imperative. **Brand consistency,** is something that every company should strive for in everything they do. Most companies will produce a brand book, which is a document that lays out the consistencies they expect everyone associated with marketing the brand to adhere to. The brand book will contain logos bearing the company name in all its iterations, colour schemes, and fonts to be used on all promotional material, both internally and externally, in all their different sizes. It will also recommend the type of imagery that the brand should be associated with and in some cases, the images they should not be seen to use. It will also feature the brand history and story behind it, its mission and the tone of voice that should be adopted when producing advertising and PR material. By maintaining a rigorous approach to their brand consistency, a company will protect the brand image from misuse and imitators.

Of course, branding is not just about logos and fonts; it can even include the product. Companies can find a point of difference with their offering and promote that to separate them from their competitors. An example is Wendy's fast-food chain in the USA, which made their hamburger patties square where all their rivals' burgers were round.

Branding on social media

While brand consistency is obviously paramount, there are some circumstances in which the marketer needs to think carefully about how the brand is being brought to the consumer. Social media adds an extra challenge. Social media sites differ not just on the types of demographics they include, but also their own favoured tone. For example, Instagram is more susceptible to an image-led, aspirational type of content while Twitter thrives on an irreverent, ironic humour compressed into its 280 characters. An example of this is Wendy's well-regarded Twitter account, which won plaudits for its funny, sometimes outrageous responses to other brand's tweets. They got the brand attention in a way that, while it didn't exactly line up with Wendy's other advertising, was very relatable and emphasized its humanity in an ironic way.

BRAND DIFFERENTIATION

This the way similar brands ensure that they don't lose their place in the market either being too much like other brands that operate in the same field or by those who target the same groups. If a company's brand becomes too generic, then their customers will find they don't particularly care if they're purchasing their product or that of a similar-enough rival. Coke and Pepsi struggled with this for decades and some would say they still haven't solved it.

Nike and Adidas are good examples of brands that have managed to define themselves differently while existing solidly in the same area,. They are both large multinational companies that provide branded sportswear and sports equipment. Nike takes a more sports-oriented approach to its branding, using international superstar athletes to embody its 'Just Do It' slogan. Adidas, in comparison, has struggled with slogans but is seen as 'cooler' because it has featured celebrities from other walks of life, for example music, in its campaigns, using its long-term association with hip hop culture to provide crossover promotions with outspoken figures like Beyoncé and Kanye West.

With food items like burgers, the actual make-up and contents of the product itself can be an opportunity for branding.

Long term rivals in sportswear, Adidas and Nike have differing approaches as fashion brands.

NEW YORK CITY is perhaps the most iconic location in the USA. It's often the first place people think of in association with the country, with endless film and television series set among the city's many iconic landmarks.

Between the 1940s and the 1960s, New York had a reputation for being sophisticated and bohemian, the centre of the USA and indeed the world in terms of art, culture – and – as it was the location of Wall Street – money. During the 1970s, economic decline led to citywide unemployment and rampant crime. Combined with events like the Vietnam War, this caused a malaise and cynicism that led people to devalue the city. Both the city and its brand began to struggle. In 1975, New York City Council ran out of money, even for day-to-day operations. It was seen as dirty, dangerous and dilapidated, it needed a bailout and to rehabilitate its image.

In 1977, the high-profile advertising agency Wells, Rich, Greene was hired to put together a marketing campaign to promote tourism in the both the state and the city, and they settled on the simple slogan, 'I Love New York'. Separately, the State Department of Commerce hired Milton Glaser to create a design based on the slogan. Glaser was an accomplished and insightful graphic designer, known for his pioneering work in psychedelic art and design. He was also a long-term New York resident who loved the city. He created the 'I (heart symbol) New York' design on a scrap of paper in the back of a taxi cab (the original of which is on display in New York's Museum of Modern Art). Glaser says it's possible he was subliminally influenced by Robert Indiana's classic pop art image 'LOVE'.

The Bronx in the 1960s showed considerable dilapidation and urban decay.

Although wilfully naïve in style people enjoyed the slogan's friendliness and simplicity. It contrasted with the cynicism and depression around the city's reputation in its darkest days, and acted like an open invitation to anyone who saw it to think about what they loved about the city.

Today, the logo has become so iconic it's difficult for modern-day audiences to appreciate the simple power of its message, one that has been endlessly co-opted and parodied by other companies and places all over the world. To contemporary

audiences, it almost seems like touristy chintz but it was enough to spearhead the rehabilitation of the city and re-establish its reputation.

Glaser didn't think the campaign would be longer than a couple of months and didn't ask to be paid for the work. But it has endured and become an inescapable symbol ,splashed across T-shirts, mugs and posters everywhere tourists are able to spend money. In 2001, he made a special alternate version with a black smudge on the heart to reflect the events of 9/11, reclaiming the symbol that has been repurposed in tourist traps in cities across the globe, making the case for it to be as representative of the city as the Statue of Liberty or the Empire State Building.

The I Love NY symbol (and its copies) is now so ubiquitous it's difficult to imagine tourist shops in New York city without it.

NAMES TO KNOW: MARY QUANT

Mary Quant not only created iconic fashion but was herself a 60s icon.

There are few designers who can have had such a profound impact on fashion and style branding than Mary Quant. She was born in Blackheath, London in 1930, the daughter of two Welsh school teachers. Educated at Blackheath High School, she then studied illustration at Goldsmiths, where she obtained a diploma in art and design. There she met the aristocratic Alexander Plunkett-Green who would become her future husband and business partner.

Mary Quant's true vocation was fashion design and, after serving an apprenticeship with a bespoke milliner, she teamed up with Plunkett-Greene to open a boutique in the King's Road, Chelsea called Bazaar, in a building he had recently purchased.

In the mid-1950s, Quant and Plunkett-Greene teamed up with a lawyer-turned-photographer, Archie McNair to launch a restaurant, Alexander's, with the boutique in the basement. This part of London was frequented by the 'Chelsea set', a group of young, influential artists, designers and film-makers, and it was a location that would prove to be pivotal in establishing the leading trends of what was to become the 'Swinging Sixties'.

At first, she sold other designers' clothes that she bought on the wholesale market, but she quickly found she was unsatisfied with the range and standards available. After attending night school to learn clothes cutting and design, she threw herself into designing, producing and selling her own clothes.

Quant soon established a reputation for creating unique and leading-edge fashions at competitive prices, and the quick turnaround meant that her offerings were always fresh for her growing band of devotees. Her designs were a refreshing contrast to the staid styles offered by post-war designers, and the experience of a visit to her boutique was in stark contrast to a department store at the time.

The fun window displays accompanied by loud music and free drinks made the shopping experience at Bazaar a big attraction to the denizens of Chelsea, who were always in search of something different. She was at the epicentre of the changing youth culture in the late 1950s and early 1960s and her designs were influenced by the young trendsetters, from street musicians to the emerging 'Mods' (short for modernists). Mary Quant went for bold colours and simple tunic-style dresses, often contrasting them with brightly coloured tights.

By 1957, she had opened her second store on the King's Road with interiors created by Terence Conran, another up-and-coming designer. She was at the forefront of everything that defined the 'Swinging Sixties', pioneering the use of unusual materials like PVC, to create dresses and thigh-length boots for her 'Wet Look' range. Mary Quant is credited with perhaps the most iconic look in fashion history, the mini skirt – a trend that took the world by storm back then and continues to make regular comebacks with high-street fashion emporiums.

However, it wasn't just her clothes that became part of her brand. She also teamed up with Vidal Sassoon, the most influential hairdresser at the time, for her defining 'A-line' bob hairstyle. She went on to launch a cosmetic brand with the distinctive 'Daisy' logo, among other ventures, and by the end of 1960s was universally recognized as the UK's most influential designer. It was estimated that up to 7 million women had at least one of her products in their wardrobe.

Dame Mary Quant has received numerous honours and awards over her long and illustrious career but perhaps, most significantly, she is inseparable from the brand she established.

As she famously said, 'Fashion is not frivolous. It is a part of being alive today.'

Mary Quant logo badges, showing the simple, understated flower symbol.

Summary

From the CEO down to the cleaner, knowing what the brand stands for and how that is expressed physically and emotionally is important. When it comes to their marketing partners, the advertising and PR agencies, taking their branding to the consumer in the right way will have a huge effect on the success of how it is promoted, and how successful it is.

As marketing guru Seth Godin put it, 'A brand is the set of expectations, memories, stories and relationships that, taken together, account for a consumer's decision to choose one product or service over another.'

Chapter Ten

ADVERTISING AND CREATIVE PROCESS

Advertising: A Brief History • How an Advertising Agency Works • The Structure of an Advertising Team • PR Agencies

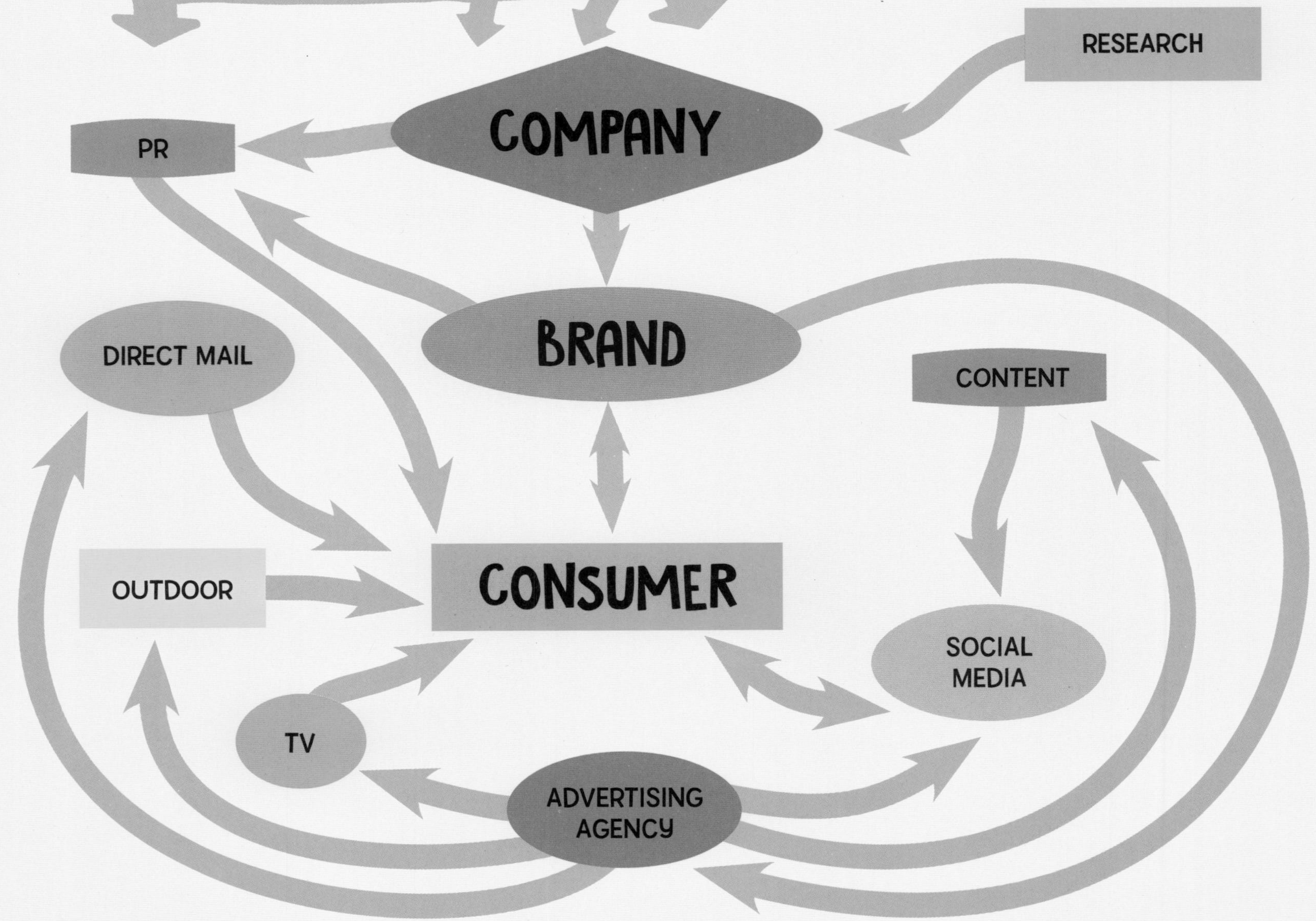

RESEARCH
COMPANY
PR
BRAND
DIRECT MAIL
CONTENT
OUTDOOR
CONSUMER
SOCIAL MEDIA
TV
ADVERTISING AGENCY

ADVERTISING: A BRIEF HISTORY

Advertising is the ultimate marketing tool. Companies apportion a significant part of their marketing budget to paid-for messages created by advertising agencies. The process is a well oiled machine in today's fast-moving market society, and the advent of the World Wide Web added even more potency and efficacy to the practice of advertising. It is often seen as the glamorous end of the business of marketing and the screening of the television series *Mad Men* did much to support the average person's view of it as such. In truth, it is a highly complex and intelligent fusion of art and science.

Every advertising campaign comes from a moment of inspiration, matched with a lot of perspiration.

Although there are many recorded instances of individuals and companies advertising their wares before the 19th century, it was at that point that marketing adopted the practice more assertively. During the early 1800s, advertising was restricted to posters, handbills and flyers, as there was a stamp duty levied on the newspapers of the time, which limited their ability to carry ads. Advertisements were not completely absent from periodicals, but they were scattered among the tightly set columns, which restricted them creatively and meant they were devoid of images.

Despite advertising being seen as a practice that wasn't respectable, and media options being limited, its influence grew as the century progressed. After establishing itself in Europe, advertising as a marketing tool soon spread to the USA, and in 1840 the world's first advertising agency was set up by Volney B. Palmer in Philadelphia. Palmer bought space in newspapers then sold it on at a higher rate to companies wanting to advertise their goods in them.

A watercolour painting of early 19th-century advertising, showing how flyposting was an epidemic.

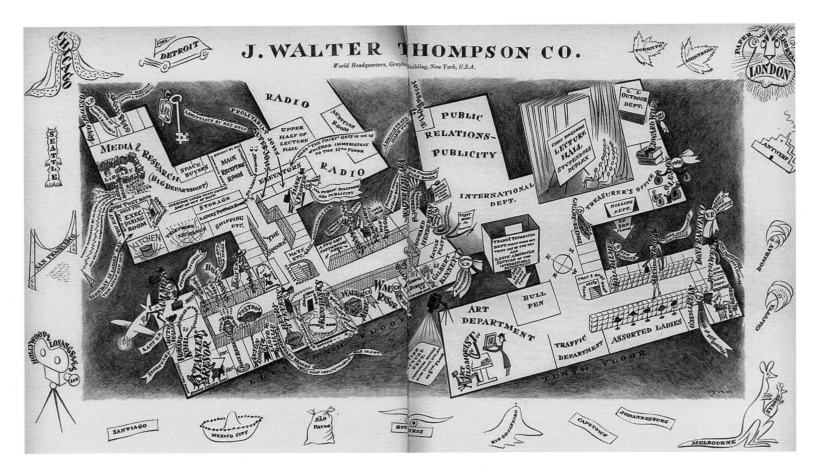

A plan of the 1940s New York headquarters of J. Walter Thompson, a household name in advertising for many years.

Arrival of the professionals

By the late 19th century, the first full-service agencies had arrived, not only placing advertisements but also creating and producing them for companies – a task that sellers had previously had to undertake themselves.

Suddenly, the level of sophistication of ads had taken a huge leap forwards, with advertising agencies employing professional writers and artists to create catchy copy and eye-catching visuals. At the beginning of the 20th century, there were established agencies like J. Walter Thompson operating internationally, with offices in New York City and London.

Advertising was becoming vital for companies' marketing efforts and agencies were not just employing creatives but also psychologists and human behavioural experts in order to better understand the consumer.

In the early 20th century, radio became a new medium for advertisers, enabling them greater reach and more creativity, with music and famous voices extolling the virtues of products. The advertising industry in the USA was already a powerful influence, and realizing the significance of radio's ability to reach the masses, it provided the funds for the growth of radio stations right across the country.

Post-war boom

During the Great Depression in the 1930s, advertising suffered in the same way as the global economy, and it wasn't until after World War II that it really started to re-establish itself as the most potent tool in the marketer's armoury. By then television was the number one medium for advertisers, with massive audiences watching their favourite shows every night. In the USA, commercial TV was already having an impact on advertising budgets. Companies were investing more and more money getting their messages across to the consumer in slickly made ads and show sponsorship.

In 1950, the total US spend on advertising had already reached $5.7 billion, with cars, domestic appliances and food accounting for the largest proportion of it. Cigarette companies were also able to advertise their products without restrictions: in 1955, a TV commercial for Camel claimed that more doctors smoked their brand than any other.

Madison Avenue in New York was the epicentre of advertising, and it was orchestrating the huge post-war boom, but the business was growing in the UK as well. In the 1960s, Britain was undergoing a cultural watershed: the music, fashion and art that was being produced was having a huge influence on young people, not just in the UK but across the globe. New agencies in London were creating advertising that reflected the experimentation going on in the arts. Collett Dickenson Pearce were at the forefront of this new wave, picking up the gauntlet laid down by American agencies like Doyle Dane Bernbach in the USA, and creating highly creative and hugely impactful campaigns for their clients. Famous ads for Parker Pens, Hamlet Cigars and Birds Eye food were scooping up industry awards both in the UK and the rest of the world.

Madison Avenue was the epicentre of the US Advertising industry, as epitomised in the TV series Mad Men.

Maurice and Charles Saatchi – brothers who managed to make their own name as famous as their clients'.

Boom and bust in advertising

Creative excellence

In 1963, The Design and Art Direction (D&AD) awards were launched, to help define the standards of excellence that the advertising industry aspired to. D&AD's Yellow Pencil went on to be the most coveted award for advertising creatives globally. New levels of proficiency, not just creatively, but with media planning and research, meant that London was the new mecca of the advertising world.

Agencies such as Saatchi & Saatchi, founded by brothers Maurice and Charles in 1970, were taking the industry by storm. It produced breakthrough creative work like the Pregnant Man print ad for the government's Health Education Council, warning about the consequences of unwanted pregnancies. Saatchi & Saatchi were also making big profits from the business, and reinvesting them into the acquisition of other agencies, allowing them spectacular growth and domination in the business.

The 1970s was a halcyon period in advertising as companies had increased their budgets and the advertising agencies were making powerful messages for them, and substantial profits from them. The standard fees were 15 per cent of the advertising budget plus mark-ups on all third-party costs, like TV commercial production and print artwork. A global recession slowed the growth of the business, but it bounced back in the 1980s, heralding a new golden age for the industry. Growth in billings were exponential, showing that companies still felt that it was the most effective way to market their products.

Apple's '1984' TV commercial, inspired by George Orwell's book, was indicative of the creative invention that agencies were now exercising on behalf of their clients. Created by American agency Chiat Day, and directed by Hollywood heavyweight Ridley Scott, it set the bar for the industry.

The internet revolution

Another recession slowed growth, but the most life changing event so far was about to hit marketing and the advertising industry in the 1990s. The World Wide Web came into people's lives and it changed the way humanity thought, lived and shopped. Its impact on marketing was immense, developing so quickly that advertising agencies have been playing catch-up since its advent. It has affected not only the way they need to talk to the consumer but the way also they run their own businesses.

Advertising agencies have never had a better opportunity to understand consumers and create content that will engage them in the most personal way. Perhaps as a result of this, recent years have seen the influence of the big multinational advertising agencies being challenged by smaller, more agile outfits, run by young creatives and shrewd business operators. Large agencies have had to adopt a more bespoke model for their clients, breaking down departments and creating specialist units to adapt to the new challenges the digital world poses for them.

In 2020, the global advertising spend was over $557 billion, but instead of most of it being spent on TV ads it is spread across a wider range of media opportunities and targeted in a much more definitive way. The global pandemic that began in 2020 will have a further impact on the way companies market their goods, and that includes advertising, but it is an industry that has always confronted the challenges set before it, and often succeeded.

BILLINGS ▶ *When a company signs up with an advertising agency, it creates an advertising budget from its marketing funds. This pays for everything from the creation and production of advertising media placement and agency fees. The industry name for it is 'billings' and agencies are ranked by the size of the billings they handle.*

FROM ADS TO HOLLYWOOD

As mentioned, Ridley Scott directed Apple's 1984 commercial, but before he found success in Hollywood, he cut his teeth making advertising spots – as did his brother Tony Scott (famous for movies like *Top Gun*), Michael Cimino (*The Deer Hunter*) and Alan Parker (*Mississippi Burning*). It has worked the other way, too, with directors who started in feature films turning their hand to TV commercials.

Many notable directors such as Wes Anderson, David Lynch and Sofia Coppola have produced spots. Even Spaghetti Western auteur Sergio Leone made one for Renault in 1985. It was to be his last ever film.

Apple's famous 1984 ad was directed by Ridley Scott and based on concepts from the George Orwell novel.

CONTENT ▶ *With the growth of digital media, a new buzzword entered the advertising vocabulary: 'content'. In order to engage with the consumer online it is necessary to talk to them in a language they are familiar with and understand. The succinct but detailed messages and information that pass from one person to another online has long been referred to as 'conten't. Marketing products online means adopting a similar, more conversational style than normal advertising copy. Content is storytelling rather than hard sell, and as such consumers are more likely to view it as information that they might act on themselves or pass on to others if it captures their imagination.*

Creative presentations are a key part of the advertising process.

How an advertising agency works

Companies wishing to market their brands through an advertising campaign first have to find the right company for the task. If they're not already in an arrangement with an agency, or are dissatisfied with what their current one is doing, they will put the account up for pitch. There are a number of registers that ad agencies affiliate to and this is where the prospective client can go to compare what's on offer and what would fit their brief. If it is a large multinational company, they might choose an agency network of similar stature to handle the task, while a local business might go for a more boutique agency who could handle their project. A competitive pitch would see a number of agencies going head-to-head for the same piece of business. The client would see presentations from each agency featuring creative, media and financial models, and then choose one based on which organization best meets their brief. Creative pitches can be costly and a bit of a lottery for agencies, but they are an accepted necessity.

Ad agencies and their clients

Campaign planning

Once a brand has chosen its new agency partner, the real process of producing an advertising campaign can begin. The client will supply the agency with all available data, research studies, sales figures, forecasts, brand specifications and so on, and with this information the agency will create a brief for the creative department. If it's a separate media agency, they will do the same but for their planners and buyers, to find the most effective channels to advertise the product or service.

Media	YEAR																					
	January				February				March					April				May				
	1	6	12	24	1	8	17	22	1	5	18	20	28	4	13	22	26	3	15	20	27	
Video																						
Newsprint and online																						
Newspaper																						
Quarter-page																						
Retail circulars																						
Home page takeover																						
SEM																						
Google																						
Paid search (text ads)																						
Social media																						
Facebook.com																						
Twitter.com																						
Digital display																						
Local and network																						
Google display network																						

An example of a media plan showing timings blocked out for various parts of the process..

Creative brief

Purpose To provide a compelling story behind an assignment that will inspire creative thinking and ideas.
Agency Name/Department
Input Brand equity/Research/Assignment brief

Date Day/Month/Year

Brand Anonymous

1 ASSIGNMENT

What do we need this work to accomplish? (Think about it in terms of a behaviour we want to change.)

This box will outline the task to the creatives, i.e. launch a new brand or create a new campaign around an existing one. It will also include the target market and the task.

3 BRAND

What must the brand do to address this tension/opportunity?

This box will talk about where the brand stands against the competition and further outline the task involved to change or reinforce the target market's views about it.

2 PEOPLE

Who are the people that matter most to us?

This box will talk about the target market and how the brand wants to talk to them.

What insight do we have into their core desire and the tension or opportunity surrounding it?

This box will talk about what the target market is thinking and feeling. It will give insights into their behaviour and the problems they might face. It will also talk about the target market's desires and what they are hoping for.

How are they behaving in the context of this desire and this assignment?

This box will talk about the target market's current habits and the challenge facing the brand in trying to convince consumers to look at it seriously.

4 FOCUS

What ONE thing must the brand communicate or do to change people's behaviour?

This box will have a USP (unique selling point) for the brand and will phrase it in a way that will inspire the creatives.

What would convince people to believe this?

This box will talk about the brand's assets and the advantages that will give the creatives something from which to create an idea.

Agency and client logos

A typical creative brief.

Creative Brief page 2

5 MOMENTS OF RECEPTIVITY

What are the moments that people are most receptive to interacting with, and experiencing the brand?

This box will talk about the best places, times and media options to effectively reach the target market.

6 EXISTING CAMPAIGNS

What is the campaign idea that this assignment will be a part of?

This box will talk about any existing campaigns or ideas for the brand and how they can be used.

7 CREATIVE

Are there any additional creative considerations or executional mandatories?

This box will cover any other thoughts on how the campaign might be created and a tone of voice for the creative work.

Always attach brand equity tool and campaign idea.

Agency and client logos

SCAMPS ▶ *When creatives are discussing ideas, the will often produce a number of quick visual renditions in rough sketch form to show their thinking. These are traditionally known as 'scamps'.*

A scamp – a rough drawing or layout to communicate an idea.

The creative brief is produced by an **account planner**, who is responsible for the communication strategy for the brand. This will include identifying the target market as well as setting the right tone of voice. The **executive creative director (ECD)** will sign off on the brief before it passes into the **creative department**. The ECD is responsible for overseeing and approving all creative work produced by the agency. They will have been a senior copywriter or art director who has worked their way up to the role. Their judgement and experience will define the creative vision of the agency. In large agencies where some brands have significant budgets, an individual **creative director** (CD) will be appointed to look after that particular piece of business. The CD will have day-to-day responsibility for the work that the creative teams working on their brand produce, but ultimately reports into the ECD for approval.

Creating the ads

Most creatives work in teams of two. This system was developed in the 1960s to speed up the creative process. Traditionally, they were made up of the complementary skills of a copywriter and an art director, who would work together to produce layouts called scamps (see left). However, with the advent of the internet, the lines between these definitive skills have become blurred and some creatives are rejecting the practice of teams and prefer to work individually or collaboratively with different creatives. They now have access to huge archives of images and information to produce their creative ideas.

Once the final creative offering has been identified and approved, it will be presented to the client by the account team involved. Even after approval, it could well undergo extensive research in consumer focus groups before it is approved for production. To produce the advertising material, whether it is a TV commercial or a digital campaign, it will be passed to a third-party production company. The final ads will then be aired to the public for a set period, until it is time to refresh the message or come up with a new campaign, and so the process continues.

Advertising agencies are a hive of fast-working creatives, psychologists and diplomats constantly working to meet the demands of their clients and help sell their wares. Ultimately, it is the creative work that will define an agency's success, because as David Ogilvy said, 'If it doesn't sell, it isn't creative.'

ADVERTISING AWARDS

Like all industries, advertising likes to reward its peers and there are literally hundreds of schemes around the globe. The merits of these schemes vary, but most of them are designed not just as a reward for excellence but as a way of keeping the bar high. The most notable of these are as follows: the Design & Art Directors (D&AD), which recognizes distinction in all forms of creative endeavour; the Cannes Golden Lions, which started as a spin-off of the famed film festival and were originally for TV commercials but now embrace all forms of creative accomplishment; and the CLIO Awards, an American award but open to creatives globally. These are the most sought-after awards, winning them will enhance a creative's reputation and increase their remuneration package. Other schemes run by industry periodicals like *The Drum* magazine, *Campaign* and *Adweek* are also influential.

The D&AD Pencil, Cannes Golden Lion and the Clios are three of the most coveted global advertising awards.

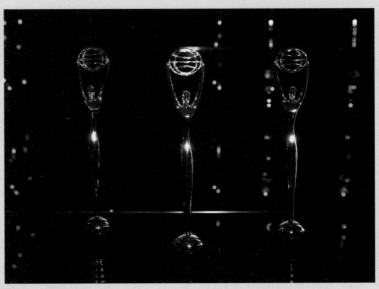

163

GLOBAL ADVERTISING SPEND PERCENTAGE

- Digital
- TV
- Newspapers
- Radio
- Outdoor
- Magazines
- Cinema

A pie-chart showing the global advertising spend in 2020.

Advertising channels

THE STRUCTURE OF AN ADVERTISING TEAM

Advertising has a number of different disciplines and agencies will hire specialists in each category.

Traditionally, ad campaigns consisted of TV, print (newspapers and magazines) and outdoor (posters) – this use of mass media to promote brands and target consumers is known as **above the line** (ATL) advertising. Brands would add pamphlets, handbills, stickers, promotions and brochures placed at **point of sale** (POS) through their shopper marketing agency. In addition, there would be product demos and samplings at shopping malls or railway stations, as well as roadshows, moving hoardings and a host of other less conventional methods, all of which would all carry the message of the main campaign. These more one-to-one activities are known, collectively, as **below the line** (BTL) techniques.

A range of disciplines

Today, agencies pride themselves on being fully integrated, so clients are able to access all disciplines. A large multinational agency will have units, like mini agencies, to service all the client's needs. Apart from the classic TV and print specialists, they will also have, direct mail, shopper marketing, sports marketing and experiential.

Digital advertising brings new challenges to the planners and creatives but also offers a different kind of opportunity. On average, brands will allocate a budget of between 10 and 12 per cent of their total spend on advertising. It's fair to say that the growth of social media advertising has been exponential since the advent of the World Wide Web and it has now overtaken TV in terms of spend globally. According to Statista, a leading provider of market and consumer data, in 2020, internet advertising accounted for 51.04 per cent of advertising budgets worldwide, followed by TV at 28.35 per cent, newspapers at 6.04 per cent, radio 5.37 per cent, outdoor at 5.31 per cent, magazines at 3.47 per cent and cinema at 0.42 per cent.

There is no doubt that the global pandemic will have had an influence on these figures, as people spent a lot of their time locked down and staring at their computers or smartphones, but internet advertising will continue to grow and dominate.

Who does what?

In terms of roles in agencies, each department will have their own specially trained practitioners. The account handling department, who interact directly with the clients, will have **account directors** who oversee the different brands. If it is a large multinational brand, there will often be an account director for each brand. Reporting to them will be **account managers**, whose role it is to work on the business on a daily basis and interface with the other departments within the agency. The role of the **account planner** is to prepare the brief that will lead to an advertising solution for a brand. Account planners will often have a background in marketing research and psychology.

Managing the account

The creative department is led by the **executive creative director** (ECD) who will provide the vision and overall guidance for the creatives. Reporting to the ECD are **creative directors**. These are senior creatives, who will lead teams. **creative teams** are made up of two individuals with complementary skills in **copywriting** and **art direction**.

The creative team

Supporting the creative department will be a **TV/radio team**, with experienced **producers** who will find production companies and help produce the TV commercials. The team also includes designers who create the finished print artwork and **art buyers**, who will source photographers, illustrators and images. All the different departments are knitted together by the **traffic department** to make sure the work flows smoothly through the agency and meets the clients' media deadlines.

Media planning and buying used to be part of a full service agency's function, but is now a separate function carried out by **media buying** agencies. They will have account directors to liaise directly with clients. They will also have **media planners**, with similar research and psychology backgrounds. Their job is to find the right avenues to the consumer, and a balanced media mix for a brand's campaign. Media buyers are responsible for negotiating with the media and broadcast companies to get the best rate for their clients.

Media planning and buying

ADVERTISING AGENCY HIERARCHY

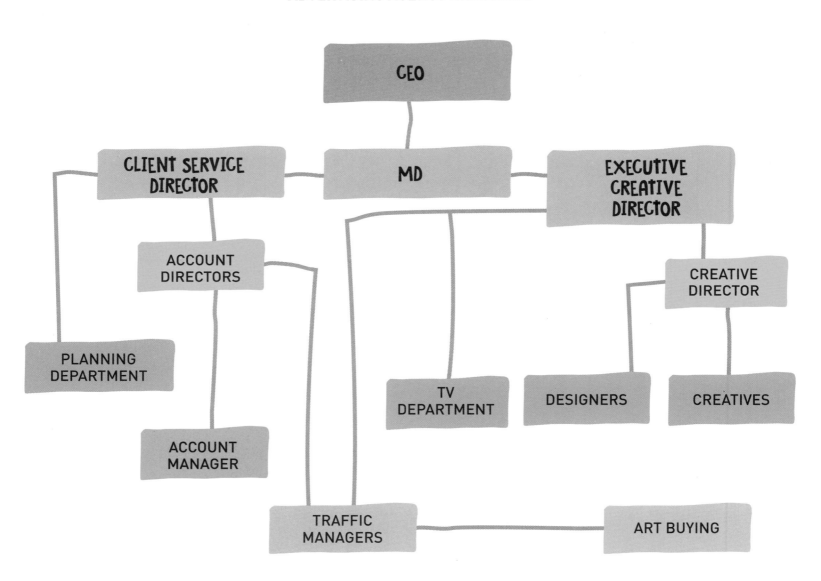

ADVERTISING MAGAZINES

To get a good insight into the world of advertising, there are a number of periodicals that are essential reading. *Campaign* has the insider's view of creative agencies and their current status, and publishes a yearly 'School Report', which ranks them by their creative endeavours and awards. *The Drum* is an influential marketing magazine that operates on both sides of the Atlantic. It has frequently been lauded for its insightful stories about advertising and marketing. *Ad Week*, prides itself on its in-depth analysis of current affairs in the business. *Ad Age* has been reporting on the important issues facing the industry for over 80 years.

Industry magazines are an important source of news and opinion.

PR Agencies

The role of Public Relations (PR) in marketing is to leverage the media channels to promote a positive perception of a product or service among consumers. The PR agency will also manage news (both good and bad) coming out of a company. It will be the PR company's role to focus on the company's brand reputation in the same way that they would for an individual. By using their contacts and associates in the news media, they are able to disseminate positive stories that will enhance a brand's status, thereby driving the consumer to feel, think and act positively towards it. Because the channels they use are not paid for, messages coming through this route will feel more independent and unreproachable. By using these channels, the stories will be picked up by a much wider audience in a more immediate way. Internet bloggers and influencers are a frequent outlet for PR stories, as they say news travels fast on the web.

Using PR to expand the audience

GUINNESS: 'GOOD THINGS COME TO THOSE WHO WAIT'

AN IRISH DRY STOUT with an almost 250-year-old history, Guinness's iconic black body and white head has been a mainstay of British pubs for centuries. For the first part of its existence, it needed no advertising, its popularity depending entirely on word of mouth. However, in response to declining sales in the 1930s, the company launched a series of bold marketing campaigns. Slogans like 'Guinness for Strength' and 'Guinness is Good For You' became ever-present on beer mats and posters, accompanied by pictures of stylized animals, most memorably a charming toucan.

However, as the 20th century wore on, Guinness's marketing efforts hit a seemingly insurmountable snag: Guinness required a double pour to ensure that the pint would not be too frothy, but this ideally took (according to the company itself) 119.53 seconds to do properly.

The appearance of a freshly poured pint of Guinness has itself become a classic brand image.

For the casual drinker, this was wasted time and therefore they began to favour quicker-pouring beverages like lager.

In 1983, the decision was made to reposition Guinness as a sophisticated 'cult' drink, something appreciated by connoisseurs and stylish young people for its quality, regardless of the time spent pouring it. In 1987, cult actor Rutger Hauer was recruited for a series of humorous, deliberately surreal ads to bolster the brand's image. This 'Pure Genius' campaign ran successfully for eight years, but still wasn't breaking through as much as hoped.

The answer lay in a simple solution: to reframe Guinness's long pouring time as a virtue rather than a drawback. It was an idea that had been considered before and the seeds of the new brand direction were planted in a well-received ad called 'Anticipation', in which a man dances comedically at the bar while waiting for his pint to be ready.

Abbot Mead Vickers won the Guinness account from Ogilvy & Mather in early 1998 with a campaign based around a new slogan, 'Good Things Come to Those Who Wait'. Its first ad, released that same year, was entitled 'Swimblack'

Interestingly, the 'Swimblack' ad was shot in a small Italian village called Monopoli.

and combined a documentary-style format with a beautifully rough aesthetic, telling the story of a now aged local sports hero's annual swim race against the pouring of a pint of Guinness. The ad was very well received, but the next one, released in 1999, was on a whole other level.

Directed, like 'Swimblack', by Jonathan Glazer, 'Surfer' was considerably more abstract and fantastical, telling the story of a group of surfers waiting for the perfect wave. With its poetic narration and visual symbolism, it elevates the act of waiting to an almost religious form of meditation, with the ultimate release and thrill of catching the perfect wave visualized in great white horses galloping as if through the surf. It was a huge success, cementing Guinness's new strategy in people's minds and sweeping the board at that year's awards ceremonies. The campaign and strategy continued for many years with other stylish and clever ads, such as one where reverse evolution takes three drinkers all the way back to the origins of life.

While none of the ads after 'Surfer' quite captured the same level of excitement, it was a very successful marketing realignment, ultimately pushing Guinness to the position of brand leader in the UK beer market. Guinness is now so tied to the idea of positive waiting that some in the media have even implied that with modern technology, the two-pull technique is no longer necessary and that it's simply kept in place for branding reasons!

The 'Surfer' ad was inspired by Walter Crane's 1893 painting Neptune's Horses.

169

NAMES TO KNOW: DAVID OGILVY

David Ogilvy, legendary advertising creative and inspirational mentor to many in the business.

David Ogilvy (June 1911– July 1999) is considered by many to be one, if not the most influential creatives in the advertising world. His path into marketing started in the research department and it was that discipline that shaped his unique approach to advertising. Born in 1911, the son of a Surrey stockbroker, David Mackenzie Ogilvy attended public school in Edinburgh then gained a scholarship to Christ Church, Oxford, to read history. The impact of the Great Depression on his father's business and his inattention to his studies meant he soon left Oxford. He trained as a chef in Paris, then sold AGA stoves in Scotland. At AGA he wrote an instruction manual **The Theory and Practice of Selling the AGA Cooker**, *for the other salesmen. This became the yardstick by which all future instruction manuals would be measured.*

The success of his first creative endeavour prompted a career change and he was invited to join advertising agency Mather & Crowther. In 1938 he persuaded the agency to send him on a secondment to the USA to work for George Gallup's Audience Research Institute. This move forged his insistence on thorough research and a grounded and realistic approach to messaging.

His career was interrupted by World War II. He worked for the Intelligence Service from the British Embassy in Washington DC, becoming a master of propaganda, tasked with ruining the reputations of businessmen supplying the Nazi war machine.

After the war, Ogilvy married and briefly spent time as a farmer in an Amish community in Pennsylvania, but a few years he gave it up and moved to Manhattan. With the backing of his former employers, Mather & Crowther, now run by his older brother Francis, David started his own advertising agency which eventually became Ogilvy & Mather.

The agency was built around David Ogilvy's principles that the consumer was intelligent and should be respected, not bombarded with brash, loud messages. In 1955, he coined the phrase, 'The customer is not a moron, she is your wife.' His reputation was for highly creative but subtle advertising based on a clear understanding of the consumer. O&M's work for brands like Hathaway Shirts and Schweppes was breakthrough. His most notable advertisement at that time and his own personal favourite was for Rolls-Royce cars with the headline: 'At 60 miles an hour the loudest noise in this new Rolls-Royce comes from the electric clock.'

An ad from Ogilvy's iconic Hathaway shirts campaign.

He also established Dove soap as the leading brand in the USA with the message, 'Only Dove is one-quarter moisturizing cream'. His agency grew in size and reputation over the next years because of his belief in creating highly creative, but also very effective, work for his clients. He was hailed as 'The Father of Advertising' and in 1962 Time magazine called him, 'The most sought-after wizard in today's advertising industry.'

In 1973, Ogilvy decided to take more of a back seat, however he continued to be involved in the network of agencies. He would turn up at agencies on designated days – named 'red braces day' after his famed fashion accessories – to inspire his employees, and his principles continued long after he left the industry. He was awarded a CBE, Commander of the Order of British Empire in 1967, and elected to the US Advertising Hall of Fame in 1977. Perhaps his most significant contribution to marketing was his dedication to the 'brand' and the building of what what he termed 'brand loyalty'. His book **Ogilvy on Advertising** *is considered a must-read for anyone entering the world of marketing and is still relevant today. Highly quoted, perhaps his most succinct and telling words are, 'The more you tell, the more you sell.'*

Summary

Advertising has its champions and detractors but its importance to a brand is measured by the fact that more money is spent on it than any other part of the marketing plan. However, treating the consumer with respect rings just as true in advertising as it does in any other marketing practice. Advertising is not just a case of endlessly bombarding the public with trite messages but talking to them as equal partners in a brand's journey. One of advertising's most influential creatives, Bill Bernbach, stated, 'Nobody counts the number of ads you run; they just remember the impression you make.'

Chapter Eleven

DIGITAL MARKETING

The Internet Explosion • Internet Advertising • Computer Game Marketing • The Covid-19 Effect • Influencers • Digital or ePosters • Search Engine Optimization • Comparison Shopping Websites • Apps

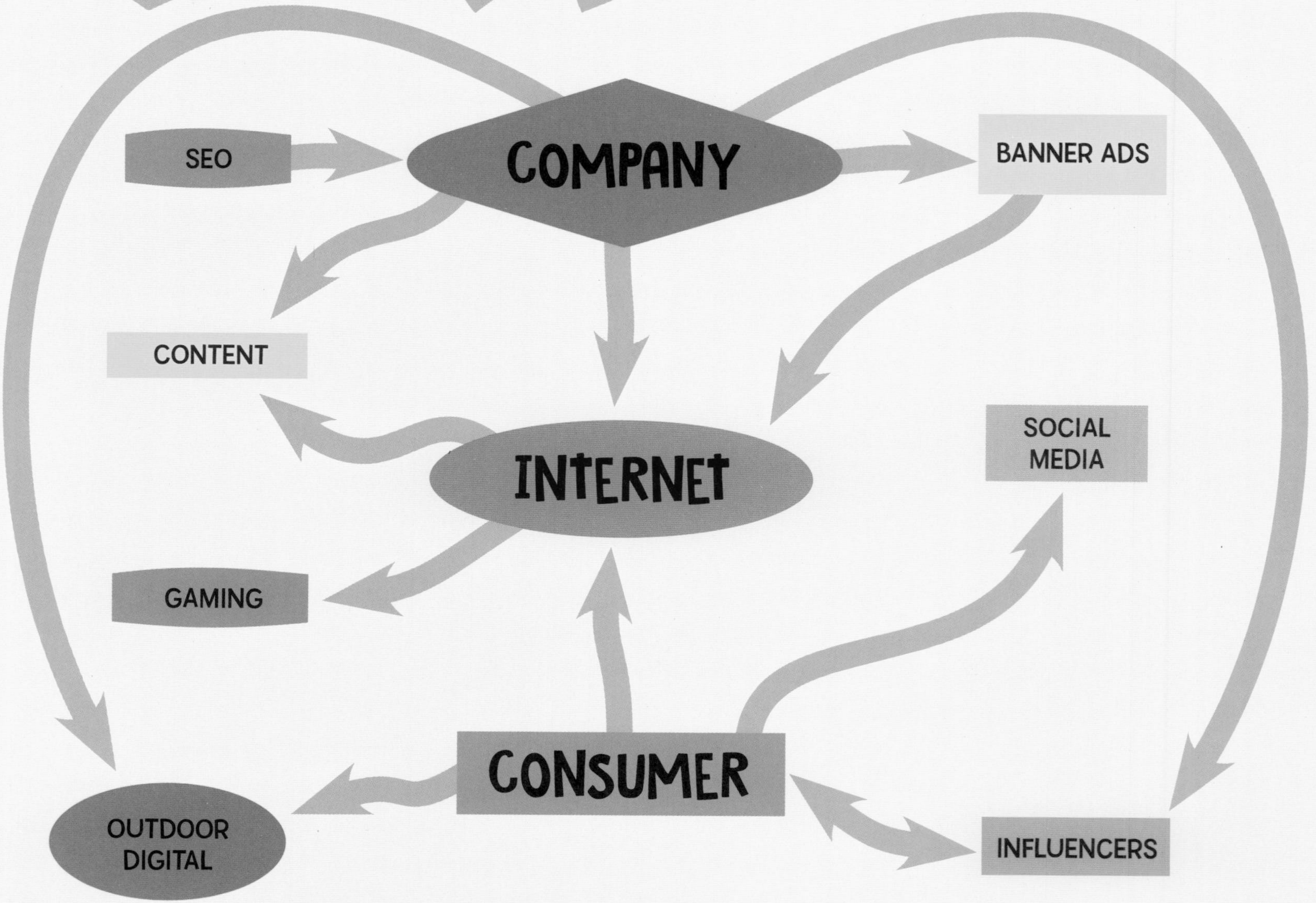
SEO
COMPANY
BANNER ADS
CONTENT
INTERNET
SOCIAL MEDIA
GAMING
CONSUMER
OUTDOOR DIGITAL
INFLUENCERS

THE INTERNET EXPLOSION

In 1980, Tim Berners-Lee created Hypertext, the backbone of what became the World Wide Web. However, it wasn't until more than a decade later that it was opened up to public use, and even then, it was slow and hard for early adopters, mostly university science departments, to use. By 1993, the web was fully available to the general public, although with only a few rather rudimentary websites available at the time – a miniscule number compared to what's available today.

The early years of the World Wide Web

Tim Berners-Lee implemented the first successful communication between a HTTP server and client in November 1989.

Founded in 1994, by 2000 Yahoo was the most popular website worldwide.

Keeping ads in mind

With the advent of data compression, streaming media and audio became much faster and the internet became easier to use. That, combined with the development of the first search engines, such as Yahoo in 1995, was when the true possibilities of marketing on the web began to dawn on those in the marketing industry. Marketers were suddenly able to see that they could access the consumer in a uniquely targeted way – it was right before their very eyes! The possibilities for this new marketing El Dorado seemed boundless, but because it was changing so quickly with every new site and search engine, understanding how to maximize their financial opportunities was to prove as mind boggling as the World Wide Web itself.

Old-school marketing methods were no longer fit for purpose, and a whole new breed of marketer was needed to get the best out of the medium. With them came new tools and techniques. Of course, it wasn't only marketers who had to rethink their approach. The regulators, who were there to make sure the marketers didn't abuse their powers and to protect the consumer, had to move as fast as the marketers and be alert to its potential for misuse.

The dilemma that pioneering internet marketers faced was that if their ads weren't noticeable enough, users would develop 'banner blindness', especially if it was an ad they had seen before. Their brain decided it wasn't important and it would completely ignore it. But if their ads were too obtrusive, like pop-ups, and scroll-over banners that would unroll and play video and sound, then the user would become irritated and have a negative response. This is why browser extensions like pop-up blockers and eventually ad-blockers were developed.

INTERNET ADVERTISING: A BRIEF HISTORY

In the 1980s, advertising was primarily banned on the packet-switching networks and bulletin boards that made up the proto-net. However, with the development of e-mail in the early 1990s came spam. The initial negative response to companies bulk posting uninvited commercial messages didn't discourage them from doing it. Unfortunately, it was immediately evident that it could be effective as a blunt tool for unscrupulous marketers. While email remains an effective marketing medium (despite newer generations viewing it as old-fashioned), it works best as a form of subscription service for information or for following up with customer service.

Bulk posting

Banner ads

In late 1994, the first ever banner ad was created. It is not surprising that a technology magazine, *Wired*, was one of the first to have a significant online presence. Called *HotWired*, the first commercial online magazine needed a way to generate revenue for their writers. Their first client, AT&T, paid $30,000 to feature their ad above the *HotWired* website for three months. Instead of simply taking the user to a standard website, the banner ad instead took them on a virtual tour of the online presences of some of the world's biggest museums. This was an attempt

While the use of pop-ups has declined, banner ads are still a popular form of internet advertising.

175

Click-through rate

to give the user an interesting experience instead of simply a commercial one. This one ad had a click-through-rate of 44 per cent, which, if you consider that the average modern click-through-rate is something like 0.03 per cent, shows what a novelty it was.

Banner ads proliferated but their newness wore off fast and people lost interest. At this point in time, it wasn't possible to incorporate any sophisticated audio or visual elements as dial-up internet didn't allow for the transfer of large amounts of data, so an alternative had to be found.

The pop-up

That alternative was the pop-up, originally generated by JavaScript, that allowed a site to open new windows. Ethan Zuckerman developed it in the late 1990s, primarily because advertisers objected to their promotions appearing on sites with sexual content. With the pop-up, a promotion could now stand separate from the page. However, it quickly evolved into a much-hated feature of online activity, considered intrusive and annoying. Within a couple of years, pop-up ads were untenable as a respectable marketing technique. So much so that by the early 2000s, the pop-up blocker had a standard feature in most browsers (see also page 178). In the contemporary internet world, the existing compromise is the hover ad, which exists as part of the page but moves as the customers scrolls to give it extra exposure. There's also a method of online advertising that is designed to seem like content that's an intrinsic part of the web-page, known as 'native advertising'. There are obviously ethical issues regarding whether this is an example of the marketer trying to deceive the viewer.

ROI tracking

A big development in the viability of banner ads was the creation of ROI tracking tools that enabled advertisers to measure how well their ads were actually doing in real time, measuring views and clicks. There also emerged digital-specific agencies who could instruct companies, who worked entirely in the online arena and could give tailored advice about how to focus their messaging on the right websites, and refine campaigns based on their reception. These developments made online advertising not just viable but very effective.

Sponsored searches

Once search engines like Yahoo and Google had entered the marketplace and made the internet easier to navigate, there was obviously scope for marketers to try to get their products and services at the top of the search list. Around 1998, early sponsored searches were possible, but the search engine companies were concerned that if people thought their results were being unfairly skewed they would lose their USP and it would negatively impact their own image and profits. Google's development of AdWords in 2000 supposedly sidestepped the issue by offering sponsored links alongside an otherwise unimpaired search. Of course, Search Engine Optimization (SEO) technology and techniques were just around the corner.

Paying for searches

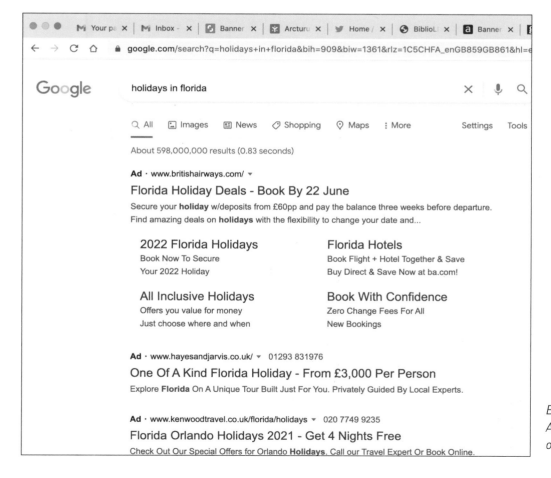

By sponsoring searches companies like British Airways can go to the top of the list without other SEO techniques.

177

Ad-blockers

The most concerning development for marketers was when software creators began building browser plug-ins and extensions designed to block online ads. This was considered by some users to be a necessary step to prevent the more disruptive advertising from affecting their online experience. From a marketer's point of view, however, these programs were a sledgehammer to crack a nut, and their use has grown and grown, to the extent that in 2016 it was estimated that 22 per cent of US consumers had an ad-blocker installed. This has been devastating not just for marketers, but for those who rely on marketing money to maintain their website or online career. It is not a problem that is going away anytime soon, and therefore marketers must be creative to reach their audience, whether it's through sponsorship, native/integrated advertising or the use of apps.

Impact of ad blockers

COMPUTER GAME MARKETING

Initial attempts at using computer games for marketing purposes were crude and often ineffective, as the companies either didn't understand the medium or were dismissive of it. In the late 1970s and early 1980s, computer games only required small teams of programmers to make them, so many companies had their own video game division, churning out cheap knock-offs starring their product. For example, in 1983, two companies tried to exploit the popularity of home consoles, like the Atari 2600, and decided to release their own promotional games. Purina Dog Food's *Chase the Chuck Wagon* (which could be mail-ordered by sending off proofs of purchase) and *Kool-Aid Man*, based on the eponymous drink mascot, were poorly made and the promotions led to the production of hundreds of game cartridges, that

Consoles like the Xbox and Playstation are now themselves widely recognized and desired brands.

were left unused. They may even have contributed to the notorious video game crash of that time.

In the 1990s, once the industry had recovered, computer game sponsorships went both ways, from blatant product placement in platform games like *Zool* (filled with giant Chupa Chups lollies) to computer game companies sponsoring real-world sports events like soccer.

Since then, the relationship between the two has grown ever more sophisticated. While product placement is still rife, it can be jarring, especially in a game that is not set in our world or current time period, as evidenced by complaints about the presence of Monster energy drink in the futuristic video game *Death Stranding*.

Types of sponsorship

Mobile gaming was once limited to simplistic arcade-like concepts such as *Snake*. In the era of smartphones, it's now a multi-billion-dollar industry and has significantly increased the percentage of female gamers in the world (although it's likely that a higher proportion of participants have been female all along and were just underserved by the male-dominated industry).

Mobile gaming and smartpones

Freemium games often use frequent in-game advertisements to justify not charging for their product, sometimes even offering an in-game reward if the user watches them voluntarily.

Some game-oriented marketing concepts have been a little too ahead of their time, for example when Pizza Hut decided to include a way to order pizza from inside the massively multiplayer online game (MMO) *Everquest 2*. In an unusual step in 2007, MI5 put an ad campaign looking for new recruits into the MMO *Splinter Cell: Double Agent*.

THE COVID-19 EFFECT

In 2020, the Covid-19 outbreak meant that large gatherings were discouraged for health reasons. One benefit to the increased popularity of MMOs such as *Roblox* and *Fortnite* is that people could simulate large gatherings inside the game's environment, whether for a promotional event or a concert or performance. These MMOs also frequently have their own in-game currency (in some cases multiple currencies) and their own virtual economies, which can sometimes be as big or bigger than actual countries, giving you an idea of the potential profit for a marketer who gets involved with them.

The definition of what a game actually is, and the boundaries between games and experiences, have worn thin, especially when people are increasingly

Fortnite's growing popularity owes as much to its sense of community as its graphics and gameplay.

using programs and apps to conduct virtual meetings, virtual events and even virtual relationships.

An interesting side-effect of the success of the internet is that marketing styles previously considered unviable for global promotion suddenly became not just useful but essential. For example word-of-mouth. While in the past word-of-mouth could spread a product's effectiveness between friends and family, or from town to town if people travelled, it couldn't stand alone as a marketing tactic. Now, in the digital age, people can communicate across the globe, either one-to-one or en masse, via various social networks and video/audio hosting sites, for only the price of the technology required. In combination with relationship marketing, this can turn a customer into an unpaid brand ambassador.

INFLUENCERS

Levels of influence

The latest and most powerful voices in the field of marketing word-of-mouth are 'influencers'. There is much debate about the actual meaning of 'influencer', and ultimately it operates as a vague umbrella term that covers a lot of different people doing different activities. Some of them are people famous for other activities offline, like actors from film and TV, sportspeople or even politicians. Others have entirely online careers, creating YouTube or Instagram content to entertain people. This could be sketch comedy or non-fiction narrative, or bringing the audience into their own lives. Sometimes, the influencers are people with genuine expertise in a particular area – like scientists or chefs or interior designers – with a fanbase who seek out their advice and emulate them.

There are different levels of influence, from mega to macro, micro and then nano, which means people with a very specific and much smaller level of influence would nonetheless be able to help a company with a niche audience. For example, if your business makes custom paint jobs for electric scooters, you would want to align yourself with an influencer in that field.

Measuring 'influence' can be as difficult as defining the word 'influencer'. YouTubers may have many views on their videos and large numbers of followers subscribing to their content, but there's no guarantee that those who are consuming their work are influenced by them to do anything. The

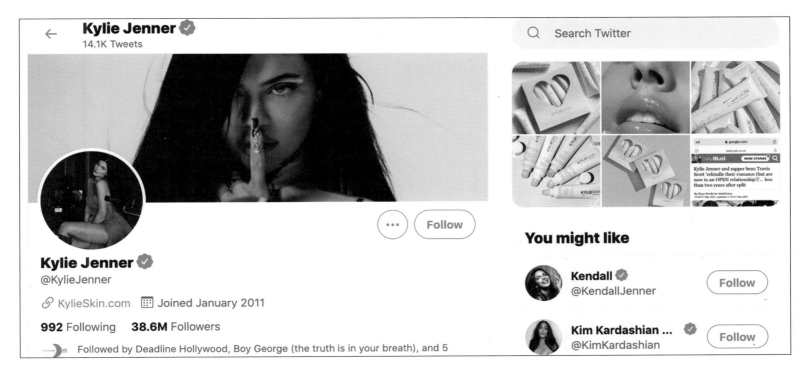

primary ways to measure this are the enthusiasm and size of their fanbase, the sales of anything they endorse, including their own merchandise, and other online metrics and measurements.

As a remarkable example of the huge power of 'mega-influencers', in 2018 the reality TV star and fashion and make-up influencer Kylie Jenner tweeted to her over 30 million followers: 'Sooo does anyone else not open Snapchat anymore? Or is it just me ... ugh this is so sad'. This one act wiped roughly $1.3 billion off Snapchat's market value. While markets *can* be very skittish and Snapchat remains popular, it does show the power influencers can wield over companies and products.

Influencers such as Kylie Jenner use their Twitter accounts both as a way to reinforce their own brand and as a way to make money with cross promotions.

DIGITAL OR E-POSTERS

These are contemporary versions of what have long been a favourite medium for marketers to advertise their product or services to the consumer. The static poster was king of the streets before radio and television turned up to steal its thunder. Companies could throw up huge, eye-catching images with snappy, memorable headlines that would capture viewers' imaginations as they passed by on foot or in their automobiles.

As the more potent influence of television took a grip it seemed that the days of the poster campaign were numbered, but then along came the digital revolution and the humble poster was

New technology for an old favourite

QR CODES ▶ *QR stands for Quick Response. Within their stylized design, they can store a great deal of data. By scanning the code with the camera on their mobile device, a consumer can interact directly with a trader or a service's website from anywhere.*

Outdoor digital posters are now a vital part of the communications landscape.

given a state-of-the-art makeover. Not only could they make posters that moved, they could talk and even interact with the consumer. Standing at a bus stop 20 years ago, a commuter would be cold, hungry and have no idea when the next bus would show up. Now, not only is there a digital readout telling them when their bus will arrive, but they can order a pizza from the interactive poster by scanning the QR code with their smartphone, and have it delivered when they get home.

Digital screens have meant that huge messages have come to life in the heart of the big cities like a scene from a sci-fi movie. Even the printing of the traditional, static poster has been revolutionized by digital production methods, allowing a cheaper, faster and more effective turnaround for the retailers to get their messages across. Travel on the London Underground and the images on the escalator posters will follow you as you move up or down. Clear Channel regards itself as one of the leading out-of-home media companies, and operates 35,000 sites across the UK, claiming to reach 93 per cent of a client's customers with a campaign. Posters are once again a powerful and exciting medium for marketers thanks to the science of numbers.

FICTIONAL TEST CASE: PIE IN THE SKY ONLINE CAMPAIGN

A popular online food vlogger decides to launch their own fresh food delivery service. They're known for their pie recipes so they devise a scheme to deliver fresh pie ingredients to customers via drone, hence the 'Pie in the Sky' (PITS) company name. This gimmicky aspect of it makes it logistically more difficult to do but they think they can create a unique customer experience. The service will have a wide choice of recipes and ideally use fresh, locally sourced ingredients (even though this may limit their distribution range). PITS will also have to fight misconceptions that the service delivers already cooked pies whereas it only delivers the makings of them.

Beyond the usual banner and social media ads (either still or animated/video), the vlogger uses their own platform to promote the service, although they have to be very clear that it is their business so as not to fall foul of laws regarding endorsements. They are also in a position to contact other influencers, whether that is other food vloggers or people in different areas. Pie in the Sky offers them sponsorship deals or simply provides them with free kits or vouchers to use the service, hoping that they enjoy it and consider it worth promoting.

Accounts on Instagram, Facebook, Twitter, TikTok and other high-profile social media sites are set up specifically for the service and boosted by the vlogger and his or her affiliates. They will engage with both current and potential customers with content designed to match the voice of the brand. Teams of people will maintain these accounts to ensure that they are posting regularly and taking advantage of memes and trends to build followings. They will have to ensure they can help and pacify unhappy customers and get out in front of any possible bad publicity.

A website is created but is not the central hub of the company's online presence due to PITS's focus on a younger millennial/generation Z market. Instead, they sidestep some of the restrictions on advertising by setting up an app for ordering and support. This app conforms to the design and voice of the brand and is easy to use but also allows for adaptability and customization.

They also think up some attention-grabbing stunts and ideas. For example, they fit the delivery drones with cameras so that the customer can watch their pie ingredients make their way to them. They also get celebrities to release videos featuring them making and enjoying the pies. They ask customers to post their own completed pies, or submit pie recipe ideas that are then compiled for access by all their fan base. Cross-promotions with online content platforms could be secured. To appeal to the ethics of the consumer, the stories of the farmers and other suppliers of the pie ingredients are told via the various outlets.

Customer support via the website, app and other social media sites are synchronized to ensure that the same level and quality of support is maintained and is consistent with the stated ethos of the brand.

Finally, they ensure that they have an understanding of SEO (see page 184) and the algorithms of the relevant social media websites, to ensure Pie in the Sky gets off the ground.

Drones were once seen as unusual but they are now so prevalent that some areas have instituted no-fly zones to avoid hazards and accidents.

SEARCH ENGINE OPTIMIZATION

SEO is a technique now considered essential to every successful web marketing model. It's a practice that helps a company filter the quality and quantity of traffic to their website. This increases the possibility that the people looking at it are the ones who have a genuine interest in its content, and therefore are more likely to become customers.

Directing customers to the right place

It's not beyond any company to attract lots of clicks to their website but if the searcher gets there and finds that although he was looking for a fan site, he's ended up listening to the latest grime track, when what he actually wanted was an electric fan, it's a wasted journey. Therefore quality of traffic is the first discipline if the marketer wants the right kind of customer. To ensure that you have to make sure that the **content** has the right **keywords** for the **crawler** on the search engine to accumulate data for an algorithm that will match it to the interested party. Once the right people are clicking through to the site from the Search Engine Results Page (SERP), then getting a high quantity of the right traffic is feasible.

Most users think it's simply some form of alchemy when they ask a question of a search engine and 'bingo!', it magically takes them right to the list of webpages they were looking for, but what's the actual process?

HOW SEO WORKS

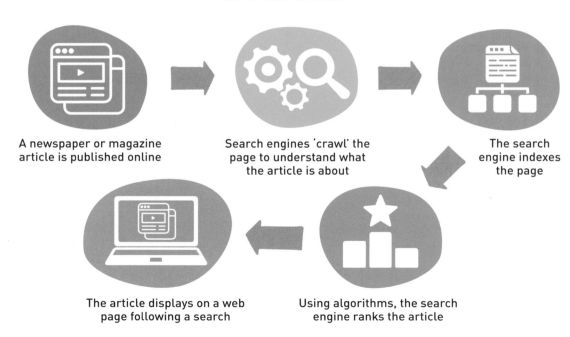

A newspaper or magazine article is published online

Search engines 'crawl' the page to understand what the article is about

The search engine indexes the page

The article displays on a web page following a search

Using algorithms, the search engine ranks the article

SEO JARGON

Keywords are simply words or a collection of words that people type into the search engine they are using when looking for something on the internet. The search engine's algorithm will then match the relevant words to a particular site, so it is important for the marketer to include the right keywords in their content in order to attract the right kind of traffic.

Crawling is a search by engine web crawlers (Bots or Spiders). They visit and download a page's content then copy its links to find extra pages. When a search engine finds changes to a page after crawling, it will update its index accordingly.

A **Bot** is an automated program that runs on the internet. Most commonly, they are web crawlers or in chat rooms. They have a mixed reputation as some people use them maliciously, disguising them as a human to gather information and then use it in nefarious ways. That is why you will often find 'I am not a robot' filters, such as CAPTCHA, on many websites.

Spiders have roughly the same function as bots or crawlers, programs that search and store information from websites.

Clickbait is a catchy phrase or headline that is meant to attract readers as they click on to something. It can be used in content to emphasise a point the author is trying to explain. However, the cynicism that the name suggests means that more often than not it can be used to mislead or entrap the reader into consuming misleading or false information.

Content is the name for personal messaging and material generated by internet users and its style has been adopted by companies to market their wares. Content marketing ideally offers the readers of anything on the internet useful and relevant information about products and services. The content is written in such a way as to engage the consumer rather than just bombard them with selling messages. At its best, it demonstrates an understanding of the consumer's needs and interests, as should be adopted by any marketing plan. The most used platforms for content on the web are blogs, social media posts and videos.

CPC (cost-rer-click)

CPC or PPC (pay-per-click) is a tool that enables marketers to measure the amount of times a customer visits their ads. Its function allows the domain where the ad is placed to calculate how much to charge the advertiser for using ad space on a particular site. For example, if the rate of CPC were 10 pence per click, the charge for 1,000 click-throughs would be £100. Based on this equation, the website publisher would negotiate a fee with the company buying ad space on a particular site, allowing for the fact that not all clicks are genuine and some are accidental, such as when the user's cursor rolls across it.

Google's doodles have honoured people from sportsmen to scientists, politicians and entertainers.

GOOGLE WAS FOUNDED IN 1996 by Larry Page and Sergey Brin at Stanford University in California. It was originally a research project nicknamed 'BackRub'. Contemporary search engines would rank pages based on how many times the searched word appeared on the page. This was simplistic and too easy for unscrupulous websites to manipulate. They theorized it would be better to rank pages based on the relationship between websites and their relative importance, i.e. the top pages would be those that have the most links to them from respected or important sources. This system was called PageRank.

In 2000, it became the default search engine for Yahoo! and introduced AdWords, a way for companies to pay for sponsored links. Google became so popular, so quickly, that the phrase 'googlin googling' became synonymous with online searches, and it entered the dictionary as a verb in 2006.

Such was Google's efficiency at charting everything online that the idea of being able to catch it out by coming up with a phrase that would only have one search result became a game known as a 'Googlewhack.'

As it grew to the incredible size it is today ($420 billion as of February 2021), it inverted usual lessons of brand consistency by championing versatility, for example, by introducing 'Google Doodles', creatively changing their front page's design to commemorate significant dates. Google's aim is to be universal, something fundamental to society, in other words an essential.

Sergei Brin and Larry Page founded Google in 1998. As of 2021 they are respectively the ninth and sixth richest people in the world.

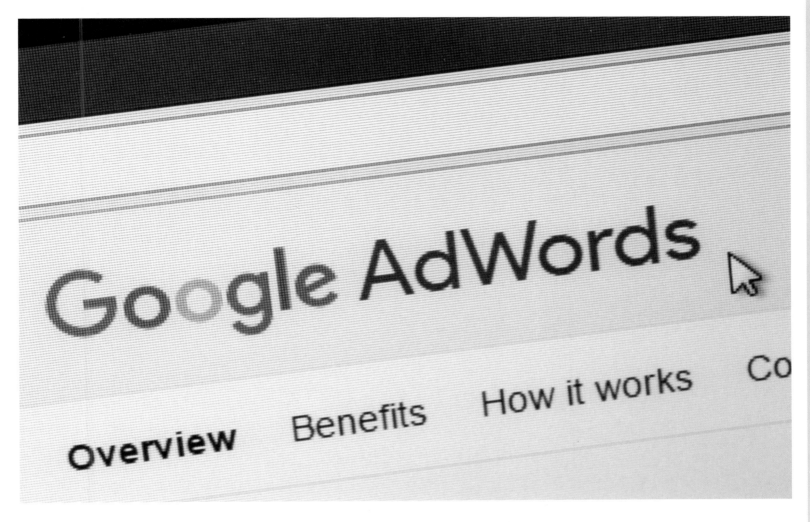

Google's massive growth means that it leads the field in most online functions. Google can organize your work and provide all the systems you need to do it, maps the world, organizes family photos and has its own custom browser, operating system and many other hardware developments. It also prides itself in innovation in future technologies such as Artificial Intelligence, Cloud Computing and both Virtual and Augmented Reality. In fact, Google's domination of people's awareness means that you probably already know all of this already. If you don't, you can always google it.

Google AdWords are now known as Google Ads and are the main source of revenue for Google's parent company Alphabet Inc.

COMPARISON SHOPPING WEBSITES

These are the product of the boom in eCommerce brought about by the rapid expansion of the internet in the last 25 years. They are a vertical search engine for consumers to browse, and find any product or service in one place, so they can compare prices or reviews without too much legwork.

The earliest example was BargainFinder, developed in the USA in 1995 by Anderson Consulting (now Accenture). Since then, comparison shopping sites have spiralled thanks to the efficacy of search engines like Google multiplying exponentially.

This has also left the door open for niche and low-quality sites claiming to be honest but that have been found to be purveyors of spam and fraud, making it hard for consumer protection bodies to regulate them. Deceptive sites can claim to be testing products rigorously when in truth all they are doing is accessing freely available information about a product or service and dressing it up as their own.

Comparison shopping is a hugely competitive market, with many of the larger companies like GoCompare and Compare the Market vying for the same customers, particularly in the financial and insurance sector in the UK. They have launched huge, sophisticated marketing and advertising campaigns to promote their brand and try to attract as many click-throughs to their site as they can. They do not charge the users anything, instead generating their income by charging a fee to the companies that list on the sites. This can either be a flat fee, a registration fee or a charge every time a customer makes a purchase through the site.

Another lucrative by-product for comparison sites is product data collection. This generates even more revenue for them as they can sell the data on to companies who need to find out the buying patterns of the consumer and design their business models accordingly. Comparison shopping sites are the new normal for the consumer and really came into their own during the Covid-19 pandemic, when the housebound shopper could find anything from a plumber to a plum pudding without leaving their front door.

Compare the Market's meerkat promotion turned a simple pun into a long-lasting successful campaign on the back of the popularity of these small mongooses.

HOW COMPARISON WEBSITES EARN MONEY

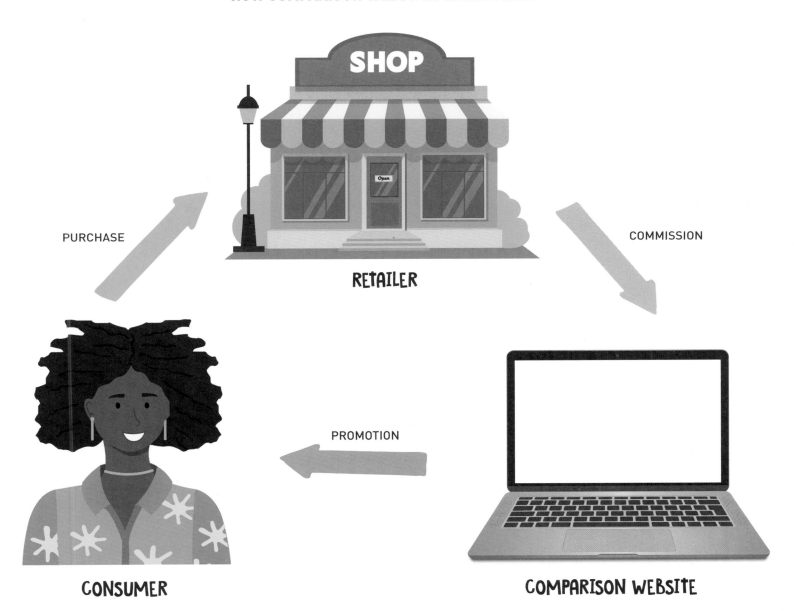

DIGITAL MARKETING MASTERSTROKE: BURGER KING WHOPPER DETOUR

WHEN IT COMES TO THE SIZE of fast-food companies there is no contest: in 2019, McDonald's were valued at $130.4 billion with its rival, Burger King, only weighing in at $7.1 billion. However, what Burger King lack in size they make up for in digital marketing nous in getting one over on the market leaders. In 2020, Burger King's advertising agency, FCB New York, came up with a very cheeky way to highjack potential McDonald's customers from right outside their rival's restaurants. The Whopper Detour, named after BK's bestselling burger, used geofencing technology, which meant that when a potential customer came within 180 m (600 ft), of a McDonald's restaurant a BK Whopper promotion was automatically unlocked on their phone, and would detour them to the nearest Burger King to redeem their prize.

All people had to do was to download the Burger King app, drive to a McDonald's and they would receive a coupon for a Whopper for the princely sum of 1 cent.

Burger King managed to geofence 14,000 McDonald's locations across the USA, and the promotion led to BK's app being downloaded 1.5 million times. It generated a staggering 3.3 billion impressions, which would be the equivalent of $37 million dollars in earned media. Half a million Whoppers were redeemed during the promotion, which was 40 times their previous digital coupon record, and BK's app rose to number one in US Google Play and Apple app stores in just 48 hours. Burger King continued to reap the rewards of this promotion with the highest increase in traffic to their outlets since 2015, and won a hatful of industry awards for their trouble. It just shows that if you use available digital marketing tools in a smart way, you can punch well above your weight.

The Burger King diversion.

APPS

The word 'app' is shorthand for 'application', which is a piece of software designed to run on a computer and, more importantly, on a mobile device. Apps are little digital shortcuts to get you to the service or game you want at the touch of a finger, and their creation suddenly added a new opportunity to the marketing mix. The situation where a company could literally be instantly connected to the consumer anywhere they happened to be, coined the term 'mobile commerce', which generates trillions of dollars globally, with the Asia Pacific market the most lucrative at nearly $2.5 trillion.

Over 90 per cent of mobile apps are free to download and there are millions available to prospective users. At last count, there were 2.87 million for Android customers and almost 1.96 million for Apple IOS users. Of course, the Covid-19 situation has had a hugely dramatic impact on app usage, with Facebook, Instagram, Gmail and WhatsApp the most popular. People, starved of personal contact, took to their devices in search of friends and family. Apps are the perfect marketing tool, and many marketers like to think of mobile commerce as 'a retail outlet in your customer's pocket.'

The sophistication of smartphones and the wide availability of wifi have meant that digital advertising can reach people wherever they happen to be.

GEOFENCING ▶ *This uses a piece of software to set up virtual perimeter for a real geographical location. It links with the GPS on a mobile device and can then send a pre-programmed message or alert to the user when they enter the geofenced area.*

Mobile commerce

Apps for everyone

Summary

Since the advent of the huge game changer that is known as the World Wide Web, marketing has been playing catch-up with this new opportunity. Just as the marketers get to grip with one new technical development, another three come along, so it could well be that by the time this book is published digital marketing might have had even more incredible breakthroughs. However, it is worth remembering that whatever technology or gizmos marketers have to adapt to, putting the consumer first is still the simple discipline that all successful marketing campaigns will follow.

Chapter Twelve
PSYCHOLOGY IN MARKETING

Why Psychology? • Scarcity Marketing • Social Proof • Authority • Unity • God Terms • Reciprocity • Commitment and Consistency • Priming • Liking

WHY PSYCHOLOGY?

Psychology is integral in marketing because a thorough understanding of consumer behaviour is the foundation on which companies will build their sales strategy.

Pre-20th century psychology was regarded as a medical or academic discipline with no real practical applications. However, the growing awareness of figures such as Sigmund Freud and Carl Jung and the growing potential customer bases that came with globalization changed the minds of many. Psychological tactics and analysis have become essential tools in marketing mixes worldwide.

There are a number of models that companies can employ to make sure their marketing plan is fit for purpose. These have been developed by some of the world's leading psychologists using extensive research of consumers to shape them. This chapter will explore the most practised of these principles.

Early psychological tactics

The brain takes 250 milliseconds to register visual cues, but it only takes 13 milliseconds to have an emotional reaction to the images.

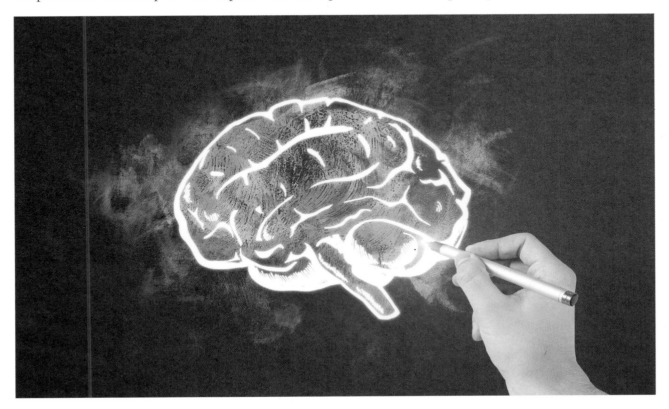

The Mona Lisa received the highest insurance evaluation in history in 1962, the equivalent of over $700 million dollars today.

SCARCITY MARKETING

Scarcity is a common psychological tactic used by marketers. Also known as 'Urgency Scarcity', it works on consumer thinking in a number of different ways. One aspect of scarcity marketing, called, FOMO or fear of missing out, was identified in 1996 by Dr Dan Herman. He defined it as a, 'clearly fearful attitude towards the possibility of failing to exhaust available opportunities and missing the expected joy associated with succeeding in doing so.' In other, simpler words, it means that people hate losing opportunities. By using statements like, 'For a limited time only!' or 'Buy now while stocks last!', the marketer gives the consumer this feeling of FOMO.

Scarcity can also mean exclusivity, for instance an elite club membership or a VIP area at a venue. The growth in the private members' club sector is down to people's need to feel part of something exclusive. The Soho House Group has grown from a single premises in the West End of London to a global network of clubs, bars and hotels, on exactly this platform.

Limited editions are often used by clothing brands for things like trainers, or by car manufacturers releasing special editions. This artificial scarcity adds value to the item, allowing the vendor to charge a premium price. The lifestyle brand Supreme has used this to market their highly sought-after merchandise, and you will often find young people queuing outside their stores to buy the latest hip-hop themed clothing.

For the consumer, buying something scarce or being part of something exclusive gives them a huge feeling of importance and is a boost to their ego. The ultimate example is the art market, and it is no coincidence that Charles Saatchi almost single-handedly created the Brit Art movement, which launched the careers of artists like Damien Hirst and Tracey Emin by employing the marketing principles he learned from his time in advertising.

Soho House locations, like this one in Istanbul, capitalize on their exclusivity.

SOCIAL PROOF

Social proof is when the action of the masses conditions people to think, 'If everyone else is doing it, it must be the right thing to do.' Marketers will often leverage this technique to ease the minds of concerned customers into thinking, 'My friend has used this service many times without a hitch so it must be OK for me to use it.'

A classic marketing tactic that uses social proof is the testimonial. By using real messages of endorsement from satisfied customers, the marketer creates ambassadors for the brand whose testimony is more powerful than anything the company itself could say about the product or service. The financial service sector is very active in using testimonials, and with social media's growing dominance in shaping people's opinions, social proof has become an increasingly used psychological tactic.

To add even more power to it, some companies will turn to a celebrity to endorse their brand. Back in the 1950s, it was at its height when almost every time you turned a page there was a Hollywood film star extolling the delights of a certain cigarette or make-up brand. Now the celebrity is more likely to relate more closely to the product, for example the use of basketball player and superstar

Far left: Marilyn Monroe also endorsed Chanel No.5, famously claiming it was all she wore in bed. Left: Ronald Reagan's acting career and endorsements actually worked in his favour when he ran for US President.

Michael Jordan's Air Jordan deal with Nike has netted him over $1.3 billion since 1984.

Using celebrities in marketing

icon Michael Jordan to promote Nike. In 1984, Jordan's prodigious ability to seemingly hang in mid air while scoring led them to create a customized trainer, the Air Jordan, to capitalize on this and channel Jordan's own brand image of aspiration and physical excellence into their own products. The decision to only produce the Air Jordans for his personal use before releasing them to the public five months after their launch was another brilliant marketing slam-dunk.

Expert endorsement has long been a useful tool for the marketer; it is a prime example of the halo effect.

The reaction to the expert testimony is, 'It must be good because they recommended it and they know what they're talking about,' or 'Maybe if I use this product I can look as good as them.'

This tactic also relates to **authority marketing**.

THE HALO EFFECT

In marketing terms, the 'halo effect' is a technique used to strengthen a brand, whereby if a consumer forms a positive impression of a product, service or spokesperson they will look at the whole offering of a company in a favourable light. For instance, it can be very simply employed by using a widely popular personality to cast their charisma over a brand. George Clooney's association with Nespresso coffee machines is a typical use of the halo effect as a marketing technique.

In 2018 George Clooney was the highest-paid actor in the world, not because of film contracts but because of his numerous endorsement deals.

AUTHORITY

Authority marketing is a form of positioning whereby marketers aim for their product or brand to occupy a space in the customer's mind as the pre-eminent example of what it represents. Authority status in people comes from being able to put honorific words like Dr, Professor or Sir in front of their name; authority branding in products comes from projecting reliability, expertise and solidity, so that the product becomes, or is seen to become, the leader in the field.

Obviously, this is not simple: a marketer can't just suddenly decide that their product is going to be the most successful and make that happen with a positioning decision. It takes careful strategizing, outmanoeuvring rivals and adapting to changing times and customer needs. Despite this, understanding the nature of authority and its appeal to consumers can be beneficial to a marketing strategy at any level.

Authority can be conveyed through official bodies. For example, since the 19th century, UK companies have been able to obtain a 'Royal Warrant'. By providing goods or services to the household of the Queen, a company is entitled to display the royal coat of arms on its products and therefore benefit from the reverence in which the Queen and other British royals are held. It can be as simple as having an endorsement from various experts in the relevant field associated with your product. For example, Audi's advertising campaign running for over 50 years, created by industry legend Sir John Hegarty, features their own engineers and the slogan 'Vorsprung Durch Technik' which means 'Progress Through Technology'. Authority can also be built up by careful referencing of previous successes. Members of successful start-ups or app launches, like Facebook, have used this as a calling card to secure finance for their next projects.

Some brands try to exert an air of authority by maintaining a voice of formality and a certain distance from the customers. However, research has shown that being extremely helpful and available to customers is the best way to establish authority, as in a crowded marketplace, being indispensable to people is the primary way to achieve genuine importance to their lifestyles.

The Royal coat of arms on a product elicits immediate respect in many UK citizens as well as worldwide.

Forms of authority

197

Collaborative activities like tug of war serve as a good metaphor for the power of unity.

Working togeather effectively

UNITY

Togetherness is a strong human instinct and unity marketing taps into this emotion in similar ways to social proof. Phrases such as, 'Join the team', 'Be one of the gang', or even 'Be part of an exclusive group', can play on people's natural urges to unite with others.

Dr Robert Cialdini, author of the bestselling book *The Psychology of Persuasion*, explains unity marketing's principles, 'It's about shared identities', he said, 'The more we identify ourselves with others, the more we are influenced by these others.'

Recruitment marketing will often use unity techniques. For example the US Marine Corps slogan 'The Few, The Proud', appeals directly to a possible recruit's desire to be part of something elite and honourable. Social media influencers are prime movers in unity marketing, with hordes of willing followers wanting to be part of their world and willing to go along with any recommendation they might make. This kind of parasocial marketing has huge potential but also massive ethical pitfalls.

PARASOCIAL RELATIONSHIPS

A term coined in 1956 by sociologists Donald Horton and Richard Wohl, 'parasocial relationships' are formed when a mass-media consumer comes to feel that a celebrity or other performer in a medium they enjoy is their friend. It's not a delusion as much as it is a subconscious feeling that evolves naturally from the nature of their job and their interaction with the audience.

While initially coined in observation of the illusion of intimacy people had developed with regard to the conversational style of chat-show hosts and radio DJs, in more recent years parasocial relationships have formed between Instagrammers/YouTubers and their audiences. This is more pronounced because in the era of monetization of videos and websites like Patreon, increased interaction with their fans is often required to keep their fanbase happy and donating money. Parasocial relationships of this kind can be unhealthy, and performers and marketers do have a duty of care to their fans.

GOD TERMS

The American literary theorist Kenneth Burke created the phrase **god terms** in his book *A Grammar of Motives* and it has found its way into marketing psychology to describe words used to inspire consumers to act in a certain way.

Words like 'free', 'save', 'love', 'happy', 'power' and so on all come under this banner, and will be seen liberally sprinkled across marketing campaigns all over the world. 'New' is probably one of the most potent god terms, as it appeals to a consumer's instinct to crave the next big thing and, as such, will drive buying habits across fields as diverse as washing powder and toothpaste to television programming and politics. The human love of novelty also combines elements of FOMO and scarcity.

Automotive industry marketing also uses the word 'new' to keep their sector moving, as they must sell their latest model in order to survive. 'The all new …' is there to motivate the consumer to react in a couple of different ways: first, to appeal to their longing for the latest thing, but also to make them feel dissatisfied with their current model and more likely to trade it in for a new one. Even the second-hand car market is changing the way it talks to possible customers, the term 'used car' being subtly replaced by phrases like 'once loved'.

The most powerful words

This sandwich board contains the most commonly used god term, 'free'.

Other common god words

Guarantee	The unequivocal endorsement of trust in a brand, continues to be effective.
Sale	A temporary period when prices are reduced, still very popular.
Promise	Similar to a guarantee but without the ultimate commitment, still well used.
Risk-free	Convincing but contentious term with possible legal pitfalls.
Now	Conveys immediacy, still in regular use in messaging.
Immediately	Sounds authoritative but usually issued with caveats or hidden terms and conditions.
Hurry	Urgency prompting, a scarcity tactic.
Instantly	Same as immediately but with even more impact, very popular in the internet age.
Going-fast	A FOMO promoting term.
Bargain	Losing popularity but still has psychological impact in supermarkets.
Bestseller	Premium evoking, often used in the book market, using authority.
Simple	In an increasingly confusing and complicated world this has strong cachet.
No-fuss	Simplicity message, ease of use.
Safe	Reassuring and most effective when used with authority marketing.
Tested	Reassurance for the consumer that the product is up to standard.
State-of-the-art	A once effective way of conveying sophisticated newness but now considered rather old-fashioned.

Hand-crafted	Bespoke and original connotations, conveys rarity.
Premium	A retro, historically charming way of suggesting quality.
Secret	Exclusivity, letting the consumer in behind the scene and inclusive.
Rare	An increasingly popular word, especially in scarcity marketing when 'blind bag' items (products with their content kept as a surprise) are offered.
Unique	A feeling that the product is one of a kind, overused.
Select	An authority term that makes the consumer feel the work of finding and choosing something of quality has been done for them.
Authentic	It must be the best and the original, much overused.
Revolutionary	Still popular as a term in fields like cosmetics and household products, but considered old hat elsewhere.
Miracle	A promise of surprising results, few products can live up to this claim.
Announcing	Using this term can give a product or service a feeling of being an event or of great importance.
Compare	A word used to challenge the consumer to seek out its efficacy, popular with cleaning products and financial services.
Challenge	This term ignites people's sense of competition and excitement, effective in unity marketing.
Discover	Prompting consumers to explore the brand.
Compelling	Often used when promoting story-based media, this word triggers feelings of interest.

Handshakes are a common symbol of reciprocity but in a post-Covid world this may shift.

Freebies

Keeping a promise

RECIPROCITY

In the 1960s, sociology professor Alvin Gouldner investigated the benefits of what happens when two people co-operate and interact. His research led him to propose the existence of a universal, generalized 'norm of reciprocity' that regulates the exchange of goods and services between all members of society, except the very young, the sick and the old.

Reciprocity marketing works on the principle that if you do something or give something to someone unprompted, they in turn will feel obliged to return the favour. So, if a company gives something free to a consumer with a no-strings-attached attitude, that person feels favoured and will be more likely to buy their products or services.

In its simplest form, this can be people standing outside an establishment offering free samples of food or cosmetic products in the hope the passer-by will then go into the shop and look at the rest of its goods. A waiter leaving sweets on the tray with the bill in a restaurant might elicit a bigger tip. The Big Tech companies apply the principle to get consumers to use their latest software with 30-day free trials, after which the recipient often feels that they have to carry on using it, so they sign up. Amazon will give free books on a Kindle, and Spotify Premium offer an ad-free trial period, after which the user is so happy to listen to music without advertising they will pay the fee.

The aim of the companies that employ this marketing tactic is not just to persuade the consumer to make a one-off purchase, but also to build a two-way, reciprocal relationship.

COMMITMENT AND CONSISTENCY

The maintenance of commitment and consistency is the aim of every company, but it's not enough to just maintain these principles, they have to be *seen* to maintain them. In marketing terms, the messaging they send out has to underline a company's commitment to these brand values. Failure to do so breaks down any trust they might have established with their consumers and the pressures on companies to stay true to these standards.

Amazon have built their vast global enterprise on a commitment and consistency platform by committing to same-day delivery and achieving it on a regular basis. Even when they don't deliver on the time promised, they have an efficient feedback service that will reassure the customer that this is an extremely rare occurrence.

Political parties will use these marketing principles when they are trying to get elected or to stay in office, and when they do fail they will roll out the propaganda machine to make sure the electorate knows how important consistency and commitment is to them.

On top of their sales messages, companies will use corporate advertising as a principal tool to show how important their brand ethos is to them.

PRIMING

Of all the psychological tools used by companies for marketing purposes, priming elicits the most debate about its ethicality. This principle involves using visual or word triggers in messaging that will 'prime' the consumer to make certain subconscious decisions or think about a product in a certain way.

For example, colour can be used as a primer in brand design to evoke particular emotions: brighter colours might project sweetness in a soft drink, darker colours can provoke feelings of power or depth of flavour in something like coffee, and light or whiter colours will promise freshness and cleanness in laundry products. The consumer will be unaware that they are being affected by these visual associations because they work on the subconscious part of the brain.

This is not just restricted to colours. Image-based primers work in much the same way. Marketers will use visual mnemonics in their messaging and repeat them to condition the way consumers react to their products. For example, the pseudoscience that is often used in advertising for women's sanitary products is accompanied by a product demonstration that is full of symbolism: soft images for comfort, bright whiteness for hygiene, even the liquid used is blue so as not to appear offensive to the viewer. On top of that, the presenter will be wearing the kind of white coat that might be found in a hospital or doctor's surgery.

Music is also used as a primer, with many ads for pasta being accompanied by an operatic piece from Puccini, even if the product is manufactured in a country other than Italy. Provenance can be suggested by the right musical soundtrack, as much as images depicting typical scenes from a particular destination.

However, in 2012, the Nobel prize-winning psychologist Daniel Kahneman sounded a warning to the marketing fraternity, saying that the practice of priming has become the 'poster child for doubts about the integrity of psychological research.'

Displays packs in window. Minimal effect on passing traffic.

Pumps smell of fresh coffee into street. Primed consumer desires coffee.

NAMES TO KNOW: ERNEST DICHTER

Ernest Dichter liked to call his wide range of focus groups his 'living laboratory'.

Born in Vienna in 1907, Ernest Dichter is sometimes called the 'Sigmund Freud of the supermarket age'. This image is something he courted, deliberately playing it up to his own advantage. He is also known as the 'father of motivational research', but although he did contribute a lot to the field, he wasn't its creator.

He began his working life as a behavioural psychologist in Austria, but the growing intolerance and anti-Semitism of the Nazi party led to his family fleeing to the USA in 1938.

Dichter was already experienced in the use of interview techniques as a form of information gathering from his time at the Psychoeconomic Institute in Vienna. He was also trained in Freudian methods of analysing the unconscious mind and people's hidden desires. He saw the potential for these techniques and ideas to be used in the marketing world and sought to provide his services in this area.

Rather than relying on surveys or other conventional quantitative marketing methods, Dichter instead suggested, among other ideas, in-depth interviews with people in a product's target markets as a way of generating deeper insights. For example, one of his first jobs was for Esquire magazine, and his techniques revealed the truth about the magazine that no one at the time felt comfortable articulating: that the readers bought it primarily to see naked women! While this seems obvious now, at the time it was a shocking revelation.

His other research ran along a similarly sensationalist path. He told Ivory Soap there was an erotic element to bathing because it was the only time during their daily routine when people gave themselves permission to touch their own bodies. He also famously compared convertible Chrysler cars to a man's mistress, while the more reliable sedan they would actually end up buying was their wife. These observations, while sexist by today's standards, revolutionized an industry that had just come out of the war and was ready to serve a society with an increased disposable income and a desire to feel good about spending it.

The simplistic advertising mantra 'sex sells' is an encapsulation of what people felt Dichter brought to marketing, although the truth is more complex. His research led to the creation of such legendary concepts as the Barbie Doll and Esso's 'Tiger in your Tank'.

Dichter's career was stalled by the 1956 publication of **The Hidden Persuaders,** a self-declared exposé by journalist Vance Packard. The book claimed that the methods used by Dichter and other marketing psychologists were tantamount to brainwashing, saying that they manipulated people via their unconscious desires.

While it's true that advertisers were seeking to use Dichter's insights to convince customers in ways that weren't always ethical, it was not brainwashing so much as using greater knowledge about consumers' habits and opinions to create more effective marketing. But the damage was already done and the public were by then convinced companies were trying to control their thoughts.

Dichter pivoted to providing motivational advice for companies and managers but his impact on the industry remains, especially in the fields of market research and branding. He died in 1991, leaving an indelible mark on the industry.

An Esso 'tiger in your tank' ad from the 1960s, influenced by Dichter's research.

IKEA

IKEA IS NOW THE LARGEST RETAILER of furniture in the world, operating 378 stores in 30 countries. In 2018, the company recorded over £32 billion in sales.

Ingvar Kamprad (who at the tender age of five was already showing his entrepreneurial skills selling matches) was only 17 when he founded Ikea in 1943. His father gave him the money to register the company as a graduation present while he created the name by using his initials, I K, adding the E – from Elmtaryd, the family farm – and A from Agunnaryd, the farm's parish in Småland.

At first, IKEA was just a direct import company, selling small items like pens and watches, but Kamprad soon realized that in order to achieve the sort of success he wanted he would have to move on to bigger things, like furniture. In 1948, the IKEA brochure offered household furnishings for the first time. Kamprad had recognized that there were a great many small furniture factories locally and his company could be the conduit between factory and consumer.

He defined his vision for IKEA as, 'to create a better everyday life for the many people'. He never looked back and neither did the company, by taking advantage of the Swedish reputation for brilliant and innovative design, it offered superbly crafted furniture at very low prices, mainly in ready-to-assemble form.

Some people have set themselves up as 'Ikea handymen', who will come to your home and construct the flatpack furniture for confused customers.

A visit to an IKEA store is like a day out for families. As the customers walk in, they are guided through a number of tasteful showcase sets featuring their furniture in lounges, bedrooms, kitchens and so on. IKEA's one-way system, called 'the long natural way', has little or no shortcuts and is designed to keep the customer moving through the building to see the entire store.

Eventually, customers end up at the racks of flat-pack furniture where, having made a note of the items they want, they load them on to trolleys and head for the checkout. Cleverly,

Building realistic rooms within their stores allows Ikea to help customers visualize how the products would look in their own homes.

Having the warehouse on the way out of the shop allows immediate purchase in a way online shopping doesn't.

IKEA position bins full of household items before the exits, a marketing technique they call 'bulla bulla', which creates an impression of volume and therefore inexpensiveness.

IKEA are without a doubt masters of every psychological marketing technique, which is why they have managed to change the way the world buys furniture. Just to put it into perspective, IKEA is responsible for 1 per cent of the entire world's commercial wood consumption.

LIKING

First outlined by Dr Robert Cialdini in 1984, the liking principle sounds almost too elementary to be worth noting. The principle is not 'if your customer "likes" your product or service they will buy it'. Instead, it analyses

MARKETING MASTERSTROKES: MARMITE, 'YOU EITHER LOVE IT OR HATE IT.'

Marmite, the dark brown and sticky spread made from yeast extract, was invented by German scientist Justus von Liebig at the turn of the 20th century. Its distinctively salty flavour and texture have long polarized opinions. Its properties, such as its high vitamin B content, mean that it is very good for small children. It was this factor that meant that many kids in the UK were brought up on it. However, this tells only half the story. While lots of people acquired a taste for it at an early age, there were many others who never took to it at all. Back in the late 1970s, the marketers

Consumers are also divided over how much Marmite to put on toast.

at Marmite even identified a North/South divide, arguing that most people from south of the Watford Gap had it when they were children and were favourably accustomed to it, whereas the folks in the North, who liked their sandwich spreads thicker, found the flavour too powerful. So common was this split opinion in the UK that the word 'Marmite' became common parlance for anything that was extremely divisive. The brand is one of the most iconic in Britain and, after seeing its share of the market starting to slip, Unilever (Marmite's parent company) decided that a bold new approach was needed to revive its flagging fortunes.

In 1996, they turned to advertising agency BMP DDB for inspiration and the brief found its way to the desk of two young creatives, Richard Flintham and Andy McLeod. During their musings, Flintham and Mcleod discovered that their opinions on the taste of Marmite mirrored the country's: Richard loved it while Andy hated it, and so the idea was born. The slogan 'Marmite. You either love it or hate it!' was adopted by

Marmite's jar design is one of the great iconic brand symbols and has barely changed since it was introduced in the 1920s.

the company and launched with two TV commercials, one focusing on the 'lovers', the other on the 'haters'. This was a fairly radical departure, not just from Marmite's marketing plans but from all that was normal in strategies, as it was pretty unheard of for a company to promote a product based on a negative. Since its launch, the Love/Hate idea has seen many incarnations but the end-line has endured to this day. It shows that using reverse psychology can be a powerful tool for marketers.

the signifiers that humans look for in other people that affect whether or not they like them. These ideas can then be applied to marketing.

For example, it's not surprising that people are drawn to those whom they find physically pleasing or attractive. On a very primitive level this is why launches of new car models invariably had women draped across the bonnet for much of the 20th century. Great progress has been made in recognizing that standards of beauty have been extremely restrictive and, in many cases, prejudiced. Despite this, the people hired to appear in commercials and other promotional materials are still invariably models or at least conventionally attractive. This principle can also be applied to the aesthetic qualities of packaging, logos, websites and any marketing materials a company uses.

It's also not surprising that people like those who pay them compliments. This doesn't mean anything as simplistic as a company going on Twitter, seeking out people and telling them they like their picture. It means engaging with customers in ways that allow them to present the company with opportunities to be positive. For example, this can be a food product's team asking for submissions for jokey competitions on social media, or a clothing brand training its customer support people to offer constructive fashion tips.

Another factor people use in determining whether they 'like' someone or not is how similar they find that person to themselves, whether through beliefs, interests or personality. Mirroring your customer's self-image in the materials you present them requires you to understand your target market. If they feel like the people running the company are 'just like them', whether they're sports enthusiasts or self-declared geeks, they will buy their products or services. For example, the supermarket chain Asda deliberately used real employees in its commercials to show that its workers were like its customers.

Marketers can also include elements that customers are culturally conditioned to like. These are aspects of the world that, although they don't see them in themselves, they are positively inclined towards. This can be a popular celebrity using your product or service, or a patriotic image or design.

However, it's also true that a company could alienate potential customers if they don't see themselves or their interests in their product or service. Therefore, concentrating only on representing their typical target markets in their brand could limit their potential customer base.

Summary

The use of psychology in marketing is probably one of the most debated topics in the industry, as it can seem to suggest that marketers are using stealth to get into the minds of the people to which they are trying to sell. However, in an increasingly competitive market society, a deeper understanding of the factors that affect everyone's lives is a legitimate and essential marketing tool, provided it is done with the correct motives. Those individuals who flout marketing ethics can find themselves on the wrong end of the regulators, who keep a very keen eye on what's going on in the marketing world.

The importance of mirroring

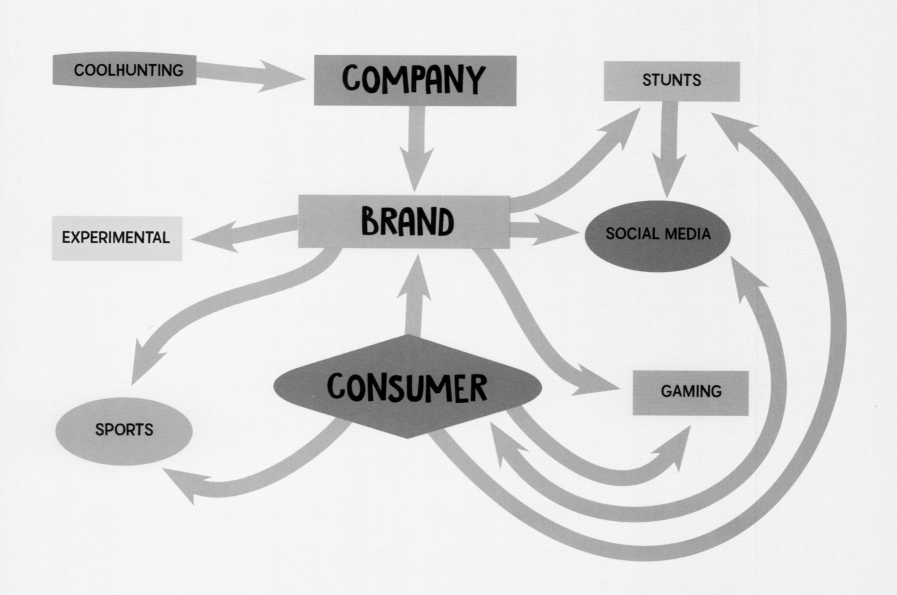

COOLHUNTING

COMPANY

STUNTS

EXPERIMENTAL

BRAND

SOCIAL MEDIA

CONSUMER

GAMING

SPORTS

GETTING CLOSER TO CONSUMERS

Engagement or experiential marketing might seem like a fairly recent development but in truth it's been around, in one form or another, for a very long time. The purpose of experiential marketing is to engage the consumer directly in a brand or product experience. By actively engaging with people, companies can get them to 'buy into' what the product or service does with a 'live' experience, and in this way the consumer will become part of the evolution of the brand and feel some ownership. It can be anything from handing out samples outside a shop to completely immersive experiences organized by a multinational mega-brand. This chapter will explore a little of the history and some of the techniques involved in what is now a vital tool for the marketer.

Engagement marketing is in some ways like a partnership between the company and the consumer with the aim of benefiting both.

Eearly experiential marketing

The Wienermobile – pictured left in its original incarnation in 1936 – is a classic example of using novelty and humour to engage the public.

ENGAGEMENT MARKETING: A BRIEF HISTORY

There is some debate as to when experiential marketing, as we know it today, actually had its first outing. Some would say that it was at the 1893 World's Fair in Chicago when William Wrigley Junior himself handed out samples of Wrigley's Juicy Fruit chewing gum to people attending the event. Others might argue that it didn't really become relevant as a marketing technique until 1924 when Macy's, the big New York department store, brought a live circus, including animals, acrobats and clowns, to the streets of Manhattan in front of 10,000 people during the Thanksgiving parade.

In 1936, the streets of Chicago were treated to the unusual sight of a sausage-shaped car driving around. Dubbed the 'Wienermobile', it was the brainchild of Oscar Mayer's nephew to promote the family's famous hot dog brand. As he drove around, he handed out whistles shaped like the vehicle to passers-by.

Procter & Gamble were early adopters, too. In the early 20th century, P&G used the learnings from live demonstrations their salesmen conducted with retailers to set up sampling events of their laundry products with consumers. In 1914, George P. Johnson, a former sailmaker, created a company to produce stands for big automobile events where consumers could put themselves behind the wheel of some fancy new cars. His early pioneering led to the GPJ establishing itself today, as an events and brand marketing multinational that prides itself on consumer interactions.

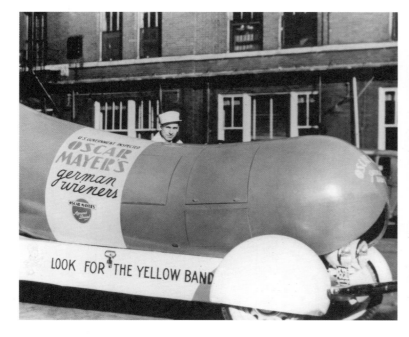

GOING VIRAL

During the 20th century, engagement marketing continued to play a huge part in companies' marketing plans, especially when they were trying to create a more personal rapport with their consumers. In the 1980s, experienced advertising creative director Jay Conrad Levinson coined the phrase 'guerrilla marketing' (see below) and, in his book of the same name, went on to describe its virtues, especially when clients had limited marketing budgets. His unconventional approach to marketing methods was summed up by his quote, 'Quality is not what you put into your product or service but what your customers get out of it.'

With the advent of the internet, engagement and experiential marketing events were able to create even more impact, challenging the more conventional media available to marketers. Not only could companies organize live interactions between their products and services and consumers, but they were suddenly able to broadcast them live around the world: the 'viral' was born. The viewers of this content would see people like them with the same interests engaging with things they liked too. Not only that, but they in turn could share it with their like-minded friends and family. Suddenly the power of 'live' engagements were accessible to audiences of millions. In this way, engagement marketing has transformed itself from a small, one-on-one experience into a powerful and vital tool for the modern marketer.

Live interaction between customer and product

GUERRILLA MARKETING

Sometimes a company has to use a high-impact, tactical campaign to maximize its budget and its message – this is known as guerrilla marketing. Named after guerrilla warfare, the idea is to catch the people by surprise with a specific message in a particular location by using imagery or text that will provoke an emotional reaction. Although often employed by companies with a limited budget, it is a tactic sometimes also used by larger organizations to make a specific point.

Now that social media has a huge role to play in the dissimilation of news, any event experienced by a few is quickly shared among millions, making guerrilla marketing an even more powerful technique.

There are a number of iterations of guerrilla marketing, including **ambush marketing**, **stealth marketing** and **street marketing**, but they all boil down to the same, unexpected, unconventional tactic. One example was an organization raising awareness of Alzheimer's disease by handing out maps of Hamburg in Germany to people in the street. When the recipient opened the map, it was devoid of street names. Another good example was when the charity UNICEF set up vending machines dispensing bottles of dirty water with labels like Typhoid, Malaria and Cholera, to draw attention to the plight of millions of children the world over and their lack of access to clean drinking water.

Exchanging collectible cards featuring footballers has been popular for decades.

SPORTS MARKETING

Because most professional sports are enjoyed live, either in a stadium or via live broadcasts watched in fan zones, bars, clubs or people's homes, sports promotion is a natural fit with engagement marketing. In the USA, the televising of live sporting events like baseball, basketball and American football has been a long-established tradition.

However, a seismic shift towards creating greater engagement with fans came with the advent of the English Premier League (EPL) in 1992. Before its formation, football had been on a downward spiral, with crumbling stadiums, hooliganism and dwindling attendances. In those days, televised sport was very limited, with a few live games and a few others covered via highlights packages. The EPL was announced with great fanfare. The competition, which replaced the old Football League Division One, would be contested by 20 clubs and the lucrative broadcasting rights were bought by Sky Television, already at the centre of the satellite revolution. Over the next few years, with more televisual opportunities for broadcasters and renewed interest from fans, revenue flooded in to the sport.

The vast sums involved meant the clubs had more money to invest in players and stadium facilities. Not only were fans watching the matches on television, but they were going to more games and enjoying a better class of live experience. The clubs were making money not just from the TV rights but also from sponsorships,

The Manchester United stadium at Old Trafford fully reflects the club's strong branding.

shirt sales to adoring fans and a myriad of other marketing opportunities. They were evolving from football teams into huge multinational brands.

Football has now become the most popular global sport, outstripping any other sporting activity worldwide. Football's regulatory bodies, FIFA and UEFA, have also profited, through deals with broadcasters, betting companies and video gaming. EA Sports' FIFA pro video game has an engagement of over 65 million games played weekly, and some of the players have become professionals, earning huge amounts of money from it. The global television rights for the EPL reached a staggering £9.2 billion in 2021 (a rise of almost 4,000 per cent since it began), adding enormous value to the clubs competing in it.

The power of football

It's not just football that had to become more accessible to sports fans to survive: athletics, aquatic sports, tennis, winter sports, in fact, just about every popular professional sport has benefitted from the huge revenues that the television networks have poured into the system.

Ripping up the rules of cricket

Another sport that has seen a phenomenal rise in popularity and found a whole new fan base thanks to television and its willingness to adapt its format to keep a fresh audience committed, is cricket. For much of the twentieth century, cricket was a game that seemed to be set in a permanent world of Victorian attitudes and cucumber sandwiches with an aging and dwindling fan base. The County Championship was seeing ever decreasing attendances, the shorter format one-day game was failing to reignite the sport's fortunes with only Test cricket keeping its head above the water. In 2003, a new format of the game was launched, Twenty20 or T20. Instead of being played over five days or even one day, the game was completed in a matter of a few hours and, as such, was perfect for TV.

A new format

The new format was received by cricket purists with mixed emotions, many of the old stalwarts thought this would signal the death knell of the game they loved. However, new fans were treated to spectacular feats of batting, bowling and fielding, either at matches or while sitting in front of their television sets. It was like the highlights of the longer game happening live, featuring the players they were used to seeing in Test matches, smashing the ball for a six or flattening the wickets in spectacular style. It breathed new life into cricket, with players taking the more aggressive style of T20 into Test cricket and the one-day game, making these more exciting and a better bet for TV networks.

Realizing the potential for the shorter format game of cricket in a country where it is worshipped, the Indian Premier League was launched in 2007, and it's safe to say that this move has had the biggest effect on the way cricket is marketed today. The IPL has attracted the biggest cricketing stars from around the world, who are subject to bidding wars, and join exotically named like the Kolkata Knight Riders and the Rajasthan Royals. It has also been a magnet for huge sums of

Shorter form cricket matches like the T-20 have breathed new life into cricket's popularity.

money, with Rupert Murdoch's Star India TV network paying $2.6 billion for the global rights. Cricket is still challenging its roots by introducing further changes like the new 'Hundreds' format, where each team is given 100 bowls to score as many as they can. This new format is even, controversially, changing the language of the game where 'balls' have become 'bowls' and 'wickets' have become 'outs'. The matches are 150 minutes long, broadcast live on Sky and YouTube and will feature both men's and women's teams.

Move over chaps!

Another notable shift in sports marketing has been the promotion of women in sports, with both women's football and cricket enjoying much greater coverage and a huge growth in popularity. Greater coverage of sports has seen new marketing sophistication, whether it is through sales of football shirts or spin-off events where fans can have greater access to their sporting heroes and heroines. Social media is also playing a part in greater engagement with players and athletes on Twitter, Facebook and Instagram, albeit with some negative consequences due to racist trolling.

Sport has seen a massive rise in engagement marketing, but this new interest has been so meteoric that the clubs, sportswear brands and broadcasters have struggled to keep pace. Money has dominated sport over the last few decades and has blinded some sports organizations as to their real purpose: the ill-fated ESL (European Super League) venture is proof of that. As in any field of marketing, sports brands need to remember who matters most: fans are their consumers and, as legendary Scottish football manager Jock Stein put it, 'Football without fans is nothing.' For football, read any sport.

The importance of fans

Argentian footballer Florencia Bonsegundo celebrating her goal in the Women's World Cup 2019.

Striking visual images like this King Kong outside the Hollywood Wax Museum draw in crowds and spread word-of-mouth via social media.

Maximizing impact

IMPACT EXPERIENTIAL MARKETING

In order to gain the maximum impact for their budget, a brand or company will sometimes need a stunt or installation that will not only impress the passer-by, but turn that engagement into a well-documented and then widely shared viral event. These experiential experiences can take any form. For example, in 2009 Volkswagen Sweden turned a much-used staircase at the Odenplan subway station in Stockholm into a working piano. This prompted more people to use the stairs instead of the adjacent escalator so that they could try to play their own tune on the way up or down. It's hard to find a natural connection between cars and pianos, but the event was seen to be fun and spontaneous, which would leave a favourable impression with the people interacting with it and those viewing it online. As well as promoting a new BlueMotionTechnologies brand, they were promoting a healthy active lifestyle, making the campaign doubly effective.

At the other end of the scale, Red Bull sponsored the world's highest parachute jump as it naturally resonated with its slogan, 'Red Bull gives you wings'. Professional skydiver Felix Baumgartner took a balloon up to 3,900 m (128,000 ft), almost into space, and jumped out. This record-breaking skydive hit over 3 million views, and Red Bull's daring promotion did a lot to underpin the properties of a stimulating drink. Marketing in this style has become increasingly popular with the advent of social media, and advertising agencies have encouraged their creative teams to embrace this form of promotion, as it punches well above its weight compared to some of the more traditional forms of advertising.

The experience is the key

Red Bull sponsorship of elaborate stunts has connected the brand with its slogan 'Red Bull Gives You Wings'

COOLHUNTING

In the early 2000s, marketing agencies were becoming increasingly aware that it was the youth market who were breaking new ground when it came to spontaneous events, and they were the ones driving the trends being adopted by consumers in general. Phenomena, such as flash mobbing, where large groups of people would suddenly and unexpectedly turn up and perform a happening or a dance; or planking, where individuals would lay flat and stiff, mimicking a 'plank' in unusual locations, were becoming widely shared on social media.

Marketing, ever keen to appropriate the latest trends, created 'coolhunting' agencies, whose purpose was to gather data via research on emerging and declining trends among young people. This was mainly done through randomly assembled focus groups, after which the gathered data was sold on to companies in search of better ways to engage this most mercurial of markets.

It's fair to say that based on this data, marketers found that traditional marketing and advertising techniques were not as effective with this demographic group and more 'out there' experiential campaigns had a far greater impact. The risk for coolhunters was always that by the time something was found to be cool, it had a very short life expectancy with the youth audience, and jumping on a particular fad could sometimes be counterproductive. Therefore, they had to try to predict these trends before they even happened, and, like meteorology, there's no perfect way to predict anything.

While flash mobs, like this international one in 2015, have fallen out of fashion, similar events are still an effective marketing tool.

MARKETING MASTERSTROKES: IKEA PREGNANCY TEST ADVERTISEMENT

In 2017, IKEA's Swedish advertising agency Åkestam Holst approached Mercene Labs, a spin-off from the Royal Institute of Technology in Stockholm, to see if they could turn a newspaper advertisement for a baby's crib into an active pregnancy tester. Mercene were a little dumbfounded at this request but, realizing it was genuine, they set about the task. The product manager at Mercene, Jonas Hansson,

IKEA's pregnancy test ad is an example of how outrageous and bold concepts can capture public imagination and motivate them to act.

worked on several different techniques before landing on the ideal solution. They combined several materials in different layers: one was a paper-like layer with large pores, so that the urine could be moved around the page quickly. That layer also contained the antibodies that interact with the hCG hormone in the urine and allow for a discounted price to appear next to the picture of the crib in red. All the reader of the ad had to do was to urinate on it, and if it came up with a positive pregnancy result, they would receive a substantial discount off the crib.

The agency took their idea to IKEA, the advertisement had the headline, 'Peeing on this ad may change your life'. IKEA has always been a company that embraced bold and innovative approaches to solve marketing problems and never shied away from controversy, so they approved the ad and ran it in December 2017 to much international acclaim.

NAMES TO KNOW: OPRAH WINFREY

Born in impoverished circumstances in Mississippi in 1954 to a single, teenage mother, Oprah (then named Orpah) moved at an early age to Milwaukee and was raised in the inner city. In her early life, she endured many hardships, including becoming pregnant and losing a child when she was just 14. She then moved to Tennessee to be brought up by Vernon Winfrey, the man she refers to as her father.

Her talent was recognized early, and she was signed up by a local radio station while she was still in high school. By the age of 19, Oprah Winfrey was working for the local evening news channel, making her the youngest news anchor and the first black

Oprah Winfrey.

woman to do the job at WLAC-TV in Nashville. Her prodigious interviewing abilities and sympathetic, often emotional engagements with people in the news saw her rocket up the broadcast ladder.

It wasn't only on live TV that she was able to demonstrate the range of her abilities; in 1985 she was cast by Steven Spielberg for the movie The Color Purple, *which saw her nominated for an Oscar.*

In the mid-1990s, Oprah Winfrey's star showed no sign of waning and she had reinvented her show as a lifestyle and culture-based broadcast. It featured art, literature, mindfulness tips and musing on spirituality with her conducting the emotional content with her customary skill. She was a great promoter and supporter of Barack Obama's presidential campaign, actions that led to her emerging as a political force, and she undoubtedly had an influence on him becoming the first African American president in US history.

In 2008, she formed her multinational basic cable TV channel the Oprah Winfrey Network (OWN) and has garnered numerous prestigious accolades and awards both personally and professionally. It's not surprising many hail her as the 'Queen of All Media'.

Such is her power and confidence that in 2004, while she was conducting one of her shows, she gave all 276 members of the audience a brand-new Pontiac car. The idea had been originally for the sponsors to donate 25 cars to be given away during her show, but Oprah had other ideas. Initially she gave out the keys to 11 cars. She then said there was one more car going and handed every member of the audience a sealed

Oprah Winfrey's boldness in giving away 276 Pontiac cars on her show singles her out as somehow who understands how to really connect with her audience.

white box, saying that one of the boxes contained the keys to the last car. Following a drum roll, everyone opened their boxes ... every one of which contained a set of keys. Cue pandemonium. Oprah began calling out to individual members of the audience with the phrase, 'You got a car! You got a car!', until she declared, 'Everyone gets a car!' to a by-now screaming audience, many of whom were also in tears. She footed the bill for the extra 251 $28,500 cars out of her own pocket but, as she now has an estimated personal wealth of $2.7 billion, her act of altruism not only served to make 276 people and their families happy, it also helped boost her status as a supreme practitioner in the art of engagement marketing.

ONLINE EXPERIENCES

While at the end of the 20th century online experiential marketing was possible, it was relatively crude and limited, operating on the level of simply clicking through to various constructed websites like a form of 'point and click' adventure game. But for some, the novelty of simply being able to be online and access websites was enough of an experience itself, as shown by the first ever banner ad providing a link to numerous web locations for international museums.

Pikachu is the most recognizable Pokemon but the brands 'Gotta catch 'em all' slogan epitomises their strategy.

However, as technology advanced and internet access massively increased, both the need and the potential for online experiential marketing exploded. One of these new experiences was alternate reality games or 'ARGs'. These were akin to detective mysteries conducted by clicking through various fictional websites, following the thread of one or many imaginary stories, sometimes combined with other audio or visual materials designed to increase the realism.

One of the earliest successful ARGs was called *The Beast* and was created in 2001 to promote the Steven Spielberg film *AI: Artificial Intelligence*. It rewarded engagement and investigation and used many of the same hooks that drive human beings to get drawn into true crime stories and, to a certain extent, conspiracy theories. It also emphazised community interaction as a large number of people collaborated to solve some of its trickier puzzles. This element set it apart from early 'quest' media, such as the 1979 book *Masquerade*, which hid the real-life location of a golden hare in a series of cryptic drawings. As *Masquerade*'s prize was monetary, it meant people would be reluctant to share their findings or collaborate, while *The Beast*'s rewards were entertainment and information and so collaboration was key. This was also true of later popular ARGs like the *Halo 2* promotional game *ilovebees*.

While they are not cheap or easy to organize, ARGs can provide a level of excitement and engagement far greater than more conventional marketing techniques.

Increasingly popular is integrating ARG-like components into other types of marketing, as well as other aspects of gamification. The rise of social media has given companies a much more convenient platform through which to use these types of techniques, as well as the development of mobile phone and tablet apps, allowing companies to literally invent their own platforms through which to create these experiences.

Augmented reality or AR is another online technology that can be used to create experiential content, whether it's putting imaginary physical objects in the real world or clever uses like Viking Footwear's app that allowed you to virtually identify a shoe from its footprint in mud (provided, of course, it was made by Viking).

Pokémon Go, ostensibly just an extension of the *Pokémon* media franchise, showed how AR computer techniques could smoothly be used to make ARG-style mechanics in the real world and this has also been embraced by some marketers to produce virtual treasure hunts to promote their offerings. As people become more technologically amphibious, living their life partially in both the online and real worlds, these kinds of experiential crossover moments will be increasingly common.

Summary

The use of psychology in marketing is probably one of the most debated topics in the industry, as it can seem to suggest that marketers are using stealth to get into the minds of the people to which they are trying to sell. However, in an increasingly competitive market society, a deeper understanding of the factors that affect everyone's lives is a legitimate and essential marketing tool, provided it is done with the correct motives. Those individuals who flout marketing ethics can find themselves on the wrong end of the regulators, who keep a very close watch on what's going on in the marketing world.

GAMIFICATION ▶ *Gamification is the act of introducing game-like elements to non-game activities with the aim of making the activity more engaging and providing motivation for those who are taking part. In a marketing contex, it can be as simple as offering customers rewards for completing various activities, like offering feedback or engaging with interactive online materials. Popular game design elements, like point systems, ranking, avatars or other representative icons or images and collective collaboration towards a shared goal are often used.*

Experiential crossover

Chapter Fourteen
MAKING A MARKETING PLAN

*Fail to Plan, Plan to Fail • Mission Statement •
Identify Target Market • Brand Properties • Decide
on Marketing and Promotional Strategies • Identify
and Understand the Competition • Marketing Plan
Goals and Objectives • Result Analysis*

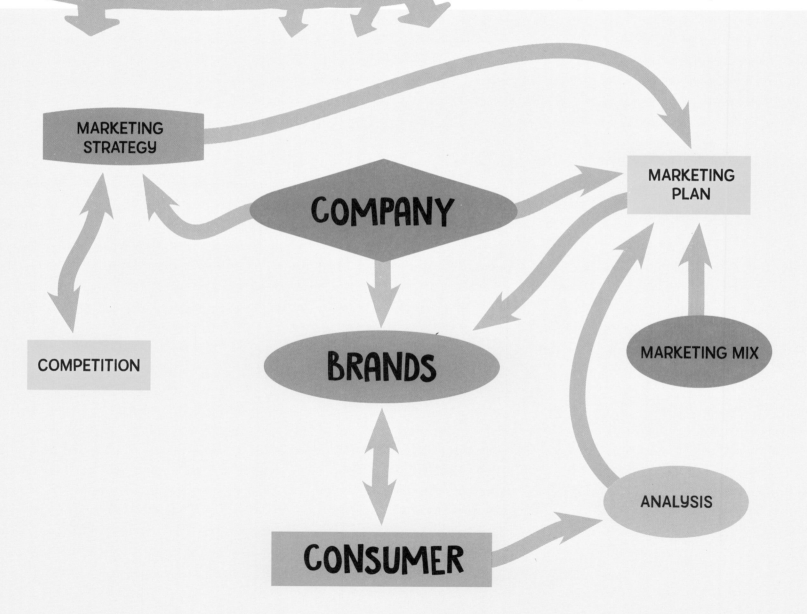

FAIL TO PLAN, PLAN TO FAIL

Before any company launches a brand, or even considers mapping out the future of their exciting products for the next year, the first vital step is to prepare a marketing plan. Without a plan, entering any market would be tantamount to stepping into a marketing abyss, and an ill-prepared plan will also severely hamper a company's ability to compete with its rivals. This chapter is an example of a commonly used, seven-stage marketing plan for a fictitious company, which will outline the right steps.

Decide where you are going

The logo is often the first place to start when creating a plan for a new product or brand.

Keep the mission statement succinct

STEP 1: MISSION STATEMENT

Writing a mission statement for the company or the brand is the first step that a marketer would take when they are preparing a marketing plan. A mission statement is the definition of a company's function and/or goal and tells the target market how they want to be perceived. It usually takes the form of one simple sentence, crafted to inspire the consumer and give an honest but favourable impression of the company.

When writing the statement, the marketer should, first of all, understand two things: what the company does and who they are marketing to. Here are a couple of examples of existing mission statements from two very different companies:

American Express *We work hard every day to make American Express the world's most respected service brand.*
Amex's mission statement wants their target market to trust them. The use of phrases such as the 'world's most respected' and 'work hard', are there to reassure the consumer that American Express's financial services are above reproach.

Patagonia *Build the best product, cause no unnecessary harm, use business to inspire and implement solutions to the environmental crisis.*
Patagonia is one of the most ethically sound companies in the world (see pages 120–1) and their mission statement

reflects that position in language they know their customers will understand. Their statement uses phrases like 'solutions to the environmental crisis' to underpin their ecologically sound credentials. But they also don't forget that they are a business and start with the phrase, 'Build the best product' so that their customers know that they will not compromise when it comes to quality.

When writing a mission statement for the fictitious company, Bee SomeBody, the first thing to do is understand at whom the message will be directed. Bee SomeBody will have to do some research into the identity of their possible target market. They would find out that the highest appeal for a brand like theirs would be among women in the A/B demographic, as the products would be sold at a premium price, due to higher manufacturing costs. This will include mothers in their 30s with children, who are aware of the natural benefits. It would also appeal to some older women, who would see the products as a way to combat the effects of the menopause on their skin. It could even filter down to teenagers, who like the environmental values of the brand.

Reflect your product

Having a firm idea of the target market is crucial to constructing a plan for the brand.

Bee SomeBody would then consider what they are offering – a range of beauty products including, soaps, hand and body moisturizers, lip balms and candles. All of the products are made using beeswax collected from a national co-operative of beekeepers, and all the other ingredients would be natural and environmentally sourced.

By understanding who they are, what they sell and who might buy it, they can choose the combination of words for their mission statement, which will in turn focus the rest of their marketing plan.

STEP 2: IDENTIFY TARGET MARKET (OR NICHE MARKET)

How would Bee SomeBody define their target market? There are a wide variety of factors to consider. They include:

- What are the basic characteristics of the product or service?
- What problem is the product solving and for whom? Is it an essential everyday item like bread or milk, or is it something purchased specially to meet a particular individual need.
- What is the pricing level, based on manufacturing, design, labour and marketing costs?
- What is the potential reach, based on where the company operates, possibilities of shipping and whether or not it's a service that requires specialized locations?
- Beyond the product or service, what particular expertise is the company offering?
- What is the target market or customer base of rival or similar products? While there are obviously going to be some differences, it's very useful to analyse this as it can also give the marketer an idea if there is room in the market for your product. They can also assess how their rivals market the product and see if it's effective, and make sure there's no crossover in approach.

Know your part of the market

A lot of these questions can be solved by drawing up a customer profile (see page 82). They may also, depending on budget, commission or conduct quantitative and qualitative research at this point (see pages 124–31). This is especially true if they have decided to aim for a niche market instead of a wider target group.

Bee SomeBody may decide that instead of aiming for A/B women in general, they want to target a particular subset of women who are interested in organic/ecological living, or alternate healthy lifestyles, or even women who see themselves as punky subcultural people who would prefer a more irreverent product. All these things will, by necessity, change the other elements of the plan.

The target market.

2

Bee Somebody

Our target market
Women who are interested in organic/ecological living, alternative healthy lifestyles.

Women who don't follow the herd but follow their own path and buy products that reflect their values.

The world is in peril, they will take the necessary steps to save it and look good doing it.

STEP 3: BRAND PROPERTIES

The third step is to explore the elements that make the brand what it is. We are not just talking about the ingredients that go into the making of the product but also other key factors associated with it. These are the unique characteristics that define the brand and make it stand out from its competitors in the market.

Define your brand

Examples of brand properties in other well-known organizations:

- **Coca-Cola** claims to be the original cola brand and therefore the best.
- **KFC** claim to have a secret recipe only known to Colonel Sanders, which gives their chicken a distinctive taste all of its own.

The product advantages.

What could be the brand properties that would set Bee SomeBody apart from its rivals, as there are other companies making products out of beeswax? First of all, Bee SomeBody would claim that they don't just source their raw material, beeswax, from anywhere, but that they have a dedicated co-operative of beekeepers supplying them. Not only that, but it is a mutually exclusive arrangement that guarantees the wax is locally sourced under sustainable conditions, which benefits the beekeepers and the bees. Even the beehives themselves are made from recycled materials. They would also point out their product is free from any additives and therefore purer than some of its competitors. They would probably add that all packaging is either biodegradable, or made from recycled materials and as such would be recyclable again. They would have done extensive research to define the product range they offer so that the fragrances and feel of their product will give their customers complete satisfaction. Lastly, their modern and tastefully designed packaging would appeal to customers and retailers alike and reflect the provenance of its natural ingredients.

3

Bee Somebody

We have a dedicated co-operative of beekeepers supplying our beeswax. It's a mutually exclusive arrangement that guarantees the wax is locally sourced under sustainable conditions that benefit the beekeepers and the bees.

The beehives are made from recycled materials. Our product is free from any additives and purer than our competitors'. All packaging is biodegradable and made from recycled materials. Our modern and tastefully designed products will appeal to customers and retailers alike and reflects the provenance of the natural materials we use.

STEP 4: DECIDE ON MARKETING AND PROMOTIONAL STRATEGIES

Once the parameters of the product or service have been strongly established, the company can begin to outline what marketing and promotional strategies are a) possible and b) preferable. Marketing strategies and plans are sometimes conflated, a situation not helped by marketing strategies sometimes being called the 'game plan'. Despite this, the strategy element is only one part of a marketing plan and without the other elements can become misdirected and aimless. The primary aim of a good marketing strategy is, in fact, to outlive its marketing plan, because it is intended to provide a structure and basis for continuing successful operations.

4

Bee Somebody

Our plan is to have an impactful online and in-store presence, grounded and not too technological. We will use stories from the beekeepers and our consumers, highlighting the importance of bee conservation.

Our online content, through bloggers who are sympathetic to the values we hold, will seek personal engagement with environmentally conscious women. The conversation will be on the theme of natural beauty, from natural sources.

We will have an unaffected feel to all our communications and marketing, not too slick, that will underpin our dedication to the causes we support.

We are going to create the right kind of buzz around **Bee Somebody**.

The key to an effective marketing strategy is finding a central concept or conceit to your brand that it can revolve around. This can come from examining your value proposition, intended message, all the previous parts of the marketing plan and even past marketing plans or strategies.

The media strategy.

For example, Tesco's strategy has for almost 30 years been built around the slogan 'every little helps'. This clever phrase is effective, explains admiring copywriter Nick Asbury, because it 'carries the everyday authority of a proverb', like a saying handed down through generations. This gives Tesco a strategic opportunity of portraying themselves as down-to-earth, wise and able to offer convenient bargains, while at the same time not as 'cheap' or budget oriented as 'lower-tier' supermarkets like Lidl and Aldi.

With this in mind, Bee SomeBody's marketing strategy should originate from its mission statement about making the world a better place for 'beauty and the bees', plus its brand and target market decisions. A great start would include an online and in-store campaign, grounded and not too technological, using the stories of the beekeepers and customers, and highlighting the importance of bee conservation. They would also seek personal engagement with environmentally conscious women, having a conversation on the theme of natural beauty, from natural sources. They would have a hand-made feel to the design of the products and to their marketing which should not be too slick, to emphasize the 'underdog' nature of the brand.

Getting it out there

STEP 5: IDENTIFY AND UNDERSTAND THE COMPETITION

In order to find Bee SomeBody's place in the market, the company would carry out research in order to find out who their main competitors are. There are a number of research tools that they could utilize in order to get the data they need for this. Anything from an in-depth SWOT analysis (see page 126 website SEO analysis (see page 184) focus groups (see page 130 or customer feedback mechanisms (although in Bee SomeBody's case the last one would not apply as they are launching themselves as a newcomer to the market). They will have also attended industry events, such as White Label Expo, Olympia Beauty London or Natural & Organic London. At these shows, they will be able to gauge how much promotional effort their rivals are employing to engage retailers and consumers.

Know your competitors

5

Bee Somebody

We need to identify our main rivals. We will attend all the major exhibitions and shows in our category so we can build an accurate picture of who we are up against. We will be reading blogs, conducting research and analysing all available data. We have already recruited staff with experience of our competitor's brands and operations. We are not just competing with the small producers with similar products, we are up against the big brands, so we must prove ourselves against them.

They would also be able to sample products and find out some of the plans that the opposition have to market their own offerings. Simple store checks would also give them a picture of what else they are up against and also which products are selling well and which are not. Combing social media sites and reading beauty blogs will give them an overview of which rival products are trending at the time.

They could consider poaching rival's staff, even though this might seem a little unethical. This would give them experienced personnel who were already au fait with the business and insider knowledge of a rival's practices and brand plans.

Identify the competition.

Bee SomeBody would see themselves as direct competitors to the high-end beauty brands, where they could claim the high ground on ethicality against the big multinationals as well as a niche product against more direct competitors, meaning that they can extol the uniqueness in the way they source the wax for their products.

STEP 6: MARKETING PLAN GOALS AND OBJECTIVES

This step will provide the company with a clear target for their plan so that they can provide direction to people involved with the brand, most typically the sales and marketing team and the promotional and advertising partners. However, it is just as important to all the other personnel, from the CEO down to the worker sticking labels on jars of the product, that the brand has a clear vision of what it wants to achieve. It is all very well to set out a really ambitious objective and hope it will inspire the company to reach for it but, in reality, the goal should be achievable and within the means of the brand to make it really effective. It needs to be measurable and have KPIs that will give you the data to measure its success. They need to fit the brand like a glove and be relevant to the product and the way it is presented to the market and, most importantly, the consumer. The goals should have a timeline so that when they reach a definitive point, the company can judge either whether it's time to redefine them or employ a new strategy.

What do you want to achieve?

6

Bee Somebody

We are ready.

We are priced competitively but we are not cheap.

We guarantee that 20 per cent of our profits will go to supporting our most important workers, the bees.

Through the 'BeeLine' our customers can tell us what they think of our products and services and we can keep them informed of our bee conservation efforts.

Our customers will be able to 'adopt a bee' and can take advantage of our free offers whenever they introduce new followers.

We are here to offer great beauty and style and to make sure there is a future for bees.

We are here to Bee **Somebody**

What makes us special?

235

Bee SomeBody would define their objectives like this:

- To launch a range of luxurious and ethically sourced beauty products, targeted at an environmentally conscious consumer, and to help save the bee from extinction.

- Bee SomeBody products will be priced competitively, but not cheaply, to reflect the high quality of their range and the unique way they source raw materials. They would point out that a proportion of their profits goes directly to support the beekeepers. This simple action would reassure the consumer that Bee SomeBody is not just a for profit organization and that they are trying to save bees from extinction.

- They would put in place a clear customer feedback system called the BeeLine so that they can create a two-way conversation with consumers that will cover all topics, from how the products are performing to environmental issues.

- They would run an 'adopt a bee' scheme that would personalize 'the most important members of their staff, the bees.'

- To encourage word-of-mouth they would offer customers free products or discounts if they introduce new customers.

Bee SomeBody will launch themselves on to the market with sound objectives that will not only enhance their reputation as an ethical and environmentally conscious brand, but also a company with a robust financial plan to make profits and grow their market share.

STEP 7: RESULT ANALYSIS

Did it work?

The final part of any marketing plan is an analysis of its success or failure. This will enable an assessment of whether the plan needs to be altered as it is being implemented or replaced with an entirely different plan. This analysis will come primarily through quantitative market research, targeted at the customers who have used the product and anyone who has been exposed to the marketing and promotional materials. Sales figures, survey results, number of clicks and other online research methods may be employed. Qualitative research may also be used to a lesser extent, though with further use in a post-mortem capacity should the plan prove ineffective.

If the plan doesn't yield the desired effect, whether it's an increase in profit, a change in image or direction, or simply to make people aware of the brand's existence, detailed analysis is important to ensure any changes can be made. If the plan is effective, analysis is also required to discern exactly why it was successful and within what metrics, to ensure that future marketing activities can try to replicate or build on these same results. With the tools that marketers have to hand in the 21st century, implementing this vital final part of the marketing plan is much easier than it used to be.

Bee SomeBody's analysis, beyond the other techniques mentioned, could centre on direct customer responses on their website and social media presence (Twitter, Facebook, Instagram etc), plus any response from retailers. They might also consider investing in further bespoke demographic research to ensure they successfully hit the correct target market.

Summary

The marketing plan is the roadmap forward for every company and at its heart are three important factors. Anyone reading it should learn a) who the company is and what they are selling, b) what its objectives are and most importantly c) the identity of the people the plan is aimed at. To quote Steve Jobs, 'Master the topic, the message and the delivery'.

KEY PERFORMANCE INDICATORS (KPIS)

▶ *In order for companies to measure and manage their progress they use KPIs to help them evaluate their chances of reaching the targets they set for themselves. High-level KPIs concentrate on the overall performance of the business, while low-level KPIs focus on work practices, sales, marketing efforts and talent management. By employing these studies and then analyzing the results, a company can get a clear picture of what is working well within the organization and anything that might be dysfunctional and need attention. It also gives them the information they need to set or readjust the targets they have set themselves. As influential business consultant Peter Drucker famously said, 'What gets measured gets done.'*

Chapter Fifteen

A WATERSHED MOMENT FOR MARKETING

An Elephant in the Room • Lockdown! • Heightened Emotions

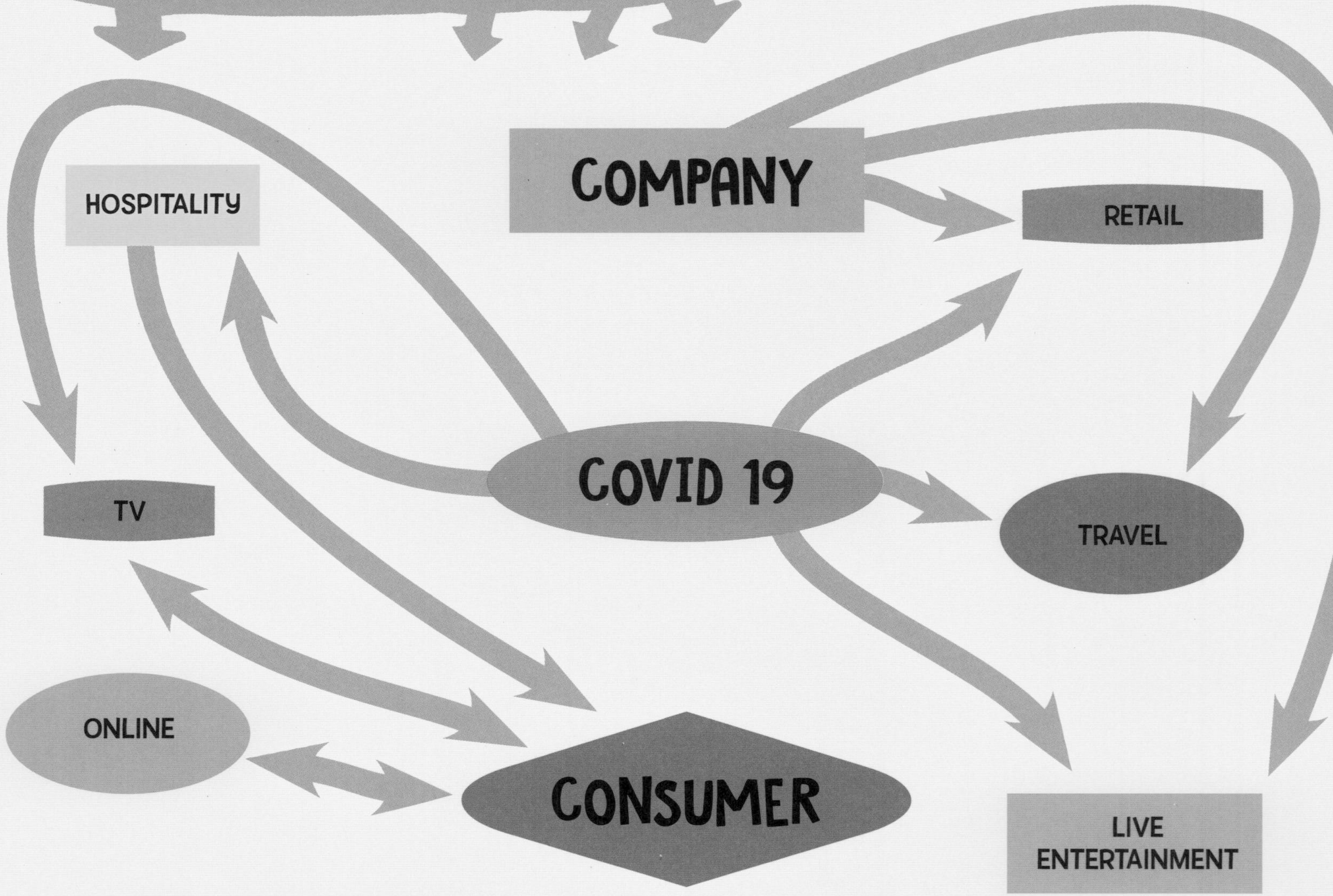

COMPANY
HOSPITALITY
RETAIL
COVID 19
TV
TRAVEL
ONLINE
CONSUMER
LIVE ENTERTAINMENT

AN ELEPHANT IN THE ROOM

There's an elephant in the marketing department that's too big to ignore. The global Covid-19 pandemic has changed everybody's lives forever, affecting the way people live, work, socialize, eat and shop. This is not a passing event: scientists predict that what was a pandemic will become endemic, something that will be part of everyone's lives for the foreseeable future. Companies have had to think on their feet and adapt their marketing plans to reflect an entirely new set of social parameters. Employers whose employees were locked down in their homes found that in many cases productivity improved where they expected it to fall. Working from home works, and many forward-thinking companies now are encouraging their staff to find a balance between coming to the office and doing their jobs from the dining room table. Of course, many industries have come off badly: entertainment, hospitality, travel and retail all took a big hit and recovery for them will be slow and painful. It will take a lot of marketing ingenuity to revive the fortunes of these sectors.

The one marketing arena that thrived because of the pandemic was the internet. For a hundred days in 2020, and again at the beginning of 2021, the safest and most efficient way for consumers to shop was via their computers and smartphones. Such was the demand that online supermarkets and shopping apps almost went into meltdown at one point. Taking all this into account, how will marketers and the brands they serve respond?

A complete re-set

Face masks have become not only a legal necessity in many situations but a fashion accessory and for some a political statement.

The emptiness of Rio de Janeiro's streets were mirrored across the globe.

LOCKDOWN!

While shopping online was already very popular, the virus made it for many the only way to buy items.

The social distancing rules imposed as a way of cutting down transmission of the virus had a huge impact on people's lives, especially when lockdowns forced them to stay in their homes unless they qualified as key workers. Transport was also restricted due to the risk of spread. Suddenly, a huge swathe of marketers' tools, from outdoor advertising to posters on train platforms, were redundant. And anyway, when people were travelling or going outside, they were afraid and tense, and not in the right frame of mind to receive marketing messages. However, if everyone's at home it means marketers and their researchers literally have a captive audience that they can access and analyse. Though, of course, they also have a responsibility not to exploit this situation.

The pandemic has forced advertising practitioners to look at the tone of voice of the messages they put out. It's not enough just to put a face mask on the actors in their commercials or create Zoom meeting ads. The very fact that people have endured something unprecedented has affected the way they perceive marketing messages. As a result, it has become clear that consumers want to see more honesty and a better understanding of what they have been through reflected in advertising.

Thinking locally

In the travel industry, the impact on people taking cruise holidays was catastrophic, but the biggest hit was on flights, which were suddenly a big health risk. It set the airline industry back 20 years. International travel was further curtailed by countries closing their borders for fear of infection spreading from one area to another. Suddenly, a global world had to think much more locally. As business travel declines due to increased use of virtual meeting technology, the airlines will have to focus their marketing efforts on consumers' leisure travel. Those that have survived have concentrated on delivering the promise of escape.

The impact of Covid-19 on the already struggling travel industry was incalculable.

Delivery couriers became essential workers, almost as important to some people's wellbeing as healthcare professionals.

Shopping habits have also changed massively. During the first lockdowns, panic buying led to scarcities of such normal essentials as toilet paper, pasta and flour. As the reality of the 'new normal' set in, the whole shopping experience changed indelibly. Newly furloughed or redundant people had to budget more for essentials than luxuries. Online ordering and deliveries became standard practice and companies like Amazon became omnipotent.

Marketers can no longer depend on in-store advertising and product design being an effective tool but instead need to consider how they can make their online presence and their delivery technique unique and interesting: perhaps

A welcome side effect of reduced human activity was reduced pollution. For example the normally smoggy conditions in Delhi were replaced by clear skies and cleaner air.

by using specially designed boxes or by including special complimentary items with the product or service they deliver. The high street was hit hard, and for a long time only the companies that had an online presence were able to shift their goods. Attracting shoppers back into shops will be the next big challenge for retailers.

New ways of thinking

Restaurants, another potential source of marketing crossover and exposure, had to close. Even universally popular chains like McDonald's felt the squeeze and had to refine their takeaway services. Companies that already had that as their model, like Domino's, had a big advantage over their rivals.

Changing habits

The 'Eat out to help out' promotion backed by the Chancellor of the Exchequer was considered successful, however, it is now up to the industry to find new ways of getting diners back into restaurants. Marketers will have to consider what makes a physical restaurant visit something people would want to repeat. It has to be a balancing act between recouping any losses and not taking advantage of cash-strapped customers, desperate for social interaction.

Benefits of a shutdown

Covid-19 has also had an impact in more unexpected ways. As fewer people were driving cars, pollution levels went down. Not only did people begin to question whether they needed a car at all, but the environmental recovery from that (and a general decrease in all polluting activity) led to increased awareness of green issues. Marketers would be wise to note this shift in public opinion, but also be aware that for some, cars are much safer than public transport from a health perspective. Cars also offer freedom, which has been in short supply.

HEIGHTENED EMOTIONS

The groundswell affection and support for the UK's National Health Service and its workers during the pandemic are demonstrated here.

The pandemic created huge frustration and anger in the populace, as grievances that had lain dormant were suddenly exposed. People could no longer be bystanders, as one slogan powerfully put it, 'Silence is compliance!'

A huge range of social issues were thrown into full focus, not just in the news but also on social media, which fanned the flames of unrest. Brands could not ignore what was going on around them as they were scrutinized by consumers to see where they stood on the ethical issues the world faced. How they move forwards in the future will be impacted by how companies reacted during this time.

The pandemic led to serious emotional issues for many people, from fear and frustrated anger to accelerated forms of depression. Marketers must keep this in mind, as well as reflecting on people's need for comfort and reassurance. They should take into account the positive feelings the public had towards those they saw as being brave or helping during the height of the crisis – people like

Captain Sir Tom Moore's popularity reflects how his selfless actions symbolized a new national togetherness.

frontline health care professionals, or 99-year-old Captain Sir Tom Moore, who did a charity walk in his garden hoping to raise a few thousand pounds. His total donations reached £32.79 million pounds, which was donated to the NHS. In light of this, marketers have to be careful that the tone of any content is respectful and not exploitative.

On the other side of the coin is people's need for something to distract them from dark times, something to make them laugh or transport them elsewhere, and meeting this need is also an important part of marketing.

Emotional investment

The pandemic proved how, more than ever, the value of a brand is not simply its price. The emotional investment in companies, their workers and customers came to the fore. It was not enough to say you cared, it had to be demonstrated. As a result, an increasing amount of messaging is coming from testimonies by companies' staff and the person on the street.

The virtual revolution

Psychological impact

The psychological impact that the pandemic has had on people has still to be fully evaluated and understood. Companies will have to assess exactly where they fit into people's lives and how they can best reflect this understanding in all their communications. It will not be enough to say, 'We're there for you', without demonstrating how.

Gyms and other health-based service providers were among the areas most at risk of spreading Covid-19. This was a huge problem for the health and welfare industry that depended on these locations as a core part of the lifestyle brand they promoted. Home health and exercise products received a boost but the whole idea of what constitutes 'a healthy lifestyle' was thrown into chaos by this unanticipated factor. Personal training has become virtual, and because of the impact on mental health, mindfulness and a more holistic approach to health and welfare has become the norm.

As people spent more time at home, companionship became a factor to combat loneliness, so more people turned to animal ownership. More animals are featuring in brands' messaging, and it's not just for cat and dog food. As a consequence, there are almost as many ads featuring animals as you find videos on Facebook.

Pets provided both an excuse for exercise and a welcome respite from loneliness and stress.

New offerings

Live engagement with consumers became non-existent during the lockdowns, but what people were able to do in the privacy of their own homes was opened up to the internet audience. Companies will start to revive their experiential programmes with caution as they will be aware that although the consumer will be desperate to re-engage with live events, it will take them a while to adjust to being in a crowd.

Not surprisingly, social media platforms became the only place people could meet and enjoy each other's company. It was also a source of original entertainment, with people demonstrating hidden acting, singing and dancing skills. TikTok, Instagram and Facebook were awash with amazing videos, so it was not long before marketers chose to follow the trend. Whether coming out of the pandemic will create another surge of new offerings remains to be seen, but marketers are sure to be better prepared to reflect the change.

Marketing follows certain patterns and rules that have been practised and perfected over decades, from branding to psychology, and all of them have been conditioned by studying the way consumers live their lives.

New media platforms like TikTok gave people entertainment and a chance to express themselves to others even while trapped indoors.

Summary

From time to time world affecting events come along and throw order into chaos, and all the tools marketers rely on need to be reset. Marketers will learn and prosper from these events as long as they put consumers first.

Let's finish with the powerful words of novelist Maya Angelou, 'I've learned that people will forget what you said, people will forget what you did, but people will never forget how you made them feel.'

GLOSSARY

Art director Traditionally part of the two-person creative team in an advertising agency, the art director concentrates on the visual and design side of the process.

ASA Advertising Standards Authority, regulating advertising across all UK media.

App Shorthand for 'application', a piece of software designed to run on a computer and, more importantly, on a mobile device. Apps are digital shortcuts to get you to the service or game you want at the touch of a finger.

BCAP Broadcast Committee of Advertising Practice, the body that oversees the UK Code of Broadcast Advertising.

Billings When a company signs up with an advertising agency, it creates an advertising budget from its marketing funds, known as billings. This pays for everything from the creation and production of advertising media placement and agency fees.

BLM Black Lives Matter, a movement protesting against incidents of police brutality and all racially motivated violence against Black people. It has become a broad coalition of movements and organizations and seeks primarily to achieve criminal justice reform.

BOGOF Buy One Get One Free is a commonly used discount promotion tactic.

Brand The perceived qualities of a particular product or service offered by a company, or sometimes the company itself. ·

Branding What a company does to present the brand to the consumer and influence choice.

Brand awareness How familiar a brand name is to the consumer.

Bricks and clicks A business model that combines a physical location with an online ordering presence. It can be implemented through a custom website, an app for mobiles or tablets, or sometimes still ordering by telephone. Most formerly retail/ physical companies have adopted this model so as to remain competitive with purely online retailers, and some retailers have abandoned their physical locations to become purely online.

Bricks and mortar A business model whereby a company sells its wares and services in a physical location, either a shop on the high street or in other locations. In the past, it would also be used to refer to a company with factories or other production facilities as well as storage warehouses. In the 21st century, it's primarily used to differentiate companies with no significant online retail presence from companies that have one.

Business models The blueprint of the structured principles and methods an organization chooses to produce and from which they receive value.

B2B or Business to Business One company interacting with another company, or doing business with another. For example, a wholesale company wanting to sell to a retailer, or a financial body aiming to sell their services to a corporation.

B2C or Business to Consumer All marketing activity that takes place when companies are in the process of offering products or services to their prospective customers.

Buyer decision process Recognizing the problem to be solved or the need to be met, evaluating all the possible options, deciding which purchase to make and then afterwards assessing whether the purchase was successful or worthwhile.

Channels In marketing a channel is the ways that goods and services are brought to customers, whether it's through groups or organizations, their staff, or activities like transportation. It can also mean media channels, means by which communication between a company and its consumers is enacted.

Content Succinct but detailed messages and information that pass from one person to another online. Content is storytelling rather than hard sell, and as such consumers are more likely to view it as information that they might act on themselves or pass onto others if it captures their imagination.

Consumers People who want or need to buy goods and or services from trading companies.

Consumer needs A specific product or service considered essential, such as food, drugs and household products.

Consumer wants A service or product that the consumer is prepared to buy but doesn't necessarily 'need'. Holidays, fashion, entertainment and luxury items all fall into this category.

C2B or Consumer to Business The least common business model but becoming increasingly relevant in the digital age. A prime example would be an online blogger encouraging companies to advertize on their page.

C2C or Consumer to consumer All marketing and sales activities between individuals, for example, if they want to sell their car or lawnmower online or even put a simple handwritten card in a shop window.

Copywriter The member of the traditional two-person writing team who concentrates on any text or writing content.

Corporate behaviour The standard that a company sets for itself as a whole and then ensures that it is adhered to at all levels and in all marketing communications.

Creative director Oversees the work of creative teams in an agency.

Desires A desire is a consumer want that may not be immediately attainable, either

Fast moving consumer goods Products that are sold swiftly and at a relatively modest price. Examples include household goods of short-term durability such as food (in packaging), drinks, confectionery, make-up and toiletries, non-prescription medication and other items that can be consumed. Also sometimes called CPG or Consumer Packaged Goods.

The four Ps The key factors to consider when constructing any marketing mix: Product (what the item or service is), Price (how much is charged for it and how much does it cost to manufacture), Place (where it will be marketed) and Promotion (what forms of advertising or other marketing techniques will be used).

The four Cs A more customer-oriented rubric, this stands for consumer wants (or meeds), cost (to the customer), convenience

(how easy is it to acquire and use the product or service) and communication (the way the company can talk to the customer and vice versa).

Franchising A business model adopted by a company that wants rapid expansion of their business or brand, and so will allow other companies or individuals to take on the licence of a service, skill or product they own and sell it themselves. Prime examples of the franchise business model are fast food companies like McDonalds and Burger King.

Freemium This denotes when a product or service is provided for no cost, with a monetary premium charged for extra elements, whether it be extra features, additional services or other actual goods.

Gamification The act of introducing game-like elements to non-game activities with the aim of making the activity more engaging and providing motivation for those who are taking part. In a marketing context it can be as simple as offering customers rewards for completing various activities, such as offering feedback or engaging with interactive online materials. Popular game design elements, like point systems, ranking, avatars or other representative icons or images and collective collaboration towards a shared goal are often used.

Geofencing This uses a piece of software to set up virtual perimeter for a real geographical location. It links with the GPS on a mobile device and can then send a pre-programmed message or alert to the user when they enter the geofenced area.

Laissez-faire economics A political philosophy frequently adopted by the free market economy. It was developed by a group of French economists (known as the Physiocrats) in the 18th century in the belief that economic success was more probable if governments stayed out of the business sector.

LGBT This stands for Lesbian, Gay, Bisexual and Transgender. It represents the interests of individuals who identify with these groups. Sometimes it is extended to

LGBTQIA+, adding Queer, Intersex and Asexual people to the group, but often the four-letter acronym is taken to stand for the totality of sexuality and gender identity.

Macroeconomics Larger economic issues up to and including the behaviour of countries, huge corporations, governments and other society spanning groups.

Market Either the possible audience or customer base for a particular product or service or the business or trade in a particular product.

Marketing mix The particular combination of marketing tactics, orientations and planning that a marketer creates or deems appropriate for their product or service.

Microeconomics Issues concerned with individuals and small organizations. This reflects the smaller nature of the amounts of demand and supply being allocated by these people or groups, based on personal budgeting.

Multi-brand A business model involving a lot of different products under different brand names to match those of a competitor or to dominate the market, in an attempt to get the lion's share of the shelf space.

Needs Items or services that are considered essential by consumers, including food, drink, clothing and household items.

OATS A marketing mix analysis tool, comprising Organize (Decide on your mix), Activate (put it into practice), Test (see if it's working) and Study (Decide if it's been effective or needs replacing)

OFCOM Office of Communications, Oversees all broadcast messages from companies and their agents.

OFT Office of Fair Trading, used to oversee the ethicality of companies' marketing practices. The FCA (Financial Conduct Authority) replaced it in 2014.

Orientation The focus of a company's output, whether product, production, marketing or other alternatives.

Pack shot The image of the packaging of a product, a key advertising tool.

Peer-to-peer A business model whereby two individuals deal directly with one another, be it sales or distribution. It can cover any number of business situations where there is direct interaction between two persons or companies without the involvement of a third party.

Platforms Methods by which people can get access to media, and marketers and other media people can communicate and sometimes interact with consumers and others. In the past, platforms tended to be one-way communication techniques like newspapers, radio, TV and cinema and billboards, as well as in-person techniques such as speeches and forums. However, in the 21st century, platforms more often mean social media sites such as Facebook, YouTube and Instagram.

Quality marks A certification granted by an independent organization the attests to certain standards for a product or service.

QR codes Digital icons that can be printed anywhere. QR stands for Quick Response. Within their stylized design, they can store a great deal of data. By scanning the code with the camera on their mobile device, a consumer can interact directly with a trader or a service's website from anywhere.

Razor and blade A business model whereby one item is sold more cheaply or even given for free in order to support sales of a complimentary product. For example, shoe polish being given to customers who buy shoes, or free software for a computer, or razors and blades, obviously.

Return on investment (ROI) An equation frequently used by companies to gauge just how much capital to invest in a product in order to make the best profit.

Scamps When creatives are discussing ideas they will often produce a number of quick visual renditions in rough sketch form to show their thinking. These are traditionally known as scamps.

Subscription/servitization A business model designed around people paying for the regular provision of a particular product or service. Telephone companies and cable and satellite television providers use these models. However, in the 1980s and beyond subscription has sometimes become servitization, the model by which product sellers can provide extras (whether it's customer support, tailored insurance or other benefits) that complement the product. Companies like Apple and Rolls Royce use this to build brand loyalty.

Supply and demand On a simple level, these are the factors that determine how organizations set their prices. In a 'perfect competition' environment, the demand for goods and services perfectly matches the supply a state that is is called 'equilibrium'. However, equilibrium is a theoretical construct as it's impossible for a perfect competition environment (where all organizations have equal access and knowledge and resources) to exist. In reality the two factors frequently fluctuate. When demand outstrips supply there is a shortage and prices increase. When supply exceeds demand it leads to a surplus and prices drop.

SWOT analysis SWOT (Strengths, Weaknesses, Opportunities and Threats) analysis is used by companies to assess these factors in a business and see how they can best use them to their advantage.

Value A term used in marketing that relates primarily to consumer perception, whereby a customer compares the costs or benefits of one product or service against another, i.e. 'value for money'.

Wants Items or services that are considered luxuries by consumers, including holidays, jewellery, fashion products. of movement across national boundaries through which migrants create meaningful social, political, and economic fields and contributions in their daily exchanges, connections and activities.

SUGGESTED READING

1. The Origins of Marketing

Kotler, P, Armstrong, G, Harris, L & He, H. (2020). *Principles of Marketing, 8th European Edition*. Pearson Education.
This comprehensive book covers a lot of ground, with interesting case studies and in-depth investigation of every aspect of marketing.
McLuhan, M (1964). *Understanding Media: The Extensions of Man*. MIT Press.
McLuhan's work, while largely theoretical, serves as the underpinning of a lot of 20th century understanding of media and how it can be (and is used).

2. The Marketing Mix

Kotler, P. (2015). *Marketing Management, 15th Edition*. Pearson Education.
Considered essential to all who study marketing, there's a reason this book is on its 15th edition and still going strong as a relevant textbook.
Lindstrom, M (2008). *Buyology: How Everything We Believe About Why We Buy is Wrong*. Random House Business.
The author is a well-respected marketing expert and journalist whose involvement with some of the world's leading brands gave him the insights and ideas that form this book.

3. Value

Doyle, P. (2008). *Value-Based Marketing: Marketing Strategies for Corporate Growth and Shareholder Value, 2nd Edition*.
Analysing and refocusing marketing through a lens of shareholder value, this book helped marketers reinvent many elements of their job.
Husemann-Kopetzky, M. *(2018). Handbook on the Psychology of Pricing*. Pricing School Press.
Practical pricing guide outlining more than 100 effects, designed for small business owners and shopkeepers but good to get a ground-level view.

4. Marketing Economics

Kay, J. (2007). *Foundations of Corporate Success: How Business Strategies Add Value*. Oxford Paperbacks.
This book looks at how different corporations weathered various economic crises as a way of teaching business theory. Despite its age it still has valuable insights.
Goldstein, J. (2020). *Money: The True Story of a Made-Up Thing*. Atlantic Books.
This book explores the origins and the future of money in a really entertaining way and will make the reader look at currency with new eyes.

5. Understanding the Consumer

Ries, A, Trout, J. (1994). *The 22 Immutable Laws of Marketing*. Profile Books.
Interesting accessible book that breaks the author's accumulated marketing down into easily digestible sections with many examples.

Shotton, R. (2018). *The Choice Factory: 25 behavioural biases that influence what we buy*. Harriman House.
Recognized by some of the most illustrious names in the marketing industry for its practical and insightful look into behavioural science and the consumer.

6. Marketing and the Law

Various. (2010). *The BCAP Code. The UK Code of Broadcast Advertising*. TSO.
The book of rules and regulations broadcast advertising is required to follow in the UK.
Packard, V. (1957). *The Hidden Persuaders*. Ig Publishing.
This book is included not as a recommendation but as an alternative view of the intentions of mid 20th century marketing, and an insight into the criticisms and challenges it faced. Its impact led towards the greater self-regulation of the industry.

7. Diversity, Ethics and Social Responsibility

Eagle, L & Dahl, S. (2015). *Marketing Ethics and Society*. SAGE Publications Ltd.
Aiming to cover a wide variety of ethical quandaries and aspects, this book explains in plain detail many of the possible pitfalls and advantages of ethical marketing.
Singer, P (2011) *Practical Ethics: Third Edition*. Cambridge University Press.
While not specific to marketing this book provides an excellent overview of ethical considerations and values in all walks of life.

8. Marketing Research

Merriam S B & Tisdell E J. (2015). *Qualitative Research: A Guide to Design and Implementation*. Jessey Base.
This is the 4th edition of a book that gives vital guidance on qualitative research models without too much jargon, which makes it very easy to understand.
Leach W. (2018). *Marketing to Mindstates: The Practical Guide to Applying Behavior Design to Research and Marketing*. Lioncrest Publishing.
A perceptive look into the minds of the most important people in marketing, the consumers. Easy and useful for those new to the world of marketing research.

9. Branding

Sullivan, L & Bennett, S. (2012). *Hey Whipple, Squeeze This! The Classic Guide to Creating Great Ads*. John Wiley & Sons.
A surprisingly hilarious yet accurate analysis of the industry and the concept of brand stories from two experienced ad-men, full of useful tips and ideas.
Neumeier, M. (2005). *The Brand Gap, The: Revised Edition*, New Riders; 2nd edition.
Highly regarded by seasoned marketing professionals and newcomers alike, and full of practical advice on brand creation.

10. Advertising and Creative Process

Ogilvy, D. (1983). *Ogilvy on Advertising, 1st Edition*. Prion Books.
The most influential book on advertising and its principles that has inspired generations of marketing and advertising professionals.
Della Femina, J. (2010). *From Those Wonderful Folks Who Gave You Pearl Harbor*. Canongate Books.
First published in 1971, this is the book that inspired the series *Mad Men*, written by a man who worked on Madison Avenue in the 1950s and 60s, when it was the epicentre of the advertising universe. Funny and irreverent.

11. Digital Marketing

Anderson, C. (2006). *The Long Tail: Why the Future of Business Is Selling Less of More*. Hyperion Books.
Written by a renowned journalist and editor of one of the leading tech magazines, Wired, this book gives fresh insights into the relationship between consumers and internet marketing.
Morrison, S. (2015). *Visitors Don't Say 'Your Website Sucks...' They Shop Elsewhere*. Mr Metric Press.
An honest and insightful guide to building, managing and marketing websites, written by someone on the front line.
Handley, A. (2014). *Everybody Writes: Your Go-to Guide to Creating Ridiculously Good Content*. Wiley. This book underpins the importance of getting content right in order to engage the consumer and does it in an inspiring, practical way.

12. Psychology in Marketing

Cialdino, R. (2007). *Influence: The Psychology of Persuasion*. HarperBus.
A classic book that unpicks the psychological elements of marketing and is honest about the more manipulative elements of the culture.
Godin, S. (2018). *This is Marketing: You Can't Be Seen Until You Learn to See*. Portfolio Penguin.
The author is seen as one of the 'go to' professionals in modern marketing and this highly rated book is testament to his theories and ideas.

13. Engagement Marketing

Schmitt, B H. (1999). *Experiential Marketing*. Free Press
From Schmitt's perspective all marketing is experiential, and this book encourages marketers to understand their craft from that perspective.
Levinson, J C (2007) *Guerrilla Marketing: Easy and Inexpensive Strategies for Making Big Profits from Your Small Business*. Houghton Mifflin.
The author of this book coined the phrase 'guerrilla marketing' and is full of ideas and techniques to maximise a marketing budget.

14. Making a Marketing Plan

Dib, A. (2018). *The 1-Page Marketing Plan: Get New Customers, Make More Money, and Stand out From The Crowd*. Successwise.
While designed for the layman this book is well regarded by industry insiders as an important read for anyone interested in getting into marketing.
Kennedy, D S. (2011). *The Ultimate Marketing Plan 4th Edition*. Adams
Another accessible and informative marketing plan guide.

15. A Watershed for Marketing

Jiwa, B. (2014). *Marketing: A Love Story: How to Matter to Your Customers*. CreateSpace Independent Publishing Platform
While written before the Covid-19 era, this book is very forward thinking in its approach, helping marketers understand how to form connections with their target audience by telling stories.

Recommended magazines

Ad Age
Campaign
Creative Review
The Drum
Lürzer's Archive
Marketing
Marketing Week
Marketing Magazine

INDEX

PICTURE CREDITS

Alamy: 13, 17 below, 19 left, 22, 38 right, 38 left, 46 left, 47 right, 70 top, 71 below, 77 right, 84, 92 below, 97, 98, 114, 118, 121 top, 121 below, 124 below, 126 left, 128, 136 below, 141 centre, 141 below, 143 left, 144, 146, 150, 154, 158 below, 170, 171, 182 right, 186 left, 186 right, 195 centre, 195 right, 196 right, 199, 205, 222, 223, 241, 242.

Getty Images: 78 below, 79, 80, 106, 148, 149, 156, 173, 196 left, 216, 243 left, 243 right, 245.

Public domain: 14, 15, 16, 17 above, 18 above, 20 below left, far left, 25, 28, 33 right, 48, 51 top, 55, 67, 72, left, 92 left, 94 top, centre, 96, 101, 103, 107, 136 left, 153 below, 163 left, 167, 175, 177, 181, 194, 204, 212 left.

Shutterstock: 6, 7, 9, 11, 12, 12, 16, 18 below, 19 right, 20 right, 21, 23, 24, 27 top, 27 below, 30, 31, 32, 33 left, 35, 37, 39, 43, 44 right, 45, 50, 52, 56, 57, 58, 59, 60, 62, 63, 64, 65, 66, 68, 70 below, 72 right, 73 top, 73 below, 75, 76, 77 left, 78 top, 81, 82, 83 top, 83 below, 85, 86, 91, 94 below, 95, 105, 108, 109, 110, 111, 112, 113, 115, 117, 119, 120, 123, 124 top, 125, 126 right, 128, 129, 130, 130, 131, 133, 135, 139, 140, 141 top, 142, 144, 145 top, 145 below, 147, 151, 155, 157 top, 158 top, 163 top right, 163 below right, 168, 174, 178, 180, 182 left, 183, 187, 188, 189, 190, 191, 193, 195 left, 197, 198, 202, 206, 207, 208, 211, 212 right, 213, 214 below, 214 top, 217, 218, 219, 220, 224, 227, 228, 229, 230, 231, 232, 233, 234, 235, 239, 240, 244, 246, 247.

Other sources: Apple 157 below. **Authors** 49, 51 below, 99, 153 top, 162. **Barbour** 143 right. **Guinness** 169. **Ikea** 221. **Kellogg's** 88, 89.